Education and democracy

Birth of Modern Britain series

General editors:

A. E. Dyson
Senior Lecturer in English Literature,
University of East Anglia

and

R. T. Shannon
Reader in English History,
University of East Anglia

Titles in the series:

Nonconformity in the nineteenth century
edited by David M. Thompson

Class and conflict in nineteenth-century England 1815–1850
edited by Patricia Hollis

The idea of the city in nineteenth-century Britain
edited by B. I. Coleman

Education and democracy
edited by A. E. Dyson and Julian Lovelock

Education and democracy

Edited by

A. E. Dyson

School of English and American Studies,
University of East Anglia

and

Julian Lovelock

Head of English,
Dulwich College Preparatory School, Kent

Routledge & Kegan Paul

London and Boston

8331

First published in 1975
by Routledge & Kegan Paul Ltd
Broadway House, 68–74 Carter Lane,
London EC4V 5EL and
9 Park Street,
Boston, Mass. 02108, U.S.A.
Set in 11 on 12 pt Bembo
and printed in Great Britain by
Unwin Brothers Limited, The Gresham Press,
Old Woking, Surrey, England.
A member of the Staples Printing Group
© A. E. Dyson and Julian Lovelock 1975

ISBN 0 7100 8016 6 (c)

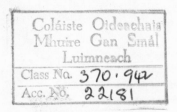

General editors' preface

The series is concerned to make the central issues and topics of the recent past 'live', in both senses of that word. We hope to appeal to students of history and literature equally, since each has much to offer, and learn from, the other. The volume editors are encouraged to select documents from the widest range of sources, and to convey the 'feel' of particular controversies when passion ran high. One problem for the modern student is hindsight: often, we fall back on over-simplified versions of history—Whig or Marxist, progressive or conservative—because we fail to imagine events as they were. We hope here to re-create situations through the passions and commitments of participants and contemporary commentators, before the outcome was known. In this way, students are encouraged to avoid both over-simplified judgments and that dull sense that whatever happened was inevitable which can so devitalise our understanding of any period's history, or its art.

We believe that this treatment of the recent past, bringing out the sense of immediacy and conflict, is also the soundest basis for understanding the modern world. Increasingly, we realise that continuity is more striking than discontinuity: nothing could be more naïve than a claim for 'modernity' which assumes that the past is 'irrelevant' or dead. It was during the age of Arnold and Gladstone, Disraeli and Tennyson, Darwin and Chamberlain that our most distinctive modern problems defined themselves—the growth of great cities and technology; the battle between individualism and collectivism; the coming of democracy, with all its implications for education, class, vocation and the ordinary expectations of living; the revolutions in travel and communication; the shifting relationships between individuals and the state. Many of the major ideas that shape our world were also born: and in the ferment of day-to-day crises and perplexities, prophetic and widely-ranging hopes and fears, we see the birth of modern Britain, the emergence of our world of today. Volume editors have been encouraged in their selection of material from contemporary sources to illuminate that density and complexity of things which is the essence of 'reality'.

The interaction between education and democracy is a central aspect of Victorian Britain. In it, we see the crisis of poverty and illiteracy which urbanisation dramatised and in large measure intensified, along with human responses of most disparate kinds. As the movement towards democracy gathered momentum, the claims of 'a truly national system of education' likewise took shape. This is part of the story of state intervention in the lives and welfare of citizens, and part of a great battle for the soul, and the future, of man. Would the heritage of the past be classified as 'aristocratic' or 'bourgeois', and tacitly or even openly denigrated, or would it be seen as a treasury now on offer to all? In this volume, the editors trace the long struggle against the privilege of class and wealth in favour of equal opportunity, along with an undercurrent of further, and far more radical, change. They see this as part of a drama still being enacted, the 'birth of modern Britain' at an especially formative stage.

Contents

Contents

A*   *ix*

Contents

Acknowledgments

The editors and publishers wish to thank the following for permission to reproduce copyright material in the documents indicated:

Allen & Unwin (84); Laurence Pollinger Ltd, Viking Press Inc. and the Estate of the late Mrs Frieda Lawrence (Epilogue); Macmillan, London and Basingstoke (98 and 99) and Macmillan, London and Basingstoke, and the Trustees of the Hardy Estate (87); and the Society of Authors on behalf of the Bernard Shaw Estate (88, 94 and 96).

Introduction

Plot and subplot

The story traced here is in outline simple. Our period starts in a society where power and privilege belong to birth, and by extension to wealth, and just occasionally to exceptional talent linked with luck. Access to high culture was restricted to the ruling minority. The majority was lucky if it learned to read. By the end of our period, it had been accepted that some degree of education must be available to everyone as a natural expectation, and that power and privilege should increasingly be related to ability and performance, and decreasingly to class. The notion of a 'truly national system of education' had ceased to be a dream and had become a reality. The ladder of ability had been constructed, and was being hoisted into place.

These educational changes were paralleled by a movement towards democracy, and certain links are easy to see. If people are to have power, they must be literate; ideally, they must be responsible custodians of the human past. In the nineteenth century, most educational thinking was sectarian in its explicit outlines, but by no means as blinkered as is sometimes made out. The implications of democracy were pondered by most intelligent people, and certain complexities, for education in particular, early emerged.

For, underneath the main plot, there is another story, which hindsight can perhaps more readily probe. While 'equality of opportunity' seems a natural child of the movement towards democracy, democracy was destined to have two children, not one, in the educational world. The second child is 'egalitarianism', at first sight very similar, yet increasingly dissimilar the more closely one looks. Even in infancy, there is tension; and might it prove, indeed, that the younger born son is hostile, and even murderous in intention towards the elder, so that 'equality of opportunity' is fated to play Abel to a fraternal Cain? At first sight, 'egalitarianism' seems almost a twin to its brother, but marked differences develop from the moment of birth. Clearsighted observers very early detected this, as some of our writers in this volume clearly prove.

The crux clarifies around the notion of 'meritocracy', which is rather a transference than an extension of power. In a 'meritocracy' the majority will still turn out to be loser, but how will this be received when the majority rules? Inherited power was, after all, a lottery, which most men could accept with relative good humour and grace. To be an earl is an accident that might have happened to anyone, so earls are not a personal judgment against less favoured men. But merited power is a very different matter, especially if everyone starts level in the race. Might the losers come to feel personally judged and diminished by failure, and therefore become angry with themselves, or with the rules of the game?

Indeed, might democracy, which is explicitly and by definition at war with arbitrary leadership, turn out to be implicitly at war with the ideal of leadership itself? Is it probable that while the ideal of 'equality of opportunity' will attend the birth of democracy, as a natural phenomenon, it will and must attract increasing enmity as the democracy matures? Men who claim equality based on merit and on fair competition in the early stages, might come to want equality pure and simple as time goes on. An allied question, of course, is whether democracy needs to be meritocratic, and if not, what scale of human values and opportunities it ideally should have. In our documents, this matter also is probed from various viewpoints, and a further range of complexities comes into view.

The great hope in the nineteenth century was that democracy would prove to be a friend to culture, lifting all men up towards riches previously reserved for a few. The great fear was that democracy would prove rather to be culture's enemy, through some inborn preference for the mediocre and small. But, behind both hope and fear lies a latent suggestion, that democracy might unpredictably mutate. If 1867 seemed to some a second and greater English revolution, it seemed to others a daring experiment rich in promise and hope. Whatever view was taken, one thing became certain; education, and its future, were now a vital concern.

General principles of selection

The possible material for this volume is limitless. We could have filled it many times over with extracts from government reports, novels, autobiographies, diaries or gossip; with statistics; with systematic philosophy or visionary intuition; with Victorian sages dreaming dreams or gripped in nightmares. It would be possible to chart schematic contrasts to well-known models—classic versus romantic, traditional versus progressive, cynical versus utopian, reactionary versus revolutionary, oligarchy versus democracy. But the debate is fluid and its lines are shifting, as most of our contributors attest. Thomas Huxley is sour about this (75), the imaginative writers are in varying ways subtle (e.g. 4, 42, 54, 76–8, 82, 87). The bureaucrats and writers of government reports are flat and cautious, moving among the complexities with discreet reserve (9, 60, 63, 74, 86). The visionaries and polemicists, too numerous to list, are less inhibited, exhorting or advising society at the tops of their voice.

Many of the complexities emerged slowly into consciousness, and in an anthology of this kind some degree of hindsight is inevitable. The century starts with piecemeal education, wholly uncentralised, financed for different motives and in different ways. The ruling classes looked after their own, and produced rulers; the rest of society fended for itself as best it could. Some were educated by the church, some by employers, some by philanthropists, some by patrons with personal motives; some were educated by no one at all (46). The church was the chief and most interested agent in education, and guarded its rights fiercely in the battles to come. By the end of the century, a National System of Education had struggled into existence, receiving its shape at last in Balfour's Act of 1902 (90–2). The long process of change is mirrored here, with the battles and setbacks and vicissitudes on the way. There were the entrenched interests, the established patterns, the smug complacencies, the rooted incredulities, the bitter threatenings and warnings—and, behind such obstacles, there was a slowly growing sense of historical inevitability, of the coming of 'the people' into their own. The voices urging reform are of remarkable diversity, whether we listen to the ruling classes or to the people themselves. Education is urged as a universal panacea or as a universal antidote; it is demanded as a necessity and as a right. We hear the arguments of those who point to crime, vice and incipient revolution, and say that the whole nation will be dragged down unless education prevails. We hear from others who speak of trade, of international competition and national efficiency, and who also think that the nation must stand or fall as a whole. But the assumption of 'two nations', the rich and the poor, remains deeply rooted, and in the late 1830s and the 1840s takes on new anger and depth. Is it really to be expected that the poor ever will be educated equally with the rich, either now or in any likely future to come? Will upper and lower classes ever really be one flesh and blood? We hear the idealism of Christian and humanist, of paternalist, of ordinary compassionate humanity and, mingling with this, the bewilderment and the anger of the oppressed. And at the same time, there are prophetic voices from both sides of society. The Marquess of Lansdowne warns his peers (28), Engels calls the workers to revolution and hate (33). There are utilitarians who say that education can shape and do almost anything (6–8), with Bentham's *Chrestomathia* (1816–17) the most influential text. But as the century progressed there were parallel idealisms, two of which proved to have special power. The first was the romantic quest for individual and unique self-fulfilment, which allied itself to primitivism and tended to reject much of the past. Rooted in the eighteenth century (though of course with more remote ancestors also) this was formulated by Blake, Wordsworth and other romantic poets, and dramatised by Victorian novelists with great imaginative force. In educational theory, it flowered in notable exponents such as Dewey (93 and 99), where it cross-fertilised with explicitly democratic ideals. A little later, the insights of psychologists such as Freud were also assimilated and 'child-centred' education became a formidable ideal. The second important idealism is more traditional and classical, and received its chief expression in Arnold's *Culture and Anarchy* in 1869 (77). This is the vision of 'culture' as a great human inheritance, notably from Jewish, Greek and Christian wisdom, which enriches individuals and keeps social anarchy at bay. Hitherto, the full riches have been available only to a privileged minority; the hope for a democracy will be to extend them to all. On balance, Arnold's view of human nature is pessimistic, and therefore anti-romantic; the 'spontaneous self' will in his view produce anarchy, not culture, if left to itself.

It is perhaps of crucial importance that while these ideals could and should have complemented one another, they too often polarised, becoming simplified and distorted in the 'traditionalist' versus 'progressive' debate. Both present vast challenges in terms of planning and resources, and an alliance would have been helpful and healing in every way. In this connection, George Eliot's contribution is illuminating (76), as an insight with very special relevance to the present time. There was a possibility that the new democracy would inherit human riches and treasure them, proving even better guardians than the élites who had gone before. But there was a possibility also that the riches would be for various reasons despised or squandered, proving too challenging or too unattractive to the majority of 'ordinary' men. Would it be understood in the coming democracy that the highest individual fulfilments require the context of human wisdom and achievement, or would 'individual fulfilment' pursue an autonomous path? Already, it was not unknown to hear 'culture' described not as a distinctively human heritage, but as a possession—a trick even—of hated oppressors from the past. Marx ascribed religion to priestcraft and to the deliberate duping of the people; perhaps art and philosophy would come to be similarly discredited in time? George Eliot foresaw that hatred or neglect of the past might emerge even without a revolution, simply as a great danger—the other side of a great hope—inherent in democracy itself.

These educational crosscurrents relate to larger social changes, which concern us only obliquely, though their impact is clear. At the start of our period, the state and the state church belong together irrevocably, lending each other sanctions and together resisting those internal and external enemies by which states are destroyed. By the end of the period, most people concede that the church and the state can often go their own ways in practical matters, even if there is no question of an official divorce. This change came about not in the ferment of revolution, but through debates on matters of pressing social concern. Much of the educational controversy in Parliament and elsewhere was explicitly religious, and had crucial bearing on the relationship between state and church. This is the context in which the assumptions of the coming democracy came gradually to colour the debate—first as a matter of marginal and almost eccentric importance, but later as the overwhelming issue in its own right.

Again, at the start of our century the state had little concern for the welfare of its citizens, and certainly not for their education or their general social health. Class distinctions were widely thought of as God-given and immutable. This view will be encountered again and again in these documents, in the early years in counterpoint with the question of extending the parliamentary franchise, and later—a very different matter—in counterpoint with the growth of 'democracy' as a dynamic ideal. Historians differ in their assessment of *laissez-faire* as a conscious English ideology, but the term describes the way in which many things in practice did most normally work. Arguably, the famous Victorians were nearly all in one context or another on the side of growing state intervention, but if so, this was often under the challenge of specific pressures and needs. Cobden himself became an interventionist on the educational question, to the scandal of a follower more purist than himself (43). In education indeed, we can follow something of the long process by which national involvement in social problems came to be seen first as inevitable, whether one liked it or not; then as a challenge that had to be made to work in practice, despite all the conflicting interests and disparate components; then as something that had to be paid for, by taxes or rates, however much of a pain and disruption this also proved; and finally, as a reality which altered the class structure and balance of power irrevocably and decisively, again whether one liked it or not. This process is paralleled, of course, in other areas of welfare, and has much to do with the industrial changes that capitalism had wrought. The novels of Dickens demonstrate the degradation to which urbanisation and poverty had reduced much of the population, the extreme urgency of the crisis, and the powerful and even irresistible tug towards reform. Some of the pressures came from human compassion where this flourished, as it did very often; some from fears and self-interests of the sharpest kind. Dickens shows the strongly stubborn and entrenched nature of the opposition to reform, and the smug stupidity rampant among all classes of people who stood in its way. If we read his novels with hindsight, we notice too his own perplexities, and the difficulty that even a man of vision had in foreseeing future solutions so far in advance. In particular, Dickens was as unable to envisage as almost any of his contemporaries would have been the welfare state as we have since come to know it—paid for by sweeping taxes, organised on a scale that would then surely have seemed visionary, and, only a hundred years later, already often thinking of itself as a 'natural right'. This immensely important process of change can be best discerned in specific issues; and our present theme of education and democracy is near the centre of the storm.

As the debate shifts and turns bewilderingly, we must remember that we confront not only battle-lines between opposing factions, but ambivalences inside individuals themselves. These inner tensions are often as illuminating as the public ones, since they reveal the human side of the complexities involved. 'Education' and 'democracy' are themselves fluctuating concepts, touching most of us at sensitive points. There is little to do with idealism or common sense, religion or self-interest, hopes or fears, or indeed the basic understanding of *homo sapiens*, which does not become engaged in the debate.

With this in mind, we have seen our theme more as a sea in flux than as a game of chess; there is an elusiveness beyond any rules. The mode of presentation is kaleidoscopic, within the prescription of chronology—perhaps because the editors are literary critics, and influenced by imagism. We have tried to represent most of the main contributors to the debate (not all, obviously), and to look for varieties of genre and tone. Various opposing views come together, setting up echoes among themselves. The chief aim has been to dramatise—to look for thought coloured by impulse and passion, thought of the kind most influential in 'getting things done' or in proving that things cannot be done. At the same time, we have remained conscious that analysis has its place in all worthwhile argument, and that very passionate ideologies can issue in logical and indeed rigid structures and forms. There was the ideology of utilitarianism, of 'fact', which pervaded so much middle-class capitalism, and which Dickens satirised savagely in *Hard Times*. There was also the less formulated ideology of 'liberty within constitutional law'—the 'English ideology', as George Watson has christened it in a recent book of that title, which throws a great deal of light on our present theme. Not least, there was the emergent Marxist ideology—blunt; anti-historical, in any terms but its own interpretation of history; drained of sensitivity and brutal with logic; an incalculable influence on every aspect of our modern world. These and other structures of ideology will be perceived in these documents, and we point to them, where necessary, in the sectional Introductions ahead.

What our method presupposes is work from the reader, who must examine tone and mood with critical care. Some of the extracts may in this aspect seem easy: no deep intuition is called for by (say) Davies Giddy (5) or A. P. Perceval (39) or George Rumsey (59). But other writers are more elusive, as John Holloway's chapters on the literary style of modern prophets in *The Victorian Sage* makes clear. Matthew Arnold, for instance (54, 77-8) woos us charmingly but insidiously with practised rhetoric, weaving his phrases as an incantation and a spell. 'Sweetness and light', 'perfection in a word', 'the young barbarians': we are eased into a mood of nostalgia tinged with apocalypse. Behind us, the lost world of religious certitude, aristocratic supremacy, culture's high summer; ahead, the coming battle in a democracy between the light and the dark. Other prophets approach us in tempest and tumult, sweeping us along as Carlyle (29) and Lawrence (Epilogue) do, in exhilaration and rage. And what do we make of a voice like that of Engels (33)? Is his anger and contempt justified as the only properly human response to intolerable injustice (the claim it makes for itself), or is his analysis over-simplified and his tone rotten with hate? Lovett (30), in contrast, is noticeably sweeter, a man more appealing in temper, though no less seriously engaged.

A few final words on selection. We have tried to include certain key statistics where they occur in the documents, rather than to abstract them; and from time to time we have allowed writers to grapple with the difficult words 'education' and 'democracy' themselves. We have chosen one or two extracts for their typical rather than for any particular significance. Disraeli's memo on a cabinet meeting (67) is a reminder of the ways in which politicians in power are likely to think on a particular day and under specific pressures; Captain Maxse RN (73) is here because when *he* has decided that change has to come, then come it must; the man and the audience tell their own tale.

Historical sketch

I

We come now to a brief and generalised sketch of the events in the period.

In the fifteenth and sixteenth centuries, an emerging middle class, realising that its existence depended on brains rather than birthright, endowed a number of schools as a shrewd act of self-preservation and advancement. Here was the beginning of many of the great grammar and public schools, destined to have chequered careers, but always to bear heavily on the nation's educational thinking, and often to stand as its supreme educational achievement. This new interest in education was paralleled by Caxton's setting up of the first English printing press in 1476, which both made possible and eventually demanded a literate population. In the 1530s, however, gifted children from poor homes received an educational setback, resulting from Henry VIII's dissolution of the monasteries. Hitherto, many had been able, like Cardinal Wolsey, to rise in this way through the church hierarchy, and to achieve academic and professional success. Such opportunities for the poor did not become available again until the earlier years of this present century, when they came as the culmination of the story to be traced here.

In the seventeenth century, Milton and Locke were both immensely influential in the development of education, the latter indeed in ways he might not have foreseen. Both of them placed great stress on moral education and notably on 'character building', a classical ideal well adapted to leaders of men. This emphasis received new impetus in the nineteenth-century public schools from Dr Arnold of Rugby and, as we shall see, proved congenial to Victorians from every social class. During our period it was everywhere in the ascendant; and the alternative morality of romantic primitivism and self-discovery, though it attracted some theorists and led to famous experiments in private education, made no serious educational challenge to it until much more recent times.

Milton's call for a revision of an outdated and over-classical curriculum was less influential, and the new learning and sciences of the Renaissance still had a hard battle to fight. Locke, on the other hand, was of crucial importance not only through his explicit writings on education but still more through his epistemology—which bore fruit in the characteristic eighteenth-century optimism about reason, and the education of reason; in the educational thinking of Helvétius; and, by way of these, in the rational utopianism of James Mill, Robert Owen and other important figures who will concern us here. At another level, Locke's thinking influenced the philosophy of democracy in America and of revolution in France, and therefore becomes part of the history of education and democracy at points where so many links between the two are forged.

In the eighteenth century, one further educational development which must be briefly noted is the success of the dissenting academies. Founded for those who were excluded from other forms of higher education on the grounds of religion, they achieved an enviable academic reputation, notably in the field of modern learning, and set standards and patterns which ensuing state education was bound to try to emulate if it could.

II

At the end of the eighteenth century, small groups of the new business and professional men (notably the Lunar Society and the Manchester Literary and Philosophical Society), thrown up by the industrial society and destined to become middle-class leaders, rebelled against the political domination of the aristocracy, and the many corrupt practices which were tolerated if not actively encouraged by British governments. They stood out against slavery; they supported the American struggle for independence and the French revolution; especially, because it concerned many of them personally, they fought for religious freedom and the abolition of the Test Acts which barred nonconformists from holding public office. And above all they believed in education—not at this stage in narrow pragmatism, education for gain, but simply and idealistically in the right of all children to fulfil their potential in every direction. Naturally they favoured a curriculum based on the sciences instead of on the classics, but unlike their immediate successors they were even more concerned about the education of the whole person, about the social, cultural, and physical aspects as well as the purely academic. With only a limited following, and with grammar schools by statute and choice persisting with classical studies to the virtual exclusion of all else, the beliefs of these early reformers about child education were tested only in the home (tutoring was one of the main forms of education, and fitted very well with the popular tenet, derived from the new romantic writing but more particularly from Rousseau's *Émile*, that a child must always be regarded and educated as an individual) and in a handful of small private schools. In the sphere of higher education they were more prominent, creating the dissenting academies which offered broader courses than had hitherto been known, and trained men to enter industry, commerce, the professions and the ministry. Many of the leading scientists of the day were in political sympathy and, if not actually involved in the founding of academies, were persuaded to serve on their staffs.

But, with the onset of the 1789 revolution, and the ensuing war between Britain and France, the position of the early radicals quickly became both popularly and politically untenable. Although prosecutions of certain of their number for offences against state and crown failed, the force of the movement was lost. The thoughts of the country turned from domestic reform to struggles abroad, and, during the years with which our period opens, English domestic policy was of a markedly reactionary and repressive kind. One of the most readable accounts of this period is still G. M. Trevelyan's *Lord Grey of the Reform Bill* (1920), which traces the pressures for and against the first great victory for franchise reform.

In the early years of the nineteenth century the fight for education was renewed. Again the pressures came largely from the business and professional men, and again the chief end envisaged was the destruction of aristocratic rule and the building of a juster and happier society. But by now, these radical thinkers were clearly identifiable with the middle classes, and their means of achieving their end were very different from those of their predecessors. Instead of concentrating on the education of the whole person, the new focus was far narrower and more utilitarian. It was argued that those who gave their country wealth should have power in it; that those who were efficient in the engine room should have a place on the bridge. The battle for political power was engaged and, since business existence centred on the making of profit and the avoidance of loss, the new educational philosophies predictably made usefulness their yardstick. In education, knowledge seemed useless and in a vacuum unless it related immediately to social needs and, specifically, to employment. Probably the most profound and lasting influence in this direction was Jeremy Bentham's *Chrestomathia*, which expounded in detail the need for *relevance* in education, and which remains the most sophisticated exposition of a very crude political theory.

Thus it was not surprising that the first main targets of the middle class were the universities and grammar schools, seats of classical learning totally removed from the everyday life of the majority of the population (in some cases quite literally, since nonconformists were all but barred from Oxford and Cambridge and from some schools). It was argued that control of the universities should be wrested from the church and put into secular hands (here James Mill was the most forthright spokesman), since the church, sensing insecurities in an age of change, was intent on preserving the *status quo*, but a 'liberal education' had to be concerned precisely with change, and with daily social realities, and so with discussion and not dogma. Educational institutions, argued Mill, had to move with the times. The need was for universities with an up-to-date and practical curriculum, which taught living languages instead of dead ones, which substituted an acquaintance with economics for the outdated classics, and which opened their doors to all who would benefit from the education offered, whether they belonged to the Church of England or not. In the event, it proved easier for the middle classes to build their own schools rather than to change overnight the traditions and prejudices of hundreds of years. In spite of fierce opposition from the church and from Oxford and Cambridge, University College, London, was granted its charter in 1836, teaching the sciences, mathematics, engineering, medicine, philosophy, law, political economy and modern languages, as well as the classics.

In the case of the grammar schools, too, the middle classes often found it easier to build rather than to change. It is true that some grammar schools did modernise their curricula in response to popular demand, but in other instances the authorities responsible for the schools pointed to their ancient statutes and argued that they could not legally teach other than the classics even if they so wanted (which, of course, overwhelmingly they didn't). Their stand was supported by the Lord Chancellor's important ruling in the 1805 Leeds Grammar School case, which forbade the school's governors from changing from a classical to a modern curriculum, on the grounds that it would be wrong 'to promote the benefit of the merchants of Leeds' at the expense of the poor, for whom the school was originally endowed. Dissatisfied with the grammar schools, some middle-class parents chose private schools as an alternative education for their children. But, although some of these certainly offered a sound modern education, others were shortlived, dependent as they were on the whims and fortunes of their owners, and others still were the model for Dickens's frightening establishments of Squeers and Creakle. In such establishments, children unwanted by parents or guardians would be left to the mercies of men sometimes vile in character and devoid of learning. And, at another level, the demand of some parents for an education wholly attuned to utility led to schools such as Gradgrind's 'In this life, we want nothing but Facts, sir; nothing but Facts!' . . . utilitarianism run mad. Not surprisingly, many parents clubbed together to found the proprietary schools, later to become boarding and then public schools, which offered to the middle class a modern education at a reasonable price.

So much for the middle classes during this period; but what about the workers? Certainly Bentham and Mill argued the case for education for all, as a kind of middle-class idealism, but the advocacy of education for the working class was in one respect, and no doubt cynically, a political ploy. First, the middle class needed the support of the working class if it was to build pressures that would loosen the stranglehold of the aristocracy on government; second, it believed that if the franchise was extended, an educated working-class voter would opt for a radical parliament with middle-class representatives, and it scarcely occurred to any of the leading reformers that the working class would want, or was entitled to, a share of power. James Mill, for example, argued unashamedly that government was the prerogative of the rich. Today, this hardly seems an enlightened sentiment, perhaps because it confronts us with ambiguities in the word 'democracy' itself. For the upper and middle classes in the nineteenth century, and sometimes today, the furthest reach of democracy was the eventual right of all men to a vote; the MPs chosen would, by definition, be articulate and (hopefully) intelligent, and they would function as representatives, not as tools of popular whim. But, for some working-class leaders, 'democracy' already had a more revolutionary aspiration attached to it, that the people would in fact come to govern themselves. 'Power to the people', as a recent pop song has it, or, in the words of today's university students applying democracy to education, 'The union general meeting is the only decision making body: the elected union executive is no more than an executive.' Here, indeed, is a dramatic confrontation between education and democracy, the dénouement of which has perhaps still to be seen.

So, how *did* the workers manage? The chief form of education open to them was the Sunday schools, run by the church, and offering moral and religious instruction, and bare literacy. Other children were able to attend the dame schools, small establishments run by unqualified ladies, and usually, as two of our extracts describe (51-2) existing in a state of bedlam. Then there were the charity schools (severely limited in number), the endowed grammar schools (which, as we have seen, were tied to a classical curriculum, and were destined anyway to be commandeered by the middle classes— and cf. extract 11), and some private schools (those that were within the purse of the workers were usually educationally worthless). In an attempt to rectify this appalling situation, Lord Brougham fought in Parliament for educational provision for all, and in 1820 introduced a bill for 'the better education of the poor in England and Wales'. But Brougham's position was a lonely one in high places, and the opposition of the church, which rightly feared that a national system of education would ultimately be a secular one, and of the aristocracy, who understandably feared for the security of their own power, doomed his bill to failure. There was also the increasing demand for child labour working against it; before the

Factory Acts, parents could send their children out to earn money while they were still infants and, given the circumstances of many of the poor, and the social setting that was normative, it is not surprising if many opted for this alternative rather than for a school. It must be noted also that some in the working classes, and perhaps a substantial number, were actually opposed to education, partly because they did not want their own children to rise above them, and partly because they mistrusted an ethos ('intellectual priggism' as Thomas Hughes called it in *Tom Brown's Schooldays*) which they either could not or did not want to understand. Lord Brougham carried on his good work outside as well as inside Parliament, as other of our extracts evidence (17–18; 27), and organised what was virtually a pressure group for universal infant teaching through unpropitious times.

However, there were minor successes. There was much self-education among adults, particularly in the 'corresponding societies'—groups of workers who joined together to make themselves and others fully conversant with current political and social problems, and to try to form solutions to them which took into account the interests of their own class. There was the founding of the secular Sunday schools for adults and children, which provided an alternative to the religious education offered by the church. There were the New Lanark schools of Robert Owen (6–7), a one-time member of the Manchester Literary and Philosophical Society. These schools, which served the families working in the local cotton industry, believed characteristically in education as a humane and not an economic necessity, and accounts of their classroom activities put them far closer to the 'child as individual' and 'learning by doing' primary schools of the 1970s than to the formality of the majority of utilitarian establishments. There were the schools set up by the early co-operative societies, with much thought and idealism underlying them (12, 14–15). There were the mechanics' institutes, some controlled by the middle class and teaching middle-class values, others controlled by the working class and now openly declaring that their aim was the emancipation of the masses. The point is clear: the working class, conscious that they were receiving no real help from elsewhere, were starting to help themselves. E. P. Thompson's *The Making of the English Working Class* (1964) has many fascinating insights; for instance:

By this time [i.e. the early 1830s] . . . the Sunday schools were liberating themselves (although slowly) from the taboo upon the teaching of writing, while the first British and National schools (for all their inadequacies) were beginning to have some effect. But, for any secondary education, the artisans, weavers, or spinners had to teach themselves. The extent to which they were doing this is attested by the sales of Cobbett's educational writings, and notably of his *Grammar of the English Language*, published in 1818, selling 13,000 within six months, and a further 100,000 in the next fifteen years (p. 734).

III

With the passing of the Reform Bill in 1832, which itself was more a Whig expedient to restabilise the balance of power and to avoid revolution on the French model than a measure based on idealism, the gap between the middle class and the working class widened. The working class was naturally angry, in its politically articulate manifestations, that its struggle alongside the middle class had resulted in the middle class winning extra power through the franchise and the working class being deprived (through property qualifications) of the few voting rights that it had had. The middle class, for its part, was now far more concerned with promoting its own interests than with philanthropy, and any further efforts to extend the franchise would certainly have to come from elsewhere. The brutal fact was that the working class provided the industrialists with a cheap and invaluable labour force, and it was not in utilitarian interests to educate this above its station. It goes without saying, of course, that many people were moved more by idealism than by class interests, but they did not add up to an effective force. And even the idealists have a double edge to their intercessions: James Kay, for example, in *The Moral and Physical Condition of the Working Classes in Manchester in 1832*, describes something of the terrible conditions in which the urban poor lived, but his plea for better conditions is based even more on fear of popular rebellion than on charity.

For the militant workers then, self-help was still more essential, and in 1836 'The People's Charter' signalled the serious start of Chartism. This demanded better living and working conditions, a shorter working day, restrictions on the employment of women and children, opportunities for education, and, above all, democracy in a meaningful sense. But although a number of acts were passed in Parliament under pressure of sometimes violent agitation, the

Radicals quickly sided with the establishment, joining forces either with the Whigs or the Tories, and often with the church, and the workers were again on their own. On the educational front, the Chartists set up their own Chartist halls and schools, but these were only oases in a still vast desert. They also took over the call for a national system of education, though there were splits on this issue in the Chartist ranks, and a shift in thinking for many about the political realities of cause and effect. Before, the call to education had seemed to most idealists an obvious prelude to political power; now, without allies, it was becoming obvious to some that the sole way to educational and indeed to any other reform was to gain power first.

The Chartist movement, always ill-co-ordinated, collapsed in the 1850s, but had ceased to be a major influence for many years before. As the 1850s advanced, the Great Exhibition era seemed set for new prosperity and even stability, but the underlying ills were not resolved. The growing distance between workers and the rest of society was a frequent theme in literature (e.g. 27, 29, 30, 31, 32, 33 among our extracts, and most of the famous novels of the decade from 1844 to 1854), and is remarked upon with regret by Thomas Hughes in 1857 (48). The 1850s, however, saw the start, however tentative and uneasy, of co-operation between workers and management. Trade unions were formed, and collective bargaining was seen as a possibly acceptable route to social progress on the one hand and to increased productivity and wealth on the other. Furthermore, the 1850s saw a rapid expansion of British trade, both because of the huge supply of raw materials available from the colonies and because better transport opened up world markets. The middle class, at the heart of the trade boom, was able to challenge further the supremacy of the aristocracy. In *Bleak House* (1852–3) Dickens compares one of the successful new self-made industrialists, an iron-master from the north, and a considerate employer within the limits prescribed by money making, with Sir Leicester Dedlock, a tenacious representative of the old aristocratic order. The industrialist is confident that the future lies with him, even though Sir Leicester cannot begin to comprehend this; and Dickens endorses the insight as an irrevocable truth.

IV

The first result of the renewed middle-class pressure for educational reform was the appointment of Royal Commissions to investigate

the running of Oxford and Cambridge universities. The die-hard
aristocrats, the church and the universities themselves were indignant,
but, although any reports were bound to advocate extensive
changes, the survival of the institutions was guaranteed by the
general recognition that, in spite of their faults, the universities had,
in their ancient traditions, a profoundly civilising influence and
consequently a vast educational potential that new institutions could
not hope to match. In the event, the commissions reported very
much along the lines that the middle-class aspirants wanted,
advocating most importantly a broadened and more specific
curriculum with opportunities for specialisation, an entry dependent
on ability instead of on connections, and an end to exclusively
clerical control.

Similarly, the Clarendon Commission, appointed in 1861 to
investigate the great public schools (namely, Charterhouse, Eton,
Harrow, Merchant Taylors', Rugby, St Paul's, Shrewsbury,
Westminster and Winchester), while exposing depressingly low
academic standards, praised the excellent character training offered
by the schools, their unrivalled preparation of young men to be
statesmen, and ensured their continued existence on almost traditional
lines (55, 63). But there was one break with tradition: the rights of
entry of the local poor were exchanged for entry based wholly on a
competitive exam. In the universities, the upper class had lost out;
in the major schools, the working class. The middle class might
smile on both sides of its face.

Then, in 1864, perhaps the most crucial of all the nineteenth-
century educational commissions started its work. The Schools
Inquiry, or Taunton Commission, studied the whole of the existing
educational provision for the middle class—the endowed,
proprietary, and private schools—and it reported back that although
the proprietary schools were doing their job well, the endowed
schools and most of the private schools were deficient in terms of
buildings, curricula, and teaching methods. The Commission's
answer to the shambles was to outline a national system of education
in which every school had a clearly defined role to play. The
system was based on the increasingly narrow class divisions which
were developing of their own accord. The upper middle class, whose
eventual aim was entry into university and subsequently government,
would have limited entry into the great public schools, into the
proprietary boarding schools (Malvern and Marlborough, for
example), and the grammar schools which were modelling

themselves on the public schools. The bulk of the middle class, the merchants and traders, would be educated in second-grade schools with a modern and practical curriculum up to the age of 16. Finally, those on the borders of the middle class, small shopkeepers and farmers and so on, would be educated in third-grade schools up to the age of 14. The differentials would be maintained by an appropriate scale of fees.

In 1869, the Endowed Schools Act was passed, and although in fact it did not incorporate as narrow a system of education as the Taunton Report had recommended, it did mean that in most areas the old school endowments no longer ensured poor children an education in their local grammar schools. Instead, free education was only open to those poor children who could win exhibitions or scholarships in competition with their social superiors. Given the conditions of their upbringing, such competition was often far from fair, and only a few working-class children made the grade. But it must be remembered that the Endowed Schools Act was a social as much as an educational measure. The exclusion of the majority of the poor from a sound education was politically necessary if the balance of power was not to be disturbed again; the inclusion of a few of the poor was, of course, politically necessary also, but for other and patent reasons.

In contrast to the wide-ranging reforms suggested by the commissions enquiring into middle-class education, the Newcastle Commission, whose brief was the condition of the elementary schools, expressed general satisfaction with what it saw; not essentially, perhaps, because the schools were excelling themselves, but because education in Britain was keeping pace with that on the continent, because child labour was still to some degree needed by the country's industry, and because radical change would, again, have unpredictable effects. One real measure alone was introduced as a result of the Commission's vast labours—that of payment by results. Grants to schools and salaries to teachers were to be made dependent upon the pupils' achievement of certain standards of competence in the basic skills. Yet far from raising standards, the step was retrogressive; human nature being what it is, the elementary schools tended to teach basic skills to the exclusion of all else, and cramming and rote learning often replaced attempts to impart true understanding. It can be remarked also that government spending on elementary education fell considerably as a result of the new scheme.

But while the middle class were achieving results on the educational front, as well as on the industrial one, the workers were also pondering their rights. The trade unions grew into a significant force—often, as our extracts from this period show, also a feared one—and the Second Reform Act of 1867, which extended the franchise to a further million people and redistributed parliamentary seats, at last put sections of large towns under the electoral control of workers, and marked the moment when a real shift in power was at last destined to come, in the fullness of time. Democracy was now more than a dream; and the result, as far as education was concerned, was inevitable. 'Though we cannot accept them as our teachers,' writes Lowe (66) of the authors of *Essays on Reform*, 'they are undoubtedly our masters,' and 'We must educate our masters' became a famous quip, often ascribed to Disraeli (Lowe, however, was not totally resigned to the passing of power from the aristocracy to the masses; the aristocracy, he argued, might hope to maintain its superiority by improving its own education and clinging tenaciously to high culture). The industrialists, too, were often coming to see that serious bargaining with their labour forces must depend on the education of the unions. In 1870, these pressures co-operated finally with all the other forces pointing towards national education, and Forster's Education Act became law. Elementary education was theoretically available to all, either in the existing church schools or in new secular establishments. The education was not yet free (except for the very poor), nor was it yet compulsory. Nor indeed, in many cases, was it yet practicable, as the absence of buildings and staff made starkly clear. There were still great battles to be fought if these advances were to become actual; but a decisive milestone in education had been reached.

V

In 1880, elementary school attendance became compulsory, though in some districts children could still leave school to go into employment at the age of ten. In 1891, the Free Education Act was passed, and although fees were not abolished completely, elementary schools were allowed to admit children free of charge and claim a state grant in lieu of fees. However, the act was not passed without protest, both from those who maintained that free education would mean taken-for-granted education and therefore a decline in standards, and from the churchmen who feared that increased state aid of voluntary schools would eventually bring them under secular control.

And so the elementary schools became normal: but once given a taste of their riches, it was natural that the working class should ask for more. It soon became customary for many children to stay on at the elementary schools after the official leaving age (usually twelve). Some schools developed 'top' classes to cope with the older pupils, and became known as 'higher grade' schools. In other areas, the school boards (locally elected bodies, which since 1870 had had control of state elementary education) founded separate and legally dubious higher grade classes, which were each fed by a number of elementary schools. In yet other areas, the school boards developed evening classes to give advanced instruction to both adults and adolescents in the whole range of subjects. But educational progress for the working classes, characteristically supported by legislation only after extreme pressure, still gave rise to resentment and fear among its social superiors. The upper and middle classes often objected that the higher grade schools were having a detrimental effect on the grammar schools, since the small but valuable (both academically and financially) streams of working-class scholars were drying up in the face of the competition of lower fees and a more modern curriculum. More crucially, they saw a threat to the comfortable socially and politically defined system of education in operation, and so to their own social and political status. At the same time, there was some official support for the higher grade schools: a minority of the 1888 Cross Commission on elementary education (the majority took the opposite line), the 1895 Bryce Commission on secondary education, and a number of leading politicians espoused their cause. And, although the schools continued to be battered by their opponents, the working class were not going to let them go. Secondary education for all became the fresh demand, supported by the Bryce Commission (86), who regarded it as a matter of first priority in the field of social legislation. The 1902 Act, far reaching in its implications but in the short term a bitter disappointment for many, was the Tory answer.

The 1902 Act had two main functions. First, it brought about a major reorganisation of elementary school management and finance. The running of the state elementary schools was to be taken away from the school boards and put into the hands of the county and county borough councils, while the voluntary schools were to be subsidised by local rates, though still retaining their independence (the foundations would appoint four out of six managers). These developments meant that the church and the upper and middle classes seemed to have won back control of the whole educational system; the measure of suspicion and hostility can be gauged from our extract 97. Although today we think of the 1902 Act as the real beginning of secondary education, it was in fact these administrative measures which were most bitterly fought, and which themselves ironically contributed to the still very slow development of secondary education for the working class. Second, the Act empowered councils to finance secondary education from rates if they thought it desirable. Predictably, few councils *did* think it desirable: the 1906 report on higher elementary schools expressed an attitude which might have sounded typical a century earlier in stating that working-class children should be educated 'to make them efficient members of the class to which they belong' and in condemning any tendency towards 'secondary' education in elementary schools. In 1907, under parliamentary and popular pressure, the Liberal government made a theoretical concession which offered a number of free places in secondary schools to suitably qualified working-class children. But when the First World War broke out in 1914, and when our period ends, secondary education for the masses was practically no more than a possibility in legislation, except for the very gifted.

VI

This necessarily brief review of the political and social situation has inevitably been simplified, since the scope is a small-scale map. Serious students must refer to the books listed in our select bibliography (itself a small cross-section of the work available) and perhaps especially to Brian Simon's *Studies in the History of Education 1780–1870* and *Education and the Labour Movement 1870–1920*. These are indispensable works of scholarship (though searchers after immutable truths *may* perceive a fashionable bias).

In tracing the fight for equality of opportunity in education, modern readers are bound to be on the side of the underdog, and not least if they are beneficiaries themselves. The upper-class establishment and the church tend to play a villainous role, on the side of reaction, and it is inevitable that this should be so. The idealism and genuine religious concern in many influential people from all classes cannot be doubted, but neither—as nearly all our documents demonstrate—can the degree to which entrenched interests, religious and social, dominated the debate.

It is important to remember therefore that those who defended the *status quo* and feared profound dangers were by no means all hypocrites, or all activated by personal self-interest in any crude sense. At the start of the nineteenth century, the alliance between church and state seemed a crucial aspect of social order, and the aristocracy believed it was defending civilisation, as well as privilege, from looming threats. The new middle classes were characterised by the production of wealth, and by ruthless efficiency, but would these qualities necessarily produce a superior world? As Arnold stressed (54), the aristocracy defended a tradition which transcended most of its members individually, and which might be far preferable to a new élitism of material success. T. S. Eliot's *Notes Towards the Definition of Culture* (1948) was no doubt born out of its time, and naïve politically, but the dangers and ugliness of meritocracy, as he exposed them, ring sufficiently true.

The working-class challenge to the established order was, on the other hand, very different, and notably in the concept of 'democracy' as truly shared power. Would it really be possible to produce a society where everyone had a share in government, and where decisions remained always intelligent and informed? Would it prove possible in practice to level up the masses to high culture, even if the fantastic resources needed, in money and manpower, could somehow be found? A society of the semi-literate might opt for a tawdry 'culture', allowing fantasy and wish-fulfilment to dominate its literature and arts. Religion itself might be watered down from its guardianship of exalted moral aspirations and the means of salvation to a mere sanction for whatever level of morality appealed to the popular mind. The process of levelling-up might be reversed decisively, and a tyranny of the commonplace (or worse) instituted, as some clearly feared (47, 64–6, 70, 76, 77, 81 and other extracts). Indeed, if one were really pessimistic, the inner logic of democracy might seem to be anti-educational—a drift towards value-free relativism in every practical sphere.

This volume presents many feats of democracy in its relations to education which are deeply thought and felt, and not merely instinctual, and which probe deeper than personal self-interest and the prejudices of class. In the final section, we relate the debate to issues still much alive in the 1970s, and to a perspective which all friends of education, and of democracy, might ignore to their cost.

Equality of opportunity versus egalitarianism

The 1832 Reform Act did not produce an explicit educational
challenge, like its 1867 successor, since most of the newly
enfranchised were well able to read and write. Indeed, middle-class
influences had long influenced the novel and most forms of
journalism, so that the 'cultural tradition' did not pass into new
hands. What the new voters lacked, of course, was that sense of
somehow possessing the treasures of the past—possessing them
literally even more than mentally and physically often—which was
so much a part of aristocratic rule. No doubt this opened the way
to new forms of philistinism, and utilitarian ruthlessness, of the kind
which Matthew Arnold defined (77) as a major cultural threat.

There were of course forebodings enough that flood-gates were
opening, and that republicanism was the inner meaning of change,
as Paine had already said (1). We trace in the 1840s in particular the
debates between those who see education as a preparation for the
responsible exercise of power and for further slow extensions of the
franchise, and those who think that revolution is needed, and that
education is an irrelevance in itself. Against the rational faith of men
like James Mill and Owen in the almost limitless power of education
to improve society, we balance the neglect of education which
characterised most truly revolutionary thought (e.g. 33, 41).

At the more pragmatic level, we observe a lot of hope being
pinned during the early years of the nineteenth century on the power
of simple literacy and sound moral and religious training to
transform individual children, and through them society, for the
good of all. It was assumed, often with good evidence, that many of
the very poor were sunk in crime, alcoholism and sensuality; and it
was assumed—perhaps with slightly less evidence?—that education
would prove to be, for these ills, a natural cure. It was urged that
when working men learned skills they would work more efficiently
and produce more wealth, to the eventual benefit of all. Arguments
for natural efficiency and international competitiveness proliferated,
and Davies Giddy's mistrust of education (5) was destined to lose
the day.

It was in this context that the notion of much more extensive
education for all emerged into consciousness, along with some sense
of the new and intractable problems that this might bring. There
must indeed have been a certain optimism or *naïveté* in those who
envisaged permanently 'tiered' education, and thought that workers

who became literate would rest happy with that. Was it likely that intelligent men would stop short at the threshold of learning, and accept permanent exclusion from positions of power and wealth? Yet the problems attendant upon universal high culture were still wholly theoretical, and hardly the pressing occasion for very close thought. Elementary education for all was the most that could be hoped for, and in the light of resources, even this seemed a visionary dream. Again, the workers had no power in politics before 1867, and very little afterwards, so the challenge to train them for responsible positions did not press too hard.

When the full Arnoldian vision crystallised in 1869, it opened new horizons, but it was still worked out as much in the face of fears as hopes and ideals. Yet hope is built into it, despite a certain realistic pessimism, and turns on the power of high culture to speak, when allowed, for itself. Arnold believed that Oxford does sing in siren voice to all who come within earshot (78)—a belief which Hardy endorsed, however bitterly, through the young Jude (87). Arnold took for granted also that 'the best that has been thought and known in the world' would indeed be honoured, at the very least by teachers, and that the citadel of culture would never be betrayed from within.

It is of crucial importance that Arnold's vision depends on the doctrine of *equality of opportunity*, which in turn implies academic selection, examination, teaching by ability, and an apparatus for matching pupils with teachers and schools attuned to their needs. This is the situation which the nineteenth century struggled to produce, against the greatest of obstacles, and which the British Labour movement by and large held (e.g. 100) and continued to hold until very recent times. At the start of our period, educational opportunities were almost always subject to class criteria; by the end of it, the right of any child of ability and good motivation to such opportunities had been in principle won. Mrs Trimmer had made very tentative claims for ability as early as the late eighteenth century (2), but she would surely not have foreseen, or approved, the full logic of the Balfour Act.

But here, we bump into perhaps the greatest of ironies attending this great change for the better, which haunted its birth, but matured only with its apparent success. In the outcome the nemesis of equality of opportunity appears to have been *egalitarianism*—a doctrine so superficially akin to it that a great many teachers as recently as the 1950s and 1960s failed to notice the difference, yet so opposed to it in essence as to prove its bitterest foe. Arguably, the capture of the Labour Party by educational egalitarianism in the 1950s will prove to be the most significant and, some may think, the most disastrous development for education for hundreds of years. Yet the possibility of such a capture was foreseen earlier, from the start of our present period almost, and accounts for most of the philosophic—as opposed to the sectarian or merely self-interested— opposition into which democracy ran.

But first, we can notice that in the early days, when 'equality of opportunity' had to struggle against its earlier bitter enemy, the belief in immutable class distinctions, a *form* of egalitarianism at a very low level could be plausibly entertained. 'If every child had the opportunity of entering a workshop', writes Kay-Shuttleworth (34) in 1847: and at this level, one reasonably could hanker after equal attainment as well as equal chance. If every child had the chance to learn a simple skill, surely every child could do it? All of us, short of special handicaps, should be capable of some skill or craft. If all of us could be taught elementary literacy and numeracy, we could mostly achieve them; and these skills, even in rudimentary form, are a prize beyond price. If all of us could be taught the basic principles of Christian doctrine and morality, perhaps we could grasp them; perhaps we could even live up to them, or do our best. Certainly the middle and upper classes were usually less sensual and drunken, less humanly stunted, than the really poor in the nineteenth century; and while this might sometimes have been as much to do with appearances as with realities, the improvement opened up by even elementary education was truly immense (27, 29, 30, 31, etc.).

At this level, yes, egalitarianism may be possible, in that you can not only give children an equal opportunity of achievement but you can hope that they will all achieve, given the level, in a competent way. The real problem sets in when you raise your hopes higher, and begin to take 'equality of opportunity' seriously in Arnold's mode. By 'seriously', we mean as a genuine long-term alternative to a class-based society; as a dynamic which might raise everyone, given time and will, to the top. This includes the top professional jobs, including those in civil service and government, and the training which would fit a born artisan for the highest posts in the land. It was Arnold who really held out this glittering prospect not just as a chimera, but as a goal which the establishment of more secondary schools, more universities, more dedication to culture might eventually achieve. The impetus of democracy certainly

pointed in this direction; and it was becoming clear that the ablest
children would most certainly not remain content with a poor
second best.

But it is precisely here that equality of opportunity ran into a new
and serious problem, of a kind pointing forward to the future, and
no longer back to the past. There was the older problem, of course,
of entrenched privilege, and the possibility that this would make a
bitter and even successful last-ditch stand. But the movement of
history was against entrenched privilege, as Arnold himself well
understood (54). There were the practical problems too of finding
men, resources and money; but, given the will, a way could usually
be found. No: the new and perhaps basic problem concerned those
who might after all fail to scale the heights when given the chance
to do so; those who, whether through laziness, or lack of inherent
talent, or wrong advice given when young, or bad environment, or
for any other cause, fall off the ladder of ability near the bottom,
and find they can never get a foot back on it again. The Arnoldian
vision demands a tiered system of secondary and higher education,
which will produce a race of Miltons only if everyone *is* a 'mute,
inglorious Milton' before the process begins. But·should some—or,
worse, most—prove non-starters, a new élite will inevitably emerge.
This might be highly cultured, or it might be merely successful;
it might, if the worst came to the worst, be not cultured at all.

And, from those who fail, there will surely be anger; and what
will happen, in a democracy, if the majority fail? Under the old
system, a peasant might accept his lot as God-given, and know that
to be a lord or an earl was simply an accident of birth. But under
'equality of opportunity' he will be haunted by a sense of personal
failure, which might be harder, and perhaps intolerable to bear.
He has been given his chance, and has failed to live up to it; what
forms of envy, fear, anger and revolution could this not breed? If
he is very virtuous and realistic he might accept the judgment; if
not, he might decide that 'the system' is wrong.

Again, under the older system, a working-class child had some
escape left open, if he had the energy and desire to attempt Smiles's
'self-help' (50). But in the new system, those who fail remain a
permanent proletariat, a pool of proven non-ability, with no further
educational ladders to climb. If you add to this the near certainty
that many who fail under pure 'equality of opportunity' will come
from upper- or middle-class backgrounds, the possibility of an ugly
and effective revolt can be clearly foreseen. The independent schools

remain, perhaps, as an invaluable safety-valve, but not all middle-class parents will be happy to pay for these.

Allied to this dilemma, there was the chance—some would think the certainty—that philistinism would prevail in a free-for-all over high culture, and that 'equality of opportunity' would lead to 'meritocracy', or to crude 'making good'. As society became richer it became visibly more grasping and worldly as well as more articulately angry, and these Victorian symptoms have stayed with us, unabated, to the present day. And here, we might suspect that one major irony rebounds upon Arnold, whose religious thinking conspired against his cultural hopes. In seeing religion as the child of 'culture' rather than as one of its parents, perhaps he proved a formidable enemy of culture himself. Could it be that the Christian values were precisely the alchemy needed by democracy, if democracy were to fulfil its ideals, and avoid the pitfall of greed? Love; acceptance of people not for their intelligence alone but for their whole inner nature; the true Christian equality hinted at among our writers here by Maurice (80) but by far too few others— are these not the values most vitally needed for the success of majority rule? Without them, culture will surely gravitate in a materialist and cut-throat direction, unless it does indeed prove to have a religious dynamic contained in itself.

What is observable in recent history is that if one enemy of 'high culture' has proved to be cultural relativism in alliance with neo-Marxist rejections of man's past religious and artistic heritage, another enemy has been the increasing obsession with technology, money-making, status, professional training as ends in themselves. These values have increasingly usurped older ideals and have been increasingly resented; if 'culture' *is* merely material goods and pleasures and the gross national product, how can an education based on such things build men up, or heal their divisions, or earn their respect?

One way and another, whether for the reasons conjectured here or for others, we seem now to have arrived at an educational crisis again. Since 1950, the comprehensive secondary schools, which were widely expected to further equality of opportunity and bring it to fruition, have proved to be tools for egalitarianism instead. This development has been paralleled by militant egalitarianism among many educational theorists, accompanied by important shifts in the understanding of 'democracy' itself. In place of universal suffrage and the rule of elected representatives, we have a new ideal of 'participation' at most levels of decision-making in human affairs. It seems possible then that while 'equality of opportunity' was born of 'democracy' while 'democracy' was still modified oligarchy, 'egalitarianism' is the true child of democracy itself.

We are familiar now with 'democracy' as a sanction for complete educational egalitarianism, and with the logic of this ruthlessly applied. There are signs that selection by ability is being outlawed, and that the very concept of ability is considered wrong. Disciplined learning is often treated with contempt and equated with 'rote-learning', while any selection for excellence becomes a rock of offence. Human achievements themselves are questioned, and made to seem relative, so that the most basic aspects of educational curricula are called into doubt. It seems indeed as if the schools which were the crowning achievement of 'equality of opportunity', the modern grammar schools, are at least as offensive to egalitarians as the original schools based solely on class. Professor Eysenck has suggested that the new ideal gravitates towards 'mediocrity'—a system where the honouring of ability, or merit, is itself a sin. We might arrive at a time when defenders of high standards in education are as much disliked as were the old defenders of class privilege, or indeed are actually confused with them, and seen as latter-day Davies Giddys attacking democracy itself.

Certainly, two possibilities of an apocalyptic kind seem to loom in the future, if the more extreme possibilities explored by contributors to this volume are driven to their ends. One is that democracy needs high culture if it is to work properly, and is the best friend of education—opening riches previously reserved for the few to the whole of mankind. The other possibility is that democracy favours the majority view always, irrespective of education, and therefore has an irrevocable bias against education built into itself.

Put another way, one might say that education has to insist, by its nature, on certain precepts, which will be popular or unpopular according to the direction that 'democracy' takes. Education must in the end insist that informed opinion is better than uninformed; that skilled work is better than unskilled; that certain achievements of men really are superior to others and humanly enriching, and that its own prime task is to lift men up towards these. In our documents, we see George Eliot's Felix Holt proclaiming this belief, despite his 'radicalism' (76); but Henry James's sensitive hero vows to destroy tradition; then falls in love with it; and then himself is destroyed (82).

Plato lived well over two thousand years ago, and knew nothing of modern society, even by guesswork, but he had a remarkable insight into the springs of human and political power. For friends of education and of democracy, a warning seems timely; does this general prophecy, from so far in the past, ring at all true?

A democratic state may fall under the influence of unprincipled leaders, ready to minister to its thirst for liberty with too deep draughts of this heady wine; and then, if its rulers are not complaisant enough to give it unstinted freedom, they will be arraigned as accursed oligarchs and punished. Law abiding citizens will be insulted as nonentities who hug their chains; and all praise and honour will be bestowed, both publicly and in private, on rulers who behave like subjects and subjects who behave like rulers. In such a state the spirit of liberty is bound to go to all lengths. . . .
It will make its way into the home, until at last the very animals catch the infection of anarchy. The parent falls into the habit of behaving like the child, and the child like the parent; the father is afraid of his sons, and they show no fear or respect for their parents, in order to assert their freedom. Citizens, resident aliens, and strangers from abroad are all on an equal footing. To descend to smaller matters, the schoolmaster timidly flatters his pupils, and the pupils make light of their masters as well as their attendants. Generally speaking, the young copy their elders, argue with them, and will not do as they are told; while the old, anxious not to be thought disagreeable tyrants, imitate the young and condescend to enter into their jokes and amusements. . . . I had almost forgotten to mention the spirit of freedom and equality in the mutual relations of men and women.
Putting all these items together, you can see the result: the citizens become so sensitive that they resent the slightest application of control as intolerable tyranny, and in their resolve to have no master they end by disregarding even the law, written or unwritten . . . the culmination of liberty in democracy is precisely what prepares the way for the cruellest extreme of servitude under a despot (*Republic*, Book 8).

A. E. Dyson
Julian Lovelock

One   1791–1831 : Sowing of seeds

We start from Tom Paine's assertion (1) that there are two forms
of government, one based on inherited privilege, the other on
'election and representation'. The first requires ignorance for its
operation, the second reason. When a 'republic' exists, then
education is clearly crucial to it, but Paine believes that the 'rights
of man' will have to be fought for, and not merely taught.

Paine's schematic simplifications are a recognisable product of
Lockean empiricism, at the point where it generated among its
ideals both democracy and revolution, and linked them with
education. If men are indeed equal at birth, coming into the world
like 'blank sheets of paper', then an egalitarianism of excellence
seems a real possibility in the truly just state. And, if we are shaped
into maturity wholly by our ability to associate ideas correctly,
and by the forces of environment, then education must be the
golden key to fulfilment and growth. The basic datum is that
environment counts for everything and heredity for nothing. This
eighteenth-century emphasis accounts for the strong strain of
educational utopianism which we meet right at the start of the
period, and in militant forms.

In contrast, Mrs Trimmer (2) assumes that social classes are
immutable—as they politically seemed to be—and that 'happiness'
includes learning to accept one's station in life. But she urges that
it is as unfair to educate children born of poor parents below their
ability as it is to educate children from richer homes above theirs.
The claims of class and the claims of ability are held in balance,
with a moderate plea for more equality of opportunity adapted
to needs.

Lancaster (3) wants children from all classes to be taught basic
skills and moral values, and realises that the strongest opposition to
this among the lower classes may come from the home. Since many
children are sent out to work as soon as they are old enough, they
should be given at least some education in their very earliest years.
He writes as a Christian, and with a certain anger, since he fears

that humanity is being eroded by motives of private gain. The meanness of some parents is matched by state meanness; there is a hint of the 'condition of England' question as it crystallises later with the Chartist revolt (28–33). Lancaster also feels that individuals have a right to personal fulfilment, of the kind which ignorance, and notably illiteracy, must permanently block.

Wordsworth (4) was born in a part of England unblighted by industrialism or class-consciousness, and found 'nature' the best of all possible teachers in this good soil. The teachings of nature were in necessary accord with 'freedom', and with the revolutionary ideals of liberty, equality and brotherhood of 1789. Nevertheless, Wordsworth early regretted that the French victors had too little respect of ancient achievements and traditions (cf. 76), and some ambivalence is detectable in all his work. He finds a spirit of republicanism, for instance, in unreformed Cambridge, in that 'talents and successful industry' are honoured above 'wealth and titles'. There are hints in our brief extract here both of radical conservatism and of revolutionary egalitarianism, the two opposing possibilities always open to such a mind. Wordsworth was to prove fertile ground, too, for later romantic primitivists, who would exalt instinct far above the merely rational mind.

Davies Giddy (5) offers a vintage instance of opposition to education, of the kind which many of our contributors knew that they had to fight. What will education achieve, he asks? It will make the poor dissatisfied and unhappy, building up highly articulate forces of unrest. To finance such ends is surely fantastic, a taxing of virtue 'for the maintenance of vice'. The arguments are characterised by a certain brusqueness, born of the inbuilt assurance that they will carry the day. Historians disagree about whether *laissez-faire* ever was an English ideology, but Davies Giddy's assumptions, whatever name we apply to them, were widely shared in the Commons in 1807.

Robert Owen (6) returns to Lockean territory, with a manifesto claiming for education almost limitless power. In this brief statement the claim has a certain starkness, which allows us to see it in more than one way. The gist is not so much that universal education will lead to democratic government (though this could be deduced from it?) as that governments have the power to manipulate men totally by educational means. If 'education' is taken in its broadest sense, does *1984* lurk in the background? Would *Education and Tyranny* be another context where this extract could appear?

Owen's essays, which formulated the New Lanark experiment in co-operation (7), develop his own variations on the basic theme. By and large, he accepts that education and environment are entirely responsible for the men who are shaped by them, and so for happiness or unhappiness in life. He modifies the complete *tabula rasa* theory, however, by recognising that certain differences between individuals are decreed by God and may be causally explained by events in the womb. His dynamic challenge is that since differences in class are wholly accounted for by social conditioning, these will cease to exist when there is education for all. Owen's hope is for a future egalitarian society in which, when all men achieve their fullest potential, any actual differences between them will prove to be of a minimal kind.

James Mill (8) takes us to the still grander claim that, if one excepts those very few people who come into the world irrevocably damaged, 'the whole of this great race of mankind' are 'equally susceptible of mental excellence'. Here, we have that signpost to a democratic and educational utopia which points along the road of intellect and rational will. The policy was tried out experimentally on John Stuart Mill, as he records in his *Autobiography*, with results that drove him to the verge of suicide in his early adult life. Mill senior waged such an effective war against the imagination and emotions—against all that was not in the Lockean sense purely 'rational'—that he left his son doubting whether he was human at all. In the long run, however, it was James Mill's polar opposites, the romantic primitivists, who were to prove the more tenacious utopians, perhaps because, for all their faults, they realised that men *are* more than machines.

The Committee of 1818 (9) allows us to see that, despite Davies Giddy, education was being taken seriously in official quarters, and that it was assumed on the whole to be a social good. The claim that many of the poor sought education and made great sacrifices for it is born out by evidence assembled by E. P. Thompson in *The Making of the English Working Class*—where Thompson stresses, however, that this quest most frequently allied itself to radical ideas:

There is a sense in which we may describe popular Radicalism in these years as an intellectual culture. The articulate consciousness of the self-taught was above all a *political* consciousness. For the first half of the 19th century, when the formal education of a great part of the people entailed little more

than instruction in the Three Rs, was by no means a period of
intellectual atrophy. The towns, and even the villages, hummed
with the energy of the autodidact. Given the elementary
techniques of literacy, labourers, artisans, shopkeepers and clerks
and schoolmasters, proceeded to instruct themselves, severally
or in groups. And the books or instructors were very often those
sanctioned by reforming opinion. A shoemaker, who had been
taught his letters in the Old Testament, would labour through
the *Age of Reason*; a schoolmaster, whose education had taken
him little further than worthy religious homilies, would attempt
Voltaire, Gibbon, Ricardo; here and there local Radical leaders,
weavers, booksellers, tailors, would amass shelves of Radical
periodicals and learn how to use Parliamentary Blue Books;
illiterate labourers would, nevertheless, go each week to a pub
where Cobbett's editorial letter was read aloud and discussed
(pp. 711–12).

One important recommendation of the 1818 Committee is that
religious instruction should be optional, since this would allow all
sects to send their children to school. The Committee is in favour
of grants to initiate education in areas where it is not yet available,
and holds out the hope that, when the buildings and teachers exist,
running expenses will be met by private charity.

The Rev. W. B. Whitehead (10) is satiric at the expense of
educational utopians, and pitches his own hopes in a lower key.
His starting-point is the two kinds of damage being done by
unsupervised education. On the one hand, dissenters are left with a
virtually free field in some parts of England, to subvert the
establishment; on the other, a free press is spreading sedition among
the newly literate poor. We encounter now the fear that bare
literacy, stopping short of any further refinement of education,
might unleash propaganda and destruction on the state. Whitehead's
perception is that good education is urgently needed to combat the
threat of this, and to harness instruction to the *status quo*.

In 1820, 'A Barrister' (11) questions the notion that there has in
fact been any educational progress, and points out that able children
from poor homes have fewer opportunities now than they often
had in the past. The grammar schools are becoming the preserve of
the 'higher orders' of society and not, as formerly, of all children in
the town they served. This trend is attributed partly to a great
increase in the 'degraded ranks' of society, and partly to 'merely

classical courses' in the schools themselves. The first development has led to a new race of paupers, the second to a basis for selection that favours the already educated class.

In 1825 the London Co-operative Society (12) proposed a scheme for guaranteeing 'the best physical and intellectual education that the present state of human knowledge affords' to its members and their children, assuming that this would maximise health and happiness *per se*. In London this scheme failed for lack of funds, but it drew on the experience of co-operative schools already established elsewhere.

Lord Brougham (13), one of the passionate advocates of education at this time in and out of Parliament, is an example of upper-class idealism at its determined best. He announces to the working class that education is indeed coming, and that they must seize the opportunity themselves. In holding up Franklin as an example of self-help he anticipates Samuel Smiles (50), and strikes a note that was to vibrate for over a hundred years. The call to develop energy and initiative, to seize opportunities and make the best of them, to work for and deserve success, united many Victorians across all barriers of class. We find it in Dr Arnold's Rugby, in the middle-class radicalism of Bright and Cobden, and in nearly all non-revolutionary working-class movements of the time. It is a theme of countless writers, sages, politicians and philanthropic idealists, a hallmark of the peculiar vitality of Britain in the Victorian years. Perhaps indeed it is a hallmark of all healthy societies, an ideal which education, in particular, can neglect only at great risk to itself. Dynamic self-help was one of the forces which certainly went into the building of democracy, and few questions were more crucial than that of whether it would, or could, survive when democracy came.

In 1828, Dr King started *The Co-operator* (14, 15) with the slogan 'Knowledge and Union are Power: Power, Directed by Knowledge, is Happiness: Happiness is the end of Creation'. He argues that since working-class solidarity requires trained intelligence, education must be a priority in the coming years. Education is made a text for some pragmatic lessons—for instance, it teaches men to work not for others' gain, but for their own. King puts much emphasis on temperance and industry, as qualities which are both incentives to education and marks of a properly educated man. Education will initiate a peaceful revolution, at the end of which class distinctions will have ceased to exist.

This section closes with a further insight into the pressures working against education (16) as the ferment which culminated in the 1832 Reform Act grows. Montague Burgoyne, writing as 'a friend of education', is nevertheless horrified by its effect in increasing crime. The poor have had their ambitions raised above their station, and have been trained for jobs superior to the ones they are likely to get. He asserts that, with proper precautions, the poor *can* be given 'a right bias to their minds' by education, and shielded from the anti-social vices common to their kind. But they must be trained to acceptance of their lot and to habits of deference; only so will education be a proper barrier against social change.

In this first section, democracy features chiefly as a lurking but remote possibility, whether it is entertained as a hope or a fear. But we see here widespread awareness of the links between education and the structure of class and even of government, and encounter ideals with an immense potential for future change.

1   Reason versus ignorance

From Tom Paine's *Rights of Man*, Part I, 1791.

Tom Paine was born in 1736 at Thetford, and after a varied and restless life he became an editor and anti-slavery campaigner in the 1770s. *Rights of Man* made him notorious. Several prosecutions followed publication, and it provoked much controversy, during the course of which he prudently stayed in France. He was the only leading English writer of his time to express the abstract doctrine of 'rights' held by the French revolutionaries, and became the hero of extreme English radicals. Died 1809.

Reason and Ignorance, the opposites of each other, influence the great bulk of mankind. If either of these can be rendered sufficiently extensive in a country, the machinery of government goes easily on. Reason obeys itself; and Ignorance submits to whatever is dictated to it.

The two modes of government which prevail in the world, are, *First*, government by election and representation: *Secondly*, government by hereditary succession. The former is generally known by the name of republic; the latter by that of monarchy and aristocracy.

Those two distinct and opposite forms, erect themselves on the two distinct and opposite bases of Reason and Ignorance. As the exercise of government requires talents and abilities, and as talents and abilities cannot have hereditary descent, it is evident that hereditary succession requires a belief from man, to which his reason cannot subscribe, and which can only be established upon his ignorance; and the more ignorant any country is, the better it is fitted for this species of government.

On the contrary, government in a well constituted republic, requires no belief from man beyond what his reason can give. He sees the *rationale* of the whole system, its origin and its operation; and as it is best supported when best understood, the human faculties act with boldness, and acquire, under this form of government, a gigantic manliness . . .

2   Educational opportunity: dangers and challenges

From Sarah Trimmer's *Reflections upon the Education of Children in Charity Schools*, 1792.

Sarah Trimmer (née Kirby) was born in Ipswich in 1741. A friend of Dr Johnson, she became an authoress with special interests in religion and education. In 1786, she was influential in establishing a Sunday school at Brentford, which started with 159 children and by 1788 had over 300, many of them dissenters. Queen Charlotte. consulted her on Sunday school education in 1786, and in the same year she published a book on the theme, *The Oeconomy of Charity*. In 1793, she formed a connection with the SPCK, and wrote many books for 'charity school children and servants'. From 1788 to 1789 she conducted the *Family Magazine* for cottagers and servants, and from 1802 to 1806 the *Guardian of Education*, an examination of children's books. An early pioneer in our field, who died in 1810.

Sunday Schools and *Schools of Industry* . . . afford instruction to unlimited numbers of children, who could not be admitted into *Charity Schools*, on account of the expense attending them; neither could such multitudes be trained up as *Charity Children* are, without great injury to society: for, however desirable it may be to rescue the lower kinds of people from that deplorable state of ignorance in which the greatest part of them were for a long time suffered to remain, it cannot be right to train them *all* in a way which will most probably raise their ideas above the very lowest occupations of life, and disqualify them for those servile offices which must be filled by some of the members of the community, and in which they may be equally happy with the highest, if they will do their duty. . . .

But there are degrees of poverty as well as of opulence; and if it be improper to educate the children of the higher classes promiscuously, it surely must be equally so to place all the children of the poor upon the same footing, without any regard to the different circumstances of their parents, or their own genius and capacity. It would be thought very cruel to send the child, or orphan, of a pious clergyman, or a respectable but reduced tradesman, to be brought up among the offspring of thieves and vagabonds in the schools so happily and judiciously founded for those most wretched of all poor children, by the Philanthropic Society; and it would appear very absurd to send a boy designed for husbandry to the Marine Society, to be educated in the art of navigation.

Yet nothing is more common than to mix poor children together in *Charity Schools*, whose separate claims to the superior advantages which these institutions hold out, are by no means equal, and whose mental abilities will bear no comparison.

It would be justly deemed very illiberal to refuse to lads of bright parts, and uncommon activity of mind, the learning which *Charity Schools* afford, and consign them to the labours of the field; but is it not equally injurious, both to society and individuals, to condemn those who are invincibly dull and stupid to literary studies, as irksome to them as the most servile occupations are to boys of quick parts and aspiring tempers?

If there be among the poor children of a parish any who have been born to good prospects, who have enjoyed in their earliest years the comforts of affluence, and who still have respectable connections, it will be an act of particular kindness to place them in *Charity Schools*, where they will receive such an education as may hereafter prove a means of restoring them to their former station. And if there be others whose bright genius breaks through the thick clouds of ignorance and poverty, reason and humanity plead in their behalf, that they should be indulged with such tuition as may enable them to advance themselves, by the exertion of their abilities, to a higher station, and fill it with propriety. It certainly would be very unjustifiable to deny such children a chance of bettering their condition.

3 Graves of genius

From Joseph Lancaster's *Improvements in Education as it Respects the Industrial Class of the Community*, 1803 (2nd edition).

Joseph Lancaster was born in 1778 in Southwark. From early years, he combined strong piety with a practical desire to help the poor to read. In 1801, he took a large room in Borough Road, and inscribed over it: 'All who will may send their children and have them educated freely, and those who do not wish to have education for nothing may pay for it if they please.' This venture attracted over 1,000 boys, and royal support.

   In 1797 he met Andrew Bell, and together they founded a system of teaching principles. They favoured a military style of discipline, and made famous the phrase, 'A place for everything and everything in its place'. In 1805, Lancaster attracted the patronage of George III, whose words 'It is my wish that every poor child in my dominions should be taught to read the Bible' became a text for the Royal Lancastrian Society. The system was highly controversial, attracting attacks from Mrs Trimmer, from church leaders and others. But Lancaster was instrumental in the founding of many elementary schools, in the growth of the monitorial system, and in formulating important teaching methods. Died 1838.

An introductory Account of the State of those Schools in which the Children of Mechanics, etc. are generally educated.

INITIATORY SCHOOLS

These are a description of schools that abound in every poor neighbourhood about London; they are frequented by boys and girls, indiscriminately, few of them above seven years of age: the mistress is frequently the wife of some mechanic, induced to undertake this task, from a desire to increase a scanty income, or to add to her domestic comforts. The subjects of tuition are comprised in reading and needlework. The number of children that attend a school of this class is very fluctuating, and seldom exceeds thirty; their pay very uncertain.

Disorder, noise, &c. seem more the characteristic of these schools, than the improvement of the little ones who attend them.

These unpleasant circumstances effectually prevent schools of this kind being opened by many females, who possess abilities and goodness of heart. While this is the case, the public will easily conceive the state they must consequently be in, and the small degree of advantage which can possibly result to the poor children who attend them. . . .

. . . Let us turn from the disgusting scene—from these graves of genius, even in its cradle; and see what they would be under proper regulations, which, modified, and carried into effect by prudent hands, would soon direct the public attention to them, as institutions pregnant with real usefulness.—It is very evident, that by the excellent modes of preparatory education, (frequent in the more respectable circles,) much invaluable time is saved, and the foundation of instruction so well laid, that when the pupil is removed to a superior school, much of the drudgery of education is over, and the pupil being ready formed to the master's hand, to good order and prompt obedience, his future progress is considerably accelerated.

Why not realize this idea among the poor, and let them partake of its benefits?—I am an advocate for this class of schools, as women manage them, and the female heart is so well qualified, by its tenderness, to sympathise with the innocent children that attend these schools, and at so early an age that they cannot be placed under better care. The infancy of their pupils requires a combination of the school and nursery, and these schools answer that description, when under proper management. . . .

But it is of peculiar importance to the poor, that these schools should be better regulated, as many children of that class have no education but what they obtain in them, and that at an early age, when totally unfit for other employ; to these, it is of consequence that they should acquire all the knowledge they can while there, for many poor children never obtain a second opportunity.—Frequently their parents are so circumstanced, that they must place them out to work as soon as they are fit for it,—and then farewel to school, to which some would never have been sent, had they been fit for any thing else. It is of consequence to all children, that no time should be spent without improvement, whether they ever attend school afterwards or not. It is of advantage in another point of view: the sober, steady, poor man, cheerfully unites with the endeavours of the benevolent, for his children's welfare: but there are others, so insensible to all idea of gratitude, that they spurn the offered benefit. This mostly happens when their children are able to assist them at work; but when they are too young for work, and are apt to be troublesome at home, their tender age requires a nurse; but nothing can be devised by their parents as a substitute for one, but sending them to an initiatory school, where they are taken care of at a small expense. This is, perhaps, the only opportunity that presents for their instruction during life. Their parents are of the lowest class, by conduct as well as poverty; and would sooner send them to a packthread ground, or other nursery for vice, where their minds are in danger of ruin, for the sake of trifling present gain, than to school, where their morals might be formed aright, and they trained to future usefulness, to themselves and to the community. . . .

. . . I conceive, the improvement children make in these schools would be greatly increased by their being placed under good regulations, supplied with proper mistresses, to whom encouragement might be extended according to merit, also to the scholars, by the same rule. They might be animated to learn reading, writing on slates or in sand, and some small portion of arithmetic, at a very early age.

. . . I cannot close this introduction, without calling the public attention to a distinct, and almost friendless part of the community. I mean the poor children who are in parish workhouses, who are often friendless, and immured in those receptacles of poverty, depression, and vice; without education and without hope; children, for whom it may be said, the sun never shines; to whom curses and ill treatment are too often substitutes for parental smiles, or maternal care. I have often viewed these poor oppressed children, when pacing, with solemn steps and downcast eye, along the streets to a place of public worship; and the settled gloom of unhappiness, visible on some of their countenances, has attracted my sorrowful attention, and forced from my eyes the unavailing tears of pity. . . . Is it not a shame, that the enormous sum of millions sterling should swell the amount of our poor's rates and charities, and yet the poor children be deprived (with some few exceptions) of even an initiatory share of education, and of almost any attention to their morals whatever?

As a citizen of the world, and a friend of mankind, actuated by no sectarian motives in my conduct, but animated by the love of my country, I see, with regret, her noble-hearted sons madly pursuing wealth, and grasping at gain, almost to perdition's door. Are not virtue, integrity, and offices of brotherly kindness, the source of all the comforts we derive from social intercourse?—Are not religion, knowledge, and good morals, the very bands of society?—Why then so eager in the pursuit of riches? and why not rather pay that attention to the infant poor, which their wants require? I wish the enormous wealth of our country may neither prove a scourge to mankind, nor a canker-worm to destroy her own bowels . . .

> Full many a gem of purest ray serene,
> The dark unfathom'd caves of ocean bear;
> Full many a flower is born to blush unseen,
> And waste its sweetness on the desert air.
>
> Gray

SECOND CLASS OF SCHOOLS

The masters of these are often the refuse of superior schools, and too often of society at large. The pay and number of scholars are alike low and fluctuating; of course there is little encouragement for steady men, either to engage, or continue in this line; it being impossible to keep school, defray its expenses, and do the children regular justice, without a regular income. Eventually, many schools, respectable in better times, are abandoned to men of any character, who use as much chicane to fill their pockets, as the most despicable pettifogger. Writing-books, &c. scribbled through; whole pages filled with scrawls, to hasten the demand for fresh books. These schools are chiefly attended by the children of artificers, &c. whose pay fluctuates with their employ; and is sometimes withheld by bad principle. . . .

4   Natural tuition

William Wordsworth's *The Prelude*, IX, 217–48, 1805 text.

Wordsworth was born in 1770 in Cumberland, and became famous as a poet. *The Prelude* traces the evolution of his views, from early radicalism to a later more cautiously conservative outlook. Though in no sense an educationist himself, his romanticism had a great influence on later progressive educationists, and also on novelists with an interest in child psychology. Died 1850.

> For, born in a poor district, and which yet
> Retaineth more of ancient homeliness,
> Manners erect, and frank simplicity,   ·
> Than any other nook of English land,
> It was my fortune scarcely to have seen
> Through the whole tenor of my school-day time
> The face of one, who, whether boy or man,
> Was vested with attention or respect
> Through claims of wealth or blood; nor was it least
> Of many debts which afterwards I owed
> To Cambridge and an academic life
> That something there was holden up to view
> Of a Republic, where all stood thus far
> Upon equal ground; that they were brothers all
> In honour, as of one community,
> Scholars and gentlemen; where, furthermore,
> Distinction lay open to all that came,
> And wealth and titles were in less esteem
> Than talents and successful industry.
> Add unto this, subservience from the first
> To God and Nature's single sovereignty,
> Familiar presences of awful power,
> And fellowship with venerable books,
> To sanction the proud workings of the soul,
> And mountain liberty. It could not be

But that one tutored thus, who had been formed
To thought and moral feeling in the way
This story hath described, should look with awe
Upon the faculties of man, receive
Gladly, the highest promises, and hail,
As best, the government of equal rights
And individual worth.

5   Ignorance is bliss, and costs less

From a speech by Davies Giddy, MP, from *Hansard*, 13 July 1807.

Davies Giddy was born in 1767 in Cornwall, of which he was High
Sheriff from 1792 to 1793. He became an MP in 1804, and was
extremely hard-working, with a strong desire to help the arts and
sciences, and especially literature. On educational matters he was no
radical, or a friend of radicals; his London home was attacked by
a mob in 1815 during Corn Bill riots.

[PAROCHIAL SCHOOLS BILL.] Mr. *Whitbread* moved the second reading
of the Parochial Schools bill. The question being put,
    Mr. *Davies Giddy* rose and said, that while he was willing to allow
the hon. gent, who brought forward this bill, every degree of credit
for the goodness of his intentions, as well as for his ability and assiduity;
still, upon the best consideration he was able to give the bill, he must
totally object to its principle, as conceiving it to be more pregnant
with mischief than advantage to those for whose advantage it was
intended, and for the country in general. For, however specious in
theory the project might be, of giving education to the labouring
classes of the poor, it would, in effect, be found to be prejudicial to
their morals and happiness; it would teach them to despise their lot in
life, instead of making them good servants in agriculture, and other
laborious employments to which their rank in society had destined
them; instead of teaching them subordination, it would render them
factious and refractory, as was evident in the manufacturing counties;
it would enable them to read seditious pamphlets, vicious books, and
publications against Christianity; it would render them insolent to

their superiors; and, in a few years, the result would be, that the legislature would find it necessary to direct the strong arm of power towards them, and to furnish the executive magistrates with much more vigorous laws than were now in force. Besides, if the bill were to pass into a law, it would go to burthen the country with a most enormous and incalculable expence, and to load the industrious orders of society with still heavier imposts. It might be asked of him, would he abolish the Poor-Laws altogether? He had no hesitation to declare he would; for, although they relieved many persons, who were certainly objects of compassion, they were also abused by contributing to the support of idleness and profligacy; and he never could admit it to be just or reasonable that the labour of the industrious man should be taxed to support the idle vagrant. This was taxing virtue for the maintenance of vice. . . .

6   Education and government

From Robert Owen's *A New View of Society*, 1813.

Owen was born in 1771 in Montgomeryshire, and became a leading socialist. On his marriage, he became part owner of New Lanark mills, and took on their government on 1 January 1800. There, his notions on co-operation and education could be given practical expression; they developed amid considerable controversy, and were formulated in *A New View of Society*. Great emphasis is placed on strength of character, notably on honesty and sobriety; Owen was influenced by the Bell and Lancaster plans, and himself claimed to be the founder of infant schools. His New Lanark institution became famous, influencing Brougham on the one hand, and the Tory government under Lord Liverpool on the other. In 1824 he helped to promote a 'London Co-operative Society', and later engaged in a variety of secular and socialist initiatives. Died in 1858.

Any character, from the best to the worst, from the most ignorant to the most enlightened, may be given to any community, even to the world at large, by applying certain means; which are to a great extent at the command and under the control, or easily made so, of those who possess the government of nations.

7 Grand and beneficial purposes

From Robert Owen's *A New View of Society*, 1813–16 (see 6 above).

From first essay (written 1812, published 1813)

According to the last returns under the Population Act, the poor and working classes of Great Britain and Ireland have been found to exceed twelve millions of persons, or nearly three fourths of the population of the British Islands.

The characters of these persons are now permitted to be very generally formed without proper guidance or direction, and, in many cases, under circumstances which directly impel them to a course of extreme vice and misery; thus rendering them the worst and most dangerous subjects in the empire.

From third essay (first printed for sale 1816)

The principle then on which the doctrines taught in the New Institution are proposed to be founded, is, that they shall be in unison with universally revealed facts which cannot but be true.

The following are some of the facts which, with a view to this part of the undertaking, may be deemed fundamental.

That man is born with a desire to obtain happiness, which desire is the primary cause of all his actions, continues through life, and, in popular language, is called self-interest.

That the desire of happiness in man, the germs of his natural inclinations, and the faculties by which he acquires knowledge, are formed, unknown to himself, in the womb; and, whether perfect or imperfect, they are alone the immediate work of the Creator, and over which the infant and future man have no control.

That these inclinations and faculties are not formed exactly alike in any two individuals: hence the diversity of talents, and the varied impressions called liking, and disliking, which the same external objects make on different persons, and the lesser varieties which exist among men whose characters have been formed apparently under similar circumstances.

That the knowledge which man receives, is derived from the objects around him, and chiefly from the example and instruction of his immediate predecessors.

That when the knowledge which he receives is true, and unmixed with error, although it be limited, if the community in which he lives possesses the same kind and degree of knowledge, he will enjoy happiness in proportion to the extent of that knowledge. On the contrary, when the opinions which he receives are erroneous, and the opinions possessed by the community in which he resides are equally erroneous, his misery will be in proportion to the extent of those erroneous opinions.

That when the knowledge which man receives shall be extended to its utmost limit, and true without any mixture of error, then he may and will enjoy all the happiness of which his nature will be capable.

That it consequently becomes of the first and highest importance that man should be taught to distinguish truth from error.

That man has no other means of discovering what is false, except by his faculty of reason, or power of acquiring and comparing the ideas which he receives.

That all men are erroneously trained at present, and hence the inconsistences and misery of the world.

That the fundamental errors now impressed from infancy on the minds of all men, and from whence all their other errors proceed, are, that they form their own individual characters, and possess merit or demerit for the peculiar notions impressed on the mind during its early growth.

That the evil and misery which arise from accidents, disease, and death, are also greatly increased and extended by man's ignorance of himself.

That when these truths are made evident, every individual will necessarily endeavour to promote the happiness of every other individual within his sphere of action; because he must clearly, and without any doubt, comprehend such conduct to be the essence of self-interest, or the true cause of self-happiness.

Here then is a firm foundation on which to erect vital religion, pure and undefiled, and the only one which, without any counteracting evil, can give peace and happiness to man. . . .

From fourth essay (first published for sale 1816)

No one, it may be supposed, can now be so defective in knowledge as to imagine that it is a different human nature, which by its own power forms itself into a child of ignorance, of poverty, and of habits leading to crime and to punishment; or into a votary of fashion, claiming distinction from its folly and inconsistency; or to fancy that it is some undefined, blind, unconscious process of human nature itself, distinct from instruction, that forms the sentiments and habits of the men of commerce, of agriculture, the law, the church, the army, the navy, or of the private and illegal depredator on society; or that it is a different human nature which constitutes the societies of the Jews, or Friends, and of all the various religious denominations which have existed or which now exist. No! human nature, save the minute differences which are ever found in all the compounds of the creation, is one and the same in all; it is without exception universally plastic, and, by judicious training, the infants of any one class in the world may be readily formed into men of any other class; even to believe and declare that conduct to be right and virtuous, and to die in its defence, which their parents had been taught to believe and say was wrong and vicious, and to oppose which, those parents would also have willingly sacrificed their lives.

The kind and degree of misery or happiness experienced by the members of any community, depend on the characters which have been formed in the individuals which constitute the community. It follows that every state, to be well governed, ought to direct its chief attention to the formation of character; and that the best governed state will be that which shall possess the best national system of education.

Under the guidance of minds competent to its direction, a national system of training and education may be formed, to become the most safe, easy, effectual, and economical instrument of government that can be devised. And it may be made to possess a power equal to the accomplishment of the most grand and beneficial purposes. . . .

. . . The time is now arrived when the British Government may with safety adopt a national system of training and education for the poor and uninstructed . . . As a preliminary step, however . . . this national system should be uniform over the United Kingdom; it should be also founded in the spirit of peace and of rationality; and for the most obvious reasons, the thought of exclusion to one child in the empire should not for a moment be entertained.

8   Education and excellence

From James Mill's contribution on 'Education' to the *Encyclopaedia Britannica*, 1815.

James Mill was born in 1773 in Scotland. He became known as a philosopher and contributor to leading journals, and around 1808 established himself as a friend and disciple of Bentham. In education, the utilitarians supported Bell and Lancaster, and Mill emerged as a bitter opponent of sectarian church education. In 1814, an association was formed to set up a school for superior education; Bentham's treatise *Chrestomathia* expounded the principles, and the foundation of London University was one notable outcome. In 1824, Mill was associated with the start of the *Westminster Review* as a radical organ. Perhaps he is most famous for the experiment in education conducted on his son, and described in John Stuart Mill's *Autobiography*. The younger Mill acquired incredible erudition in his early years, but was emotionally stunted, and later came to the verge of suicide. James Mill died in 1836.

M. Helvétius says, that if you take men who bring into the world with them the original constituents of their nature, their mental and bodily frame, in that ordinary state of goodness which is common to the great body of mankind,—leaving out of the account the comparatively small number of individuals who come into the world imperfect, and manifestly below the ordinary standard,—you may regard the whole of this great mass of mankind, as equally susceptible of mental excellence; and may trace the causes which make them to differ. If this be so, the power of education embraces every thing between the lowest stage of intellectual and moral rudeness, and the highest state, not only of actual, but of possible perfection. And if the power of education be so immense, the motive for perfecting it is great beyond expression. . . .

One of the causes, why people have been so much startled, by the extent to which Helvétius has carried the dominion of education, seems to us to be their not including in it nearly so much as he does.

They include in it little more than what is expressed by the term schooling; commencing about six or seven years of age, and ending at latest with the arrival of manhood. If this alone is meant by education, it is no doubt true, that education is far indeed from being all-powerful. But if in education is included every thing, which acts upon the being as it comes from the hand of nature, in such a manner as to modify the mind, to render the train of feelings different from what it would otherwise have been; the question is worthy of the most profound consideration. It is probable, that people in general form a very inadequate conception of all the circumstances which act during the first months, perhaps the first moments, of existence, and of the power of those circumstances in giving permanent qualities to the mind. . . .

It is evident how much it imports the science of education, that these circumstances should, by careful and continued observation, be all ascertained, and placed in the order best adapted for drawing from them the most efficient practical rules. This is of more importance than determining the question, whether the prodigious difference, which exists among men ordinarily well organized, is owing wholly to the circumstances which have operated upon them since the first moment of their sensitive existence, or is in part produced by original peculiarities. Enough is ascertained to prove, beyond a doubt, that if education does not perform every thing, there is hardly anything which it does not perform: that nothing can be more fatal than the error of those who relax in the vigilance of education, because nature is powerful, and either renders it impossible for them to accomplish much, or accomplishes a great deal without them: that the feeling is much more conformable to experience, and much more conformable to utility, which ascribes every thing to education, and thus carries the motive for vigilance and industry, in that great concern, to its highest pitch. This much, at any rate, is ascertained, that all the difference which exists, or can ever be made to exist, between one *class* of men, and another, is wholly owing to education. Those peculiarities, if any such there be, which sink a man below, or elevate him above the ordinary state of aptitude to profit by education, have no operation in the case of large numbers, or bodies. But large numbers or bodies of men are raised to a high degree of mental excellence; and might, without doubt, be raised to still higher. Other large bodies, or whole nations, have been found in so very low a mental state, as to be little above the brutes. All this vast distance is undeniably the effect of education. This much, therefore, may be affirmed on the side of Helvétius, that a prodigious difference is produced by education; while, on the other hand, it is rather assumed than proved, that any difference exists, but that which difference of education creates.

9   The poor anxious for education

From *Third Report from the Select Committee on the Education of the Lower Orders*, June 1818.

Your Committee have the greatest satisfaction in observing, that in many schools where the national system is adopted, an increasing degree of liberality prevails, and that the church catechism is only taught, and attendance at the established place of public worship only required, of those whose parents belong to the establishment; due assurance being obtained that the children of sectaries shall learn the principles and attend the ordinances of religion, according to the doctrines and forms to which their families are attached.

It is with equal pleasure that Your Committee have found reason to conclude, that the Roman Catholic poor are anxious to avail themselves of those Protestant Schools established in their neighbourhood, in which no catechism is taught; and they indulge a hope, that the Clergy of that persuasion may offer no discouragement to their attendance, more especially as they appear, in one instance, to have contributed to the support of schools, provided that no catechism was taught, and no religious observances exacted. . . .

Your Committee are happy in being able to state, that in all the Returns, and in all the other information laid before them, there is the most unquestionable evidence that the anxiety of the poor for education continues not only unabated, but daily increasing; that it extends to every part of the country, and is to be found equally prevalent in those smaller towns and country districts, where no means of gratifying it are provided by the charitable efforts of the richer classes.

In humbly suggesting what is fit to be done for promoting universal education, Your Committee do not hesitate to state, that two different plans are advisable, adapted to the opposite circumstances of the Town and County districts. Wherever the efforts of individuals can support the requisite number of schools, it would be unnecessary and injurious to interpose any parliamentary assistance. But Your Committee have clearly ascertained, that in many places private subscriptions could be raised to meet the yearly expenses of a School, while the original cost of the undertaking, occasioned chiefly by the erection and purchase of the schoolhouse, prevents it from being attempted.

Your Committee conceive, that a sum of money might be well employed in supplying this first want, leaving the charity of individuals to furnish the annual provision requisite for continuing the school, and possibly for repaying the advance.

Whether the money should be vested in Commissioners, empowered to make the fit terms with the private parties desirous of establishing schools, or whether a certain sum should be intrusted to the two great Institutions in London for promoting Education, Your Committee must leave to be determined by the wisdom of Parliament.

In the numerous districts where no aid from private exertions can be expected, and where the poor are manifestly without adequate means of instruction, Your Committee are persuaded, that nothing can supply the deficiency but the adoption, under certain material modifications of the Parish School system, so usefully established in the Northern part of the Island, ever since the latter part of the seventeenth century. . . .

10   Good education for driving out bad

From W. B. Whitehead's *Letter to Rt. Hon. the Viscount Sidmouth*, 1820.

The Rev. W. B. Whitehead described himself as 'Vicar of Twiverton, Somerset and late Fellow of Worcester College, Oxford'. His letter concerned the 'expected Parliamentary provision in furtherance of general education suggested by the Reports of the Education Committee of the House of Commons'.

Your Lordship well knows, that it is the fashion, with all the more philosophically reforming philanthropists of the day, to felicitate themselves upon the rapid approach of a new era of light and refinement. . . . Animated by the apparent dawn of this brilliant day, they

c

already enjoy in anticipation the virtuous delight with which they expect, ere long, to have to rebuild the antiquated fabric of society. . . . They console their followers under present disappointments, by telling them, that they will have to curb their impatience for a little while only, until the sun of renovated intellect, which is now rising, shall have dissipated the mists of ignorance, prejudice, and bigotry.

These, my Lord, are believed to be the expectations of a large body of modern reforming illuminati, religious as well as political; and the present appearances of popular education amongst us have greatly contributed to raise them. These unquiet visionaries see the flood wide and powerful, but the banks which should restrain its impetuosity, and the safe channels which should direct its course, weak in quality, and few in number; and thus they are led to hope, that, instead of fertilising the land, as we ardently wish it might, by spreading over it in refreshing and regular order, it may, ere long, involve all our present vitiated systems in one resistless and renovating inundation.

My Lord, it is certainly the opinion of many experienced observers of the times, that there is, in the causes which excite these criminal hopes, something to hold out the promise of their realisation. It is evident everywhere, that the propagators of erroneous opinions of all kinds are using education, under its improved plans, which are too often apt to cultivate the mind too much and the heart too little, as their most favorite instrument of conversion and future strength; while it is equally clear, that the really beneficial instruction of the people, in the least disordered parts of the kingdom, is greatly obstructed, if not nearly prevented, by the want of adequate means to support it, even on the smallest scale. In the populous towns and districts, it is true, the exertions of dissent have been most zealously and liberally met by the friends of established religion and order, under the beneficent auspices of the 'National Society'; but, in these apparently charitable, though, in a great measure, also party rivalries, the external advantages are at present inconsistently equal on both sides. The State, at present, regards with an equal want of protection the efforts of both, and these struggles, therefore, in which the vital interests of the country are at issue, are too apt to be considered by the indolent and the thoughtless, as mere contests for superiority between indifferent opinions, or between equally beneficial charitable establishments. Private patriotism, in the mean time, however zealous, must relax, whilst the hopes of sectarianism must proportionably rise under this unseemly, and impolitic, and too disinterested impartiality.

But the progress of that spirit of error and disorder which spreads

54

on all sides, from the populous centres of dissenting education, is absolutely unprovided against by any systematic instruction in the great majority of the agricultural parishes of the kingdom; and thus, in those large districts in which, beyond all others, with a little exertion, the minds and feelings of the people might be preserved orthodox in principles, and patriotic in attachments, they are at present left exposed, without any means of self-defence, to the first attempted encroachments or seductions, or schism, or sedition.

But, whilst such disastrous prospects are opened by this misdirected excitement of the popular mind, there is an engine in league with those who indulge in them, vast in its power, which is constantly adding to and taking advantage of that excitement. The licentiousness of the press, as its valuable liberty, has, in too many instances, become, and has, indeed, for some time, been proving itself to be, the most powerful instrument which disaffection ever had to work with among an ill-educated people. It is sedulously endeavouring, as your Lordship too well knows, to fasten its destructive fangs upon every mind in the community which is at all released from the fetters of ignorance, and to render its sweetened poison acceptable wherever education has communicated even the least relish for literary employment.... An unprincipled press and injudicious or irregular education are, in this manner, working together in the cause of religious and social disorganisation; the one preparing the soil, which the other renders fertile in every noxious produce....

It is considered, I will assume, by the Legislature, that irreligion, and vice, and opinions hostile to the fundamental institutions of the State, are alarmingly prevalent in the community, occasioned by much popular ignorance, on the one hand, and a wrong education of the lower orders of the people, on the other. As the official and sworn guardians of all the great national interests, the Legislature, under these circumstances, wisely determine, that the right education of the people would be the best remedy for the growing evils; and they fix, of course, the established principles of Church and State, as the basis of that education, because, as I have already endeavoured to prove, they could not, as conscientious men, confiding in the excellent tendencies of their own belief, and as conscientious legislators, under exclusive institutions, give the smallest facility to the dissemination of other or anti-constitutional doctrines. They, accordingly, appropriate a portion of the general public revenue, or the produce of special local taxes, paid equally, in each case, by persons of all civil and religious persuasions, to the establishment and support of such a system of general instruction. What is there in this, my Lord, I venture to ask, bordering even upon hardship towards Dissenters? The legislature, by so acting, force not their instruction upon those who cannot conscientiously receive it; neither do they contract, in the smallest degree, the privilege of all persons to educate their children in their own way, and at their own expense. They only offer, in the strict discharge of their most momentous duties, without prejudice to any right, or necessary injury to any conscience, the means of gratuitous education to the people at large, in the ancient and recognised principles of their country; principles, which they know will make them, if sufficiently inculcated, good Christians, and good subjects.

11   The new race of paupers

From a tract by 'A Barrister' entitled *Grammar Schools Considered, with reference to a case lately decided by the Lord Chancellor*, 1820.

This anonymous pamphlet concerned a suit in Chancery 'instituted by the inhabitants of Bingley, Yorks, in administration of their Free Grammar School'.

It is probable that by the operation of the poor laws and by taxation, the lower orders have retrograded into a state in which the founders of these schools did not calculate on so many of the excluded by condition ever being in existence.—There was once a time when the lower ranks presented more members to the Church than now, in consequence, without doubt, of their being competent to attend these schools in their boyhood joined to greater facilities of rising being open to them when these posts were less anxiously sought for by the higher orders. . . . The terms which, at an earlier period, would embrace all the inhabitants of a town as candidates, or leave the excluded, as exceptions only to a general invitation will now fall short, and not reach the new race of paupers, the circumstances attendant on whose poverty will so frequently shut them out of the Grammar School. . . . Perhaps the increase of population has taken place most considerably among the degraded ranks. . . . Without entering here on the controversy upon the right of admission it may be remarked, that to allow the degraded ranks to be *indirectly* unfit candidates for Grammar Schools, by no means implies the higher orders to be sole proper occupiers of their forms; yet, to this event does the exclusive adherence to merely classical courses threaten to be carried.

12   To all children, the best

From the Manifesto of the London Co-operative Society, *Article XII*, 1825.

In 1821, some printers started the Co-operative and Economical Society, which set up a community at Spa Fields. Several artisan families lived together, sharing their incomes, educating their children, and producing various articles for sale, with an emphasis on quality of workmanship. The first London Co-operative Society was set up in 1824, and its educational policy is contained in this extract from the Manifesto.

To all the children entering the Community, or born within it, we guarantee the best physical and intellectual education that the present state of human knowledge affords, *an advantage for which our peculiar arrangements afford facilities not to be obtained by any exertion of toil, or sacrifice of wealth, in the present state of society*. To maintain uninterrupted health during the longest possible life, and to render that life the most happy, diversified by all the innocent pleasures of sense, of active exertion, of knowledge, of sympathy, and mutual benevolence, with every variety and combination of these enjoyments will be the great objects of the general education of the whole Community. The *mode* of education, combining always practice with theory, the Community will hereafter determine. To individual parents, and those teachers in whom they confide, the teaching of their peculiar religious tenets is assured: with religious instruction the general teachers are forbidden to interfere.

13   Not whether, but how

From H. Brougham's *Practical Observations upon the Education of the People*, 1825.

H. Brougham was born in 1778 in Edinburgh. He set out to become a lawyer, but his restless talent and versatility led him in other directions. In 1802 he helped to found the *Edinburgh Review*, which became for many years his chief vehicle. He entered the Commons in 1810, and became a peer, and Lord Chancellor, under Grey in 1831. After 1820, he was much concerned with education, and, with Dr Birkbeck, helped to set on foot several mechanics' institutes. In 1825, he published the tract from which this extract comes, which ran into many editions. Also in 1825, he helped to found the Society for the Diffusion of Useful Knowledge (see note to 17 below). For the next fifteen years he was continually active in this field, and conducted what was virtually a pressure group in the interests of infant education. Died 1868.

To the Upper Classes of society, then, I would say, that the question no longer is whether or not the people shall be instructed—for that has been determined long ago, and the decision is irreversible—but whether they shall be well or ill taught—half informed or as thoroughly as their circumstances permit and their wants require. Let no one be afraid of the bulk of the community becoming too accomplished for their superiors. Well educated, and even well versed in the most elevated sciences, they assuredly may become; and the worst consequence that can follow to their superiors will be, that to deserve being called their *betters*, they too must devote themselves more to the pursuit of solid and refined learning; the present public seminaries must be enlarged; and some of the greater cities of the kingdom, especially the metropolis, must not be left destitute of the regular means within themselves of scientific education.

To the Working Classes I would say, that this is the time when by a great effort they may secure for ever the inestimable blessing of knowledge. Never was the disposition more universal among the rich to lend the requisite assistance for setting in motion the great engines of instruction; but the people must come forward to profit by the opportunity thus afforded, and they must themselves continue the movement once begun. Those who have already started in the pursuit of science, and tasted its sweets, require no exhortation to persevere; but if these pages should fall into the hands of any one at an hour for the first time stolen from his needful rest after his day's work is done, I ask of him to reward me (who have written them for his benefit at the like hours) by saving threepence during the next fortnight, buying with it Franklin's Life, and reading the first page. I am quite sure he will read the rest; I am almost quite sure he will resolve to spend his spare time and money, in gaining those kinds of knowledge which from a printer's boy made that great man the first philosopher, and one of the first statesmen of his age. Few are fitted by nature to go as far as he did, and it is not necessary to lead so perfectly abstemious a life, and to be so rigidly saving of every instant of time. But all may go a good way after him, both in temperance, industry and knowledge, and no one can tell before he tries how near he may be able to approach him.

14   Education and working-class power

From *The Co-operator*, October 1828.

The Co-operator was edited for the Co-operative Movement by
Dr King of Brighton, who described working men as mere counters
'in the power of the capitalists'.

This mistrust of *laissez-faire* was not, of course, exclusively
radical. *Blackwood's* argued in April 1830 that the workers were
regarded merely as 'beasts of burden' by Whig economists, and the
belief that Whig bankers were disrupting the older class harmony
of Britain was held by many Tories, long before Disraeli made it
famous in *Sybil* (1845).

But the main attack on capitalism naturally came at this period
from radicals, along—very importantly—with practical efforts and
organisations of the kind advocated by King.

THE CO-OPERATOR

KNOWLEDGE AND UNION ARE POWER:
POWER, DIRECTED BY KNOWLEDGE, IS HAPPINESS:
HAPPINESS IS THE END OF CREATION.

No. 6	OCTOBER 1, 1828.	1d.

A CO-OPERATIVE SOCIETY; OR WORKING UNION.

ITS PRINCIPLES, RULES AND MANNER OF FORMATION.

1. THE OBJECTS.—The objects of such a Society are, first, the mutual
protection of the members against POVERTY: secondly, the attainment
of a greater share of the COMFORTS of life: thirdly, the attainment of
INDEPENDENCE by means of a common capital. . . .

5. UNION and DISUNION are the two pivots upon which turn the
happiness and misery of the world. Disunion is the natural fruit of
ignorance and barbarism. Ignorance is the condition of incipient
existence; it is therefore, also the condition of men in a rude and
uncivilized state. . . .

11. Hence a Working Union, having the same object as a Benefit Union—namely, comfort and independence—endeavours to obtain that object by different means. The minds of the members are more enlightened, and therefore their means are more enlightened. Their knowledge is farther advanced, and they accordingly use more intelligent measures: they see that the old methods do not succeed sufficiently—they therefore search for new ones. . . .

18. QUALIFICATIONS OF MEMBERS.—The members of such a Society should be carefully chosen.

I. They should be all of the working class. The reason of this rule is—first, that labour is the only source of wealth: and capital is of no use till it is converted, by labour, into the comforts and luxuries of life. Secondly, in the present state of society, the different classes do not easily amalgamate: they are jealous of each other. The higher person is apt to look down upon the lower with some degree of contempt, and cannot bear to converse with him as an equal. . . .

. . . II. The members should all be good and skilful workers—able to earn a certain sum per week, to be settled by the rules: the most useful trades should be chosen; and there should not be too many of the same trade.

III. They should be persons of good character—industrious, sober, steady and quiet.

IV. They should not be ignorant and prejudiced persons, but as well informed as their rank in life admits of, and desirous of adding to their knowledge and improving their minds, as far as their circumstances and opportunities allow. . . .

. . . XI. The Society should meet in their own room once a-week, for the mutual instruction and improvement of the members in the principles of such Unions. The subject of the evening's conversation should be given out at the preceding meeting. Books on the subject may be read, and their arguments considered. One member should preside as chairman, and the office should be filled by rotation.

XII. On the other evenings of the week, those members who have leisure, should meet at the room and form themselves into classes for mutual instruction. As the societies will consider labour to be the source of all wealth, and therefore be called Working Unions, so they will perceive that labour must be directed by KNOWLEDGE, and therefore they will acquire all the useful knowledge they possibly can.

XIII. Agreeably to this principle, they will begin to pay particular attention to the education of their children. They should select the best school the neighbourhood affords; and agree to send their children to the same, on condition that the members of the society may visit the school and notice the progress of the children. But a still more desirable plan would be, to have a school of their own, and employ a master, at a salary.

XIV. This school should combine learning with industry, that the children should not acquire either pride or laziness, but habits of active carefulness. . . .

15   The power of reading

From *The Co-operator*, December 1828. See 14 above.

KNOWLEDGE

13. Many circumstances have occurred within the last year, nay within the last few months, to show that the working classes are approaching towards the knowledge and practice of co-operation. The great obstacle in the way of co-operation is the ignorance of the working classes. This ignorance is fast dissipating. Knowledge in general has accumulated among men of science and the upper classes, to such an extent, that it has necessarily spread to the workman. The complicated relations of society compel every man, however low his rank, to acquire some portion of knowledge. A workman or servant cannot fill his situation without reading and writing. The power of reading is followed by the use of it. The reading of absurd and useless trash gradually gives way to a taste for something useful and improving, and even books of science have reached the hands and are comprehended by the minds of the working classes. No man ever lost the love of knowledge when once acquired, neither will the working classes undervalue that which will assuredly lead them to independence. As their knowledge increases, they will know the principles of co-operation, and to know them is to ensure their being acted upon.

14. This knowledge, those of the working classes who begin to understand co-operation, will endeavour to acquire as far as their leisure permits. It will be one of their first principles, because they will perceive that it is only ignorance which leaves a man to do so foolish

a thing as to work for another instead of himself; and that it is only knowledge which enables a man of capital to live without work.

16   Education for deference

From Montague Burgoyne's *Address to the Governors and Directors of the Public Charity Schools*, 1830 (2nd edition).

Burgoyne was born in 1750 in Bedfordshire; he held a profitable sinecure under Lord North, and was also for many years verderer of Epping Forest. His main enthusiasm was for the allotment system, but he contributed pamphlets to various debates. Died 1836.

Your Lordships must be fully aware of the powerful effects produced by the education of the lower ranks upon the interest and welfare of the Society at large. If a good direction be not given to the knowledge afforded by the few to the many . . . then our Altars, our Throne, and the just property of individuals will be soon trampled on. If one part of the instruction given, be not to learn truly to *labour*, to get their own living, and to do their duty . . . I very much fear that the result of the Education given, will be discontent, idleness, and vice. Though sincerely disposed to give my neighbour every species of knowledge, I have been alarmed by an omission of labour and industry in most of our Public Schools. I have observed their good effects when introduced, and the fatal consequences when omitted.* . . . It is not uncommon to observe, boys and girls of the age of 14, on quitting Public Schools, well instructed in Reading, Writing, and Arithmetic, sometimes in History and Mathematics; the boys competent for the situation of a Clerk, a Writing-Master, or an Engrosser; the girls qualified for Governesses or upper servants; but, unfortunately, the market is overstocked with these superior qualifications; and when they are called for, one is chosen, and forty-nine are disappointed. What is the consequence of the disappointment? Discontent, perhaps idleness and vice. The unfortunate young persons have aspired too high. Happy

* The place to which the Author alludes, is the Town of Brighton.

would it have been for the boys if they had made more use of the plough, the spade, the awl, and the needle, and less of the pen. The situation of the females is still more to be deplored: unaccustomed to works of labour, and the menial offices of housewifery, they are unwilling to apply their hands to such low employments; they expect higher situations, and finding them not, they at last fall a prey to vice and misery. I have seen children, after quitting the Public Schools, singing ballads in the streets, and having recourse to all manner of idle and wanton tricks, for want of employment. Their parents have boasted to me of their attainments, but deplored their profligacy. It is a melancholy fact, as notorious as it is extraordinary, and as unexpected as it is appalling to the Friends of Education, that with all the pains taken to instruct and improve the lower ranks of Society, the March of Intellect has been attended with an increase of crime. In vain may we shut our eyes to this dismal result of our labours in the cause of Education. In vain may we attribute it to the increase of our population; it is far beyond the proportion. Let us consult the Judges of Assize; let us examine our Calendar; let us ask those to whom the custody of our criminals and malefactors is committed. Nay, let us consult our own experience and observation in the different walks of life; do we find more or less industry, more or less anxiety in the labouring classes, to provide for themselves without being an expensive burthen to their neighbours? Alas! the poors' rates speak volumes, and, if not speedily reformed, must involve the kingdom in ruin and confusion. But, with the increase of expense, occasioned by the wants of the Poor, do we find more respect to their superiors and gratitude to their benefactors? Do they order themselves more lowly and reverently to their betters? If these questions cannot be answered according to our wishes, there must be something radically wrong in our System of Education. . . .

But, God forbid that these difficulties should damp our zeal, or form an obstacle in the way of Education; or to our desire to expand and develope the human mind. . . . Numberless instances occur in this nation, and particularly in the metropolis, where benevolent individuals are employed in administering relief to distress under every shape which it assumes. But the higher and noble aim of preventing those calamities which lead to idleness and crimes, and produce poverty and misery, by guiding and properly directing the early conduct of the lower orders of the community, and by giving a right bias to their minds, has not, as yet, generally attracted the notice of those who move in the more elevated walks of life. . . . The prosperity of every state depends on the good habits, and the religious and moral instruction of the labouring people. By shielding the minds of youth against the vices that are most likely to beset them, much is gained to society in the prevention of crimes, and in lessening the demand for punishments. The laws have done much to punish offences: It remains yet to do much for prevention. This desideratum, of such incalculable importance to the great interests of society, is best attained by giving proper instruction to the inferior classes in early life.

It is not, however, proposed by this institution, that the children of the poor should be educated in a manner to elevate their minds above the rank they are destined to fill in society, or that an expense should be incurred beyond the lowest rate ever paid for instruction. Utopian schemes for an extensive diffusion of knowledge would be injurious and absurd. A right bias to their minds, and a sufficient education to enable them to preserve, and to estimate properly, the religious and moral instruction they receive, is all that is, or ought ever to be, in contemplation. To go beyond this point would be to confound the ranks of society upon which the general happiness of the lower orders, no less than those that are more elevated, depends; since by indiscriminate education those destined for laborious occupations would become discontented and unhappy in an inferior situation of life, which, however, when fortified by virtue, and stimulated by industry, is not less happy than what is experienced by those who move in a higher sphere, of whose cares they are ignorant, and with many of whose anxieties and distresses they are never assailed.

Two   1831–1860: Crisis and evolution

We come now to the start of our main story, which spans the years between the two great Reform Acts of 1832 and 1867, and has its climax in 1870. In this period, the movement in English society is towards democracy, and the education debate takes new point and edge. Dreams and nightmares continue and intensify, but there is much practical thought and planning as well. Most of our writers are well aware of social fluidity and crisis, and of major changes destined to come, whether they like them or not. In this present section, the emphasis is on crisis. First, there are the years of poverty and unrest which produced the Chartist uprisings, and the bleak social analyses of the 1840s. The working classes discover that the new middle-class voters whom they helped to power in 1832 have no answering gratitude, and that the lot of the poor is becoming worse. Then later, there is the first decade of the Great Exhibition era and of the new *laissez-faire* ascendancy—more apparently stable, as Asa Briggs has argued (in *Victorian People*), but with the forces of change still potently at work.

In 1831, Lord Brougham's Society for the Diffusion of Useful Knowledge launched the *Quarterly Journal of Education*, which identified the education of the educators as its primary task (17). When the poor do become literate, what will they learn? With luck, the new quarterly decides, a number of lessons—though by no means the ones envisaged by Dr King (15). They will learn, for instance, that private property is a blessing to all classes of society, whether propertied or otherwise, and that this is a foundation and immutable truth. They will learn of the dangers of anarchy; of the power of machines to produce wealth for everyone as long as no one smashes them; and of the pressing need to limit the size of families among the poor. We stand or fall together as one nation, and the poor must be encouraged to see this as clearly as do the rich.

A modern reader will find the Malthusian argument for population control familiar, though in the context of contraception—free, or even compulsory—rather than of disciplined celibacy and self-restraint. Whether this change is judged to be progress, regress, technological adjustment or mere irony, may affect a reader's response to the extract as a whole.

In 1832, we come to J. Phillips Kay (19), who on his marriage ten years later became James Kay-Shuttleworth, and who was to be one of the great educational thinkers of his time. He links the ill fortunes of education with 'commercial restrictions', which deter capitalists from co-operating with the better education of their workers, as they surely otherwise would. Some of his arguments recall the previous extract, but there is a more subtle and sensitive mind at work. In urging that the human heritage of great art and literature should be on general offer he anticipates Matthew Arnold (77), and the vision of universal education with no upper levels prescribed. Again, he anticipates George Eliot (76) and other writers of the 1860s in seeing that a merely semi-literate populace might be raised to revolution, and sweep all past achievements away in a general wreck. In a period marked by political ferment, he urges the need for popular consent in government, if not popular rule. Any government needs to have informed public opinion on its side for major decisions, if it is to rule effectively without depending upon tyranny or naked power.

This is more searching than anything we have previously encountered, and various questions hover in the air. It is still an attempt to ally the *status quo* to popular education, but Kay no doubt realises the implications for long-term change. If education really produces, in time, a fully literate electorate, further extensions of the franchise will surely follow as a matter of course? Most early nineteenth-century educationists envisaged working-class education as the three Rs and basic morality, but with nothing over and above these that could lead workers to real cultural equality with the rich.

John Stuart Mill's piece from 1832 (20) is equally seminal, if in a somewhat different way. He welcomes the coming rule of the people, but only if this is exercised through their representatives and is not direct. If the democracy should ever decide that all men's opinions are *in fact* of equal value, it would become anti-educational in an irrevocable sense. Uninformed opinion would claim equality with informed opinion, and mass ignorance would win the day. Ideally, the democracy will choose men of trained ability for the business of ruling, and respect their judgment even when public opinion swings the other way. But Mill sees that pressure groups will flatter the new sovereign power, the people, as they once flattered oligarchs, appealing to popular prejudice over their elected rulers' heads.

This raises a problem that is touched on much later by Bagehot (81) and Shaw (96) among others, and that is clearly still crucial today. Will Burke's doctrine that MPs are the electors' representatives and not their tools be carried over into democracy, or will democracy press for 'participation' whenever policy decisions are at stake? Will the democracy opt for equality of opportunity, and respect for educated opinion, or will it opt for egalitarianism at whatever level the enfranchised majority achieves? Mill couldn't foresee (no doubt) that MPs might become the tools of Cabinets, or of constituency workers or of party conferences, but he could foresee the pressure from public opinion direct. This in turn raises the question of whether the majority ever *will* achieve excellence (as Mill's father had so confidently expected), and of what might happen to 'excellence' if they don't? The fight for excellence would obviously be a long, uphill battle; but what if genetic reality were enlisted in the enemy camp?

In 1833, Roebuck (21) also prophesies the coming of popular rule. As a Benthamite radical, he assures MPs that though few of them will understand the importance of educational issues, he is infallibly interpreting for them the signs of the times. His chief moral is that education will be a vital factor in the coming democracy, since the people will not otherwise know where their true happiness lies.

The *Quarterly Journal of Education* of 1834 (22) seeks to refute the argument that increases in crime are due to education (e.g. 16) by offering the maladministration of the Poor Laws as an alternative cause. It argues that, in favourable conditions, education produces better workmen and more harmonious industrial relations, and that no causal connection between the new literacy and the new rioting exists. The Rev. H. C. Curtis is quoted as saying that the 'natural . . . distinction of the higher from the lower class consists in their intellectual attainments', and as envisaging a kind of race towards improvement, with the upper classes leading the way. When all have reached 'the highest point of improvement which in the present dispensation is possible to man', social classes will presumably continue to exist, unaltered in structure, but at a much higher level of general attainment than at the start of the race.

In 1835, the *Quarterly Journal of Education* (23) again offers educational progress as the one path leading to a happy society, stirring together a number of now familiar ideas. It picks out sectarianism as the chief enemy of progress—a view which the Rev. J. Gilderdale refutes in 1838 somewhat starkly (24), taking for granted 'the scanty opportunities of the poor'.

In 1839, J. Phillips Kay now dramatises the challenge (25). When the labouring poor were dispersed through England in isolated cottages, their ignorance had been no threat to society, but neither did the conditions for alleviating it exist. Now, the accumulation of population in cities makes ignorance socially dangerous, but provides the opportunity, also, to build schools. Kay has an eye to the needs of all classes, including the lowest, and expresses a 'confident belief' that 'every hour increases the anxiety of all friends of our constitutional liberties and national institutions, to preserve both by the education of the people'.

We come now to a caution, from Dr Arnold (26). The truly educative factor, he says, is property ownership; men without property are likely always to be reckless, and hard to predict. He confesses that cause and effect are difficult to distinguish in such matters, and that it is perplexing to know where to begin.

At our stage of history in the 1970s, Arnold's point might have a bizarre appearance, but it links with a fairly general uncertainty about the way ahead. Which should come first, property, or the power that goes with it; which should come first, education or the vote? On 29 September 1838, J. E. Taylor had written in the *Manchester Times*: 'Let the people have a good education, and, with the habits it would induce, the bribe of the intoxicating draught would be less powerful. Till then the elective franchise could not with safety be extended.' Sir Benjamin Heywood had a similar message in 1840 when he addressed the Mechanics' Institution at Manchester. Speaking of the ambition of workers to raise their condition, he said 'they must do it by exerting themselves for their own moral and intellectual improvement. Instead of seeking, in the first instance, an extension of their political privileges from the legislature, let them seek a system of rational and liberal education for themselves and their children.' The Chartists, on the other hand, were unimpressed by this ordering, as Henry Vincent's programme for election at Ipswich in 1842 showed. His formal address, published in the *Suffolk Chronicle* on 13 August 1842, included among its aims first, the endeavour to obtain electoral reform upon the basis of complete suffrage, and second, the provision of a more widespread education in order that 'the child of the honest poor man should have its mind trained in everything requisite for the

promotion of its spiritual, moral, political and social interests'.
A statistic for 1839 given by G. D. H. Cole and Raymond Postgate
(in *The Common People*) highlights the dilemma: 'The percentage of
illiterates was 41·6 in 1839 (men 33·7 and women 49·5) and it
remained virtually unchanged until 1846 and probably later.'

It was in the late 1830s that the Chartists appeared on the scene,
making the crisis no longer chronic but acute. (Asa Briggs, indeed,
has argued in *Chartist Studies* that the Whigs started to go ahead
with plans for educational reform in 1838, a little before Chartism
emerged as a major force, for fear that agitation should be fostered
for educational ends.) In 1839, we find Lord Brougham summing
up the extreme frustrations suffered in Parliament by those who
have fought for education (27), and reasserting that infant education
is now a crying social need. There is a brusque warning, too, from
the Marquess of Lansdowne (28), whose concern is decidedly more
with social stability than with infant rights.

In 1840, Carlyle (29) names and crystallises the 'condition of
England' question, saying that it appears, and to him 'has for many
years appeared, to be the most ominous of all practical matters
whatever. . . .' He diagnoses working-class violence as a madness,
and asserts that however the madness is interpreted, a remedy for
it must urgently be found. The analysis which he then makes is
one which is to be heard again and again in the next decade, from
political figures as diverse as Disraeli and Engels, and from novelists
and social prophets alike. The older unity of the English people—
however partial it was, and based on whatever inequalities—seems
to have disappeared, leaving a population in which the great
majority are permanently oppressed and uneducated, and at the
mercy of a minority with position and wealth. England has become,
in Disraeli's famous phrase, 'two nations, the rich and the poor';
and these two nations are at war with one another in their social
relationships and locked in mutual antagonism, even though England
is bound to stand or fall as one nation in the end. In *Sybil* (1844)
Disraeli pointed to two ancient roots of the catastrophe. The first
was the dissolution of the monasteries by Henry VIII in the 1530s,
which had shattered an older feudal harmony and sacrificed religion
to human greed. The second was the growing power of the Whig
bankers, notably after the 1689 revolution, and the coming of a
form of capitalism into which principles of inhumanity and social
divisiveness were deeply built. In the 1840s, Disraeli and the Young
England Movement half hoped for a new alliance between

aristocracy and workers, ranged together in mutual independence against the new capitalist middle classes. Possibly this romantic notion had some basis in social history and observable psychology (indeed, this is virtually certain), but it was unlikely to solve the crisis of the times. For the next few years, the reality of class warfare was continually dramatised in fiction by writers wholly different from each other in temperament, in political views, and in their search for solutions. The novels include *Vanity Fair*, *Dombey and Son*, *Shirley*, *Mary Barton*, *Bleak House* and *Hard Times* to name only the most famous, all of them produced in the decade from 1845 to 1855.

From the Chartists themselves, we reproduce here an extract from Lovett (30), that gentle and self-taught cabinet-maker whose prose glows at times with charity, despite its polemical edge. Like Carlyle, he believes that knowledge is a human heritage, not a class prerogative, and that its blessings should be transmitted to all men as of right. But he sees that little is to be hoped for from Parliament or from the elected government, partly because ignorance is not confined to the working class. The upper classes are profoundly short-sighted in tolerating injustices whose consequences will destroy perpetrators, as well as victims when the reckoning comes. The middle classes chase illusory goods—wealth, status and material possessions—forfeiting that true happiness which lies quite another way.

Samuel Wilderspin (31) echoes Brougham's views (and indeed whole paragraphs of his writing: cf. 27) writing as an experienced teacher of infants; Dr Arnold (32) insists that 'some degree at least of intellectual and spiritual cultivation' must be on offer to all. And in 1844 Engels (33) says the things they are nearly all afraid of: that the middle classes have no desire to help the workers; that slavery is still the lot of the majority, as it always has been; that a class war is raging, and has to be fought to the death. Engels's analysis is marked by hatred of the past, sanctioned by a passionate ideology of social justice which will prove itself prepared to write off all human religion and perhaps all human art and achievement as a ruling-class trick. In effect, he sees education as an irrelevance, unless it stirs the workers to revolution and issues in a total break with society as it has hitherto been. Engels's book was not translated into English till many years in the future, but its tenor was a potent factor on thinking in the years to come.

In 1847, Kay-Shuttleworth (34) draws attention to the condition

of schoolmasters, returning the debate to practicalities, and to
immediately pressing affairs. His depiction of the worst kinds of
school teaching is a reminder of Dickens's vivid portrayals of
Squeers in *Nicholas Nickleby* (1838–9), of Creakle in *David
Copperfield* (1849–50) and many more. And—on the other side of
the picture—the voices of short-term self-interest are still audible.
The Rev. B. Parsons (35) warns in 1847 of the iniquity of taxes,
and asks if men are really to be their brothers' keepers, at such a
price? Thomas King (36) urges that the rights of individuals to
education coincide with national self-interest, and wonders whether
England is to fall behind foreigners, and even Russians, in the
civilised scale.

In 1847, *The Labourer* (37) considers education in the context of
political in-fighting, and detects deep duplicity in Russell's
approach. The Whigs, who have been cast in a villainous role by
the Rev. B. Parsons (35) for having anything to do with school-
houses, are now trounced with equal gusto from the other side.
The anonymous writer urges that it is a government's duty 'to do
as the majority of the male adult population will they should do',
and takes for granted that this *de facto* exercise in democracy would
tell for efficient education on a national scale. The reference to new
methods of rote learning no doubt draws attention to the
Lancaster/Bell system, which according to Cole and Postgate
(op. cit., p. 308) tended to replace the teaching methods of many
dame and parish schools, bad though these had often been, with a
wholly mechanical chanting of questions and answers. The founders
themselves had said of this discovery that it could 'with great
propriety' be called 'the Steam Engine of the Moral World', and it
is presumably an ingredient in the merciless fact-grinding which
Dickens depicted so vividly in *Hard Times* (1854).

In David Stow (38) we come across a far more humane view of
education, allied to the now familiar sense of crisis. By this point
in the 1840s, many writers believe that national education is
essential, and that it will and must come eventually, but they are
correspondingly aware of obstacles blocking the path. The Rev.
A. P. Perceval (39) might be considered as one such obstacle
incarnate; and we follow his grave constitutional warning with
three brief and tangential aspects of the educational scene. First,
boarding-school accounts (40) with their down-to-earth costing,
from a Pembrokeshire farmer who sent his son as far afield as
Bristol to school. Then, a further indication of the low priority of

education in the Marxist scheme of things, from *The Communist Manifesto* (41).

And third, an extract from *Wuthering Heights* (42) which outlines Heathcliff's educational plans in a context far removed from democracy or from national schools. Heathcliff's policy is to take a naturally gifted child and to brutalise him, and to take a naturally ill-fated child and make him shine. His motive is hatred and his aim mischief, yet he believes in education as firmly as Robert Owen or James Mill.

Is this relevant to our present story; or would *Education and Tyranny* again be the more fitting home? At least it shows that education *need* not be allied to high ideals or even to sane self-interest, and that it *need* not seek as its end any 'higher good'. It suggests that a war might be declared between genetic potential and environmental conditioning, for reasons of a recognisably human, if capricious, kind. Part of our story here is the progress towards a national system of education—and while few people, as yet, wanted the state to have a monopoly of education, the connection between monopoly and tyranny was well understood. Heathcliff is no doubt a bizarre and unusual figure, and not least in his attempt to oppose and reverse natural gifts. Yet, if some such impulse lurks in egalitarianism and if egalitarianism is 'democratic', our inclusion of Heathcliff may have more than a glancing point. Modern readers can take some comfort from Heathcliff's 'fiendish laugh', since this at least marks him off from egalitarians of the idealistic kind. And perhaps it is worth noting that Emily Brontë records the failure of his system; the good and bad in human nature prove too strong for education to change.

In 1852, the Rev. B. Parsons (43)—at the opposite pole to educational monopoly and to *that* aspect of tyranny—defends voluntaryism and *laissez-faire* to the death. Cobden is taken to task for failing to live up to himself on the educational question, and urged to renounce state interference in any shape or form. Now that the golden age of market forces is dawning, should education not be trusted to look after itself? In contrast with most of the testimony assembled in this, or in any possible collection, Parsons draws a glowing picture of educational advances in the early nineteenth century on the voluntary base. The working classes are merely waiting for an end to state interference in order to liberate themselves into the sturdiest educational self-help. In conclusion, he interestingly perceives a new conspiracy between tory and radical, and between 'despots and certain *soi-disant* democrats', working against the 'rational liberty' represented by no government sponsored education at all.

Also in 1852, Mill (44) reflects on the need for quantity as well as quality in education, and—emancipated at last from his father's rigid utilitarianism—points to the awakening of 'imagination' as an important aim. He asserts that a society in which wealth is more equally distributed is desirable, but stresses that working-class self-discipline and social conscience must be the other side of this coin. Free and equal discussion across class barriers is the 'best instruction' (an insight with which Thomas Hughes, 48, agrees). Finally from 1852, two sharply contrasting pieces: Newman's vision of the inherent worth of university training as an ideal to aspire towards (45), and Dickens's depiction of one of the really poor in the London streets (46).

In 1856, Bagehot (47) brings into the open the thought that democracy and education might yet prove incompatible partners, especially if a 'tyranny of the commonplace' is the destined child of their match. In 1857, Thomas Hughes (48) regrets that the classes are growing further apart through pursuit of riches and status, and sees healthy muscular exercise as a better leveller than most. True equality exists, he suggests, only in real relationships; yet how many of us see in the 'lower orders' the same flesh and blood as our own?

Mill's piece from *On Liberty* (1859) is another insight of the kind which has become more, not less, relevant with the passage of time (49). He argues that the state has the duty of enforcing education, but that it has no right to establish a monopoly itself. The dangers of educational monopoly are as great under a democracy as under aristocracy or any other form of government; education can become a mere contrivance for moulding people to be exactly like one another, an instrument in state tyranny or in the reduction of man. In the same year, Samuel Smiles's *Self-Help* (50) champions sturdy individualism, in the faith that merit and hard work *can* earn their due reward. He greatly admires Dr Arnold's ideal, notably touching the development of character, and grasps that this is appropriate for men of all classes and in all kinds of need. 'Character is power': in expounding this precept, Smiles might be thought too sanguine about the actual state of his own society, but it is arguably the foundation for any education deserving the name.

This would be a hopeful note on which to end this present section; but we add two reminders (51 and 52) that all was far from

well in many schools. Dr Hodgson is giving evidence to an official
committee; Dickens is writing of a fictional past, set in the 1820s,
but certainly with an eye—as Hodgson demonstrates—to the
contemporary scene.

17 Educating the educators

From *Quarterly Journal of Education*, 1831.

This journal was set up as an organ for the Society for the
Promotion of Useful Knowledge (see note to 13 above). The
Society sponsored penny magazines, penny cyclopedias, etc., but this
new journal was clearly intended more for the middle-class liberal
idealists who promoted the Society and its aims than for the workers
themselves.

The Society attracted hostility equally from traditionalists and
radicals. A writer in *Blackwood's Edinburgh Magazine* of 1834 attacked
the Society for its secularism, saying 'it is religion which must form
the basis of every system of education which is to be really
beneficial, and if that one ingredient is wanting, all that is mingled
in the cup will speedily be turned to poison.' From the other side,
Thomas Hodgskin had said of such enterprises as early as October
1823, in the *Mechanics' Magazine*: 'Men had better be without
education, than be educated by their rulers; for their education is
but the mere breaking in of the steer to the yoke.'

The new journal's views can be judged also from 18, 22 and 23
below.

It is the opinion of the Committee that the general education of those
classes of the community, who, from their station in society, have the
control over that of the poorer classes, is the most important object to
which they can direct their attention. They do not intend to neglect
either the statistics of the education of the poorer classes, or the books
which are used for their instruction, nor any other fact of any kind
that concerns so large a part of the population. But the education of
that class, on which depends the education of all the rest, demands
their especial attention.

18   Showing the poor their real interests

From *Quarterly Journal of Education*, 1831. See 17 above.

Hitherto it would seem as if those who have promoted the education of the poor imagined they had done quite enough when they taught them to read and write. But though this much be indispensable, still it is certain that the education which stops at this point is most incomplete, and may, indeed, be perverted to the very worst purposes. A knowledge of the arts of reading, writing, and arithmetic may, and frequently does, exist along with the most profound ignorance of all those things as to which it is most essential that the poor should be informed; it opens an inlet to truth, but so does it to error and sophistry; and it is the bounden duty of the rulers of every country, at least if they would make sure of their own safety, and provide for the welfare of their people, to take especial care, not only that the avenues to knowledge shall be opened to the poor, but that they shall be instructed in the mode of distinguishing what is true from what is false—at least in so far as their leading interests and those of society are involved. . . . They should, first of all, be made acquainted with the motives which have induced every society emerging from barbarism to establish the right of property; and the advantages resulting from its establishment, and the necessity of maintaining it inviolate, should be clearly set forth. The sophisms of those who contend that property is instituted only for the advantage of the rich should be exposed; for though it cannot be shown that the institution of private property has made all men rich, it may very easily be shown that it has done ten times more than all other institutions put together to produce that effect; and that were it subverted, the rich man would very soon become poor, while he that is at present poor would become still poorer. The circumstances that give rise to those gradations of rank and fortune that actually exist ought also to be explained: it may be shown that they are as natural to society as differences of sex, of strength, or of colour; and that though such a revolution were to take place as should overthrow all that is exalted . . . the equality thus violently and unjustly brought about could not be maintained for a week; and that infinite misery would be inflicted on society without obtaining any countervailing good whatever.

The next object should be to make the poor fully acquainted with the various benefits resulting from the employment of machinery in industrious undertakings; and they should be shown, that though such employment may sometimes appear to lessen the demand for labour, its real effect is *always to increase it*; and that their interests are invariably promoted by the adoption of every device that can in any way add to the powers of production.

But it is, above all, necessary that the labourers, and indeed that every class, should be acquainted with the circumstances that determine the rate of wages, or with the plain and elementary principles respecting population and the demand for labour. We certainly have no wish to extenuate the faults of the rulers of any country; but to ascribe, as so many do, all the poverty and distress abroad in the world to the agency of government, argues either the most deplorable ignorance or the most barefaced knavery. . . . Wherever the number of labourers, as compared with the demand for their services, is redundant, wages will be low, whatever be, in other respects, the situation of such country; and wherever labour is not redundant as compared with the demand, wages will be good. The important and undoubted truth ought, therefore, to be early impressed upon the poor, that they are themselves, in a great measure, the arbiters of their own fortune; that the means of subsistence and of comfort are in their own hands; and that what others can do for them is but as the small dust of the balance compared with what they can do for themselves. Frugality and forethought are the virtues which they should be taught to cultivate; and it is principally by their cultivation that man is distinguished from the lower animals. The former teaches to husband our present means, while the latter warns us not to expose ourselves to the risk of lengthened privations hereafter for the sake of immediate gratifications. Notwithstanding no effort whatever has at any time been made to open the eyes of the poor as to what is so essential to their welfare, their natural sagacity has led them to act in the way that is most beneficial for themselves. The difficulty of providing for the wants of a family being far greater here than in America, marriages amongst us are generally deferred to a later period, and many find it expedient to lead a life of celibacy. Now if the natural and untutored sagacity of the people has made them so far control their passions, can it be doubted that this control would have been far more effective had all classes been made fully aware of the importance of moral restraint? And to do this would not certainly be a very difficult task; it would not require any very great cogency of reasoning to convince even the most obtuse that it is their duty to provide for the support and instruction of the beings they bring into the world; and that to discharge this duty they should decline marrying until they have made some little provision against contingencies, or obtained a reasonable prospect of being able to support themselves and their families. We do not pretend that this, or indeed that any instruction would prevent all improvident unions; but it is not possible to doubt that it would have a very powerful and salutary influence.

Such are the leading subjects with respect to which it is of the last importance that the poor should be thoroughly instructed. If we show them clearly wherein their real interest consists, if education be made to embrace objects of undoubted utility, and if they be explained with that clearness, and enforced with that earnestness, which their superior importance requires, we shall have done the most that can be done to ensure the tranquillity of the country, and the prosperity of the higher as well as of the lower classes. . . .

19　Ignorance twice a curse

From J. Phillips Kay's *The Moral and Physical Condition of the Working Classes Employed in the Cotton Manufacture in Manchester*, 1832.

J. Phillips Kay, born in Rochdale in 1804, has been called the founder of the English system of popular education. He was a medical student at Edinburgh, where he first became interested in the condition of the poor. His philanthropic efforts brought him to the notice of the government (perhaps ironically) as one specially fitted to introduce the new Poor Law of 1834. For some years, he injected into the working of this law, as one of its servants, more humanity than (say) Dickens's Oliver Twist encountered; and he published a valuable government paper on the training of pauper children in 1841.

From 1839, he devoted himself to introducing a 'national system of education'. In 1839, he was appointed first secretary of a Committee to administer government grants for education, and continued to display a special concern for pauper children in the metropolis. In pioneering such fields as teacher training, the public inspection of schools, the pupil-teacher system, the balance between religious instruction and liberty of conscience, and the financing of education he was, as Dr Arnold said, a key figure. In 1842 he married Janet Shuttleworth, and assumed the name by which he later was known—James Kay-Shuttleworth—by royal licence.

We believe that no objection to a reduction of the hours of labour would exist, amongst the enlightened capitalists of the cotton trade, if the difficulty of maintaining, under the present restrictions, the commercial position of the country did not forbid it. Were these restrictions abolished, they would cease to fear the competition of their foreign rivals, and the working classes of the community would find them to be the warmest advocates of every measure which could conduce to the physical comfort, or moral elevation of the poor.

A general and efficient system of education would be devised—a more intimate and cordial association would be cultivated between the capitalist and those in his employ—the poor would be instructed in habits of forethought and economy; and, in combination with these great and general efforts to ameliorate their condition, when the restrictions of commerce had been abolished, a reduction in the hours of labour, would tend to elevate the moral and physical condition of the people.

We are desirous of adding a few observations on each of these measures. Ere the moral and physical condition of the operative population can be much elevated, a system of national education so extensive and liberal as to supply the wants of the whole labouring population must be introduced. Ignorance is twice a curse—first from its necessarily debasing effects, and then because rendering its victim insensible to his own fate, he endures it with supine apathy. The ignorant are, therefore, properly, the care of the state. Our present means of instruction are confined to Sunday Schools, and a few Lancasterian and National Schools, quite inadequate to the wants of the population. The absence of education is like that of cultivation, the mind untutored becomes a waste, in which prejudices and traditional errors grow as rankly as weeds. In this sphere of labour, as in every other, prudent and diligent culture is necessary to obtain genial products from the soil; noxious agencies are abroad, and, while we refuse to sow the germs of truth and virtue, the winds of heaven bring the winged seeds of error and vice. Moreover, as education is delayed, a stubborn barrenness affects the faculties—want of exercise renders them inapt—he that has never been judiciously instructed, has not only to master the first elements of truth, and to unlearn error, but in proportion as the period has been delayed, will be the difficulty of these processes. What wonder then that the teachers of truth should make little impression on an unlettered population, and that the working classes should become the prey of those *who flatter their passions, adopt their prejudices, or even descend to imitate their manners.*

If a period ever existed, when public peace was secured, by refusing knowledge to the population, that epoch has lapsed. The policy of governments may have been little able to bear the scrutiny of the people. This may be the reason why the fountains of English literature have been sealed—and the works of our reformers, our patriots, and our confessors—the exhaustless sources of all that is pure and holy, and of good report, amongst us—*have not been made accessible and familiar to the poor.* Yet, literature of this order is destined to determine the structure of our social constitution, and to become the mould of our national character; and they who would dam up the flood of truth from the lower ground, cannot prevent its silent transudation. A little knowledge is thus inevitable, and it is proverbially a dangerous thing. Alarming disturbances of social order generally commence with *a people only partially instructed*. The preservation of *internal peace*, not less than the improvement of our national institutions, depends on the education of the working classes.

Government unsupported by popular opinion, is deprived of its true strength, and can only retain its power by the hateful expedients of despotism. Laws which obtain not general consent are dead letters, or obedience to them must be purchased by blood. But ignorance perpetuates the prejudices and errors which contend with the just exercise of a legitimate authority, and makes the people the victims of those ill-founded panics which convulse society, or seduces them to those tumults which disgrace the movements of a deluded populace. Unacquainted with the real sources of their own distress, misled by the artful misrepresentations of men whose element is disorder, and whose food faction can alone supply, the people have too frequently neglected the constitutional expedients by which redress ought only to have been sought, and have brought obloquy on their just cause, by the blind ferocity of those insurrectionary movements, in which they have assaulted the institutions of society. That good government may be stable, the people must be so instructed, that they may love that *which they know to be right*.

The present age is peculiarly calculated to illustrate the truth of these observations. When we have equally to struggle against the besotted idolatry of ancient modes, which would retain error, and the headlong spirit of innovation, which, under the pretence of reforming, would destroy . . . shall we hesitate to guide the vessel of the state, by the power of an enlightened popular opinion? The increase of intelligence and virtue amongst the mass of the people, will prove our surest safeguard, in the absence of which, the possessions of the higher orders might be, to an ignorant and brutal populace, like the fair plains of Italy, to the destroying Vandal. The wealth and splendor, the refinement and luxury of the superior classes, might provoke the wild inroads of a marauding force, before whose desolating invasion, every institution which science has erected, or humanity devised, might fall, and beneath whose feet all the arts and ornaments of civilized life might be trampled with ruthless violence.

Even our national power rests on this basis, which power is sustained 'not so much by the number of the people, as by the ability and character of that people';* and we should tremble to behold the excellent brightness and terrible form of a great nation, resting, like the 'image' of the prophet, on a population, in which the elements of strength and weakness are so commingled, as to ensure the dissolution of every cohesive principle, in that portion of society, which is thus not inaptly portrayed by the feet which were part of iron and part of clay.

The education afforded to the poor must be substantial. The mere elementary rudiments of knowledge are chiefly useful, as a means to an end. The poor man will not be made a much better member of society, by being only taught to read and write. His education should comprise such branches of general knowledge, as would prove sources of rational amusement, and would thus elevate his tastes above a companionship in licentious pleasures. Those portions of the exact sciences which are connected with his occupation, should be familiarly explained to him, by popular lectures, and *cheap treatises*. To this end, Mechanics' Institutions (partly conducted by the artisans themselves, in order that the interest they feel in them may be constantly excited and maintained) should be multiplied by the patrons of education, among the poor. The ascertained truths of political science should be early taught to the labouring classes, and *correct* political information should be constantly and industriously disseminated amongst them. Were the taxes on periodical publications removed, men of great intelligence and virtue might be induced to conduct journals, established for the express purpose of directing to legitimate objects that restless activity by which the people are of late agitated. Such works, sanctioned by the names of men distinguished for their sagacity, spirit, and integrity, would command the attention and respect of the working classes. The poor might thus be also made to understand their political position in society, and the duties that belong to it—'that they are in a great measure the architects of their own fortune; that what others can do for them is trifling indeed, compared with what they can do for themselves; that they are infinitely more interested in the preservation of public tranquillity than any other class of society; that mechanical inventions and discoveries are always supremely advantageous to them; and that their real interests can only be effectually promoted, by displaying greater prudence and forethought.'†

* Cobbett's Cottage Economy. Introduction.
† McCulloch, on the rise, progress, and present state of the British Cotton Manufacture. Edinburgh Review, No. 91.

20   When the people are wrong

From John Stuart Mill's editorial comment in *The Examiner*,
15 July 1832.

John Stuart Mill, born in 1806, is too famous as a philosopher to
require notes. Under his father's tuition (see note to 8 above) he
was one of the most precocious children ever; he inherited, but
later humanised his father's utilitarianism, and indeed spent much
time attempting to incorporate tests of quality as well as quantity
into the calculations of hedonism. This early piece is one of his
many contributions to *The Examiner*, with which he shared the aim
of keeping radicals from becoming a mere extreme wing of the
Whigs. In its apprehension of future problems, it seems far ahead
of its time. Throughout his life, Mill's socialism was tempered by a
lively sense of the dangers as well as the opportunities of democracy.

For our part, we avow, that when the Tory prints accused the Reformers of seeming to set up a government of mere numbers, instead
of one of intelligence, *our* denial of the imputation was sincere. Such
never was our object. A government of honesty and intelligence was
all we sought, and our quarrel with the old government was, that its
character was the very reverse. We know that the will of the people,
even of the numerical majority, must in the end be supreme, for as
Burke says, it would be monstrous that any power should exist capable
of permanently defying it: but in spite of that, the test of what is right
in politics is not the *will* of the people, but the *good* of the people, and
our object is, not to compel but to persuade the people to impose, for
the sake of their own good, some restraints on the immediate and
unlimited exercise of their own will. One of our reasons for desiring a
popular government was, that men whom the people themselves had
selected for their wisdom and good-affections, would have authority
enough to withstand the will of the people when it is wrong. And it is
surely some presumption that the people are in the wrong, if they
cannot find any man of ability who will do as they wish him, without

being pledged to it. We ourselves do not think that the public opinion, except where it has adhered to the impressions of early education, has often gone far wrong heretofore; but this is because the people have for the most part acted upon our principle, and have not yet learnt the doctrine that they are to hear appeals on all subjects, from the decision of the most competent judges. We must recollect, however, that the people are now the sovereign: as such, it is they who will now be the objects of flattery; it is to them that the interested, the discontented, and the impatient, will henceforth carry their complaints. Every factious minority, every separate class, every adventurer who seeks to rise by undermining those above him, will endeavour to obtain, not as before from the oligarchy, but from the people, what has been refused by the people's representatives: and the grand instrument of success will be, persuading the people, that no thought, no study, no labour, give any superiority in judging of public measures, and that the question immediately on the *tapis*, whatever it be, no matter how complicated, is level to every man's capacity. Where the popular mind is not kept steady by confidence in superior wisdom, these tactics will frequently succeed. The man who says, Judge for yourself, you are wise enough, has an immense advantage over him who can only say, I speak from study and experience, and I know better than you. An ignoramus in politics may deem lightly of this danger; all things appear easy to him, because he sees little in them, and cannot conceive that anything is to be seen, except what he can see.

21   The multitude full of a new spirit

From John Roebuck's speech in the Commons, *Hansard*, 30 July 1833.

John Arthur Roebuck was born in Madras in 1801, and called to
the bar in 1831. He was a disciple of Bentham, a friend of John
Stuart Mill, and a leading radical. Returned for Bath in 1832 to the
reformed Parliament, he early showed his strong contempt for the
Whigs. In 1852, he was to write of the Whigs that they 'have ever
been an exclusive and aristocratic faction, though at times employing
democratic principles and phrases as weapons of offence against
their opponents. . . . When out of office they are demagogues; in
power they become exclusive oligarchs.' In 1853, his motion for
secular education was rejected by 156 to 60. Died 1879.

[National Education.] Mr. Roebuck rose to move a Resolution in
conformity to his notice, that the House would, with the smallest
delay possible, consider the means of establishing a system of National
Education; and spoke as follows:—Although the subject to which I
am now about to solicit the attention of the House, can be surpassed
by none in the importance of its influence upon the well-being of
society; although none even at this time more imperiously demands
consideration from the rulers of the people; yet all this, notwithstanding, I dare not, in the present temper of the political world,
request the House to listen to anything like a complete exposition of
my opinions and my plans respecting it. Men's minds are now in a
ferment on matters solely of immediate import—the interest of the
day, the pressing urgency of the present moment, are those alone which
can command the consideration of the existing race of politicians. It
would, therefore, be idle to hope, that a subject like general education
could engage their favour, or even occupy their thoughts. Its results
are distant—the benefits to be expected from it can only be attained
by the slow operation of time, patience, and industry. There is nothing
to raise the wonder and admiration of the ignorant many—no party—
no individual purposes can be served by promoting it—nought can
be obtained by its assistance, but the pure unalloyed benefit of the

D

community at large—no wonder, then, that it has been so long, so steadily, so pertinaciously neglected. . . .

. . . Education means not merely the conferring these necessary means or instruments for the acquiring of knowledge, but it means also the so training or fashioning the intellectual and moral qualities of the individual, that he may be able and willing to acquire knowledge, and to turn it to its right use. It means the so framing the mind of the individual, that he may become a useful and virtuous member of society in the various relations of life. It means making him a good child, a good parent, a good neighbour, a good citizen, in short, a good man. All these he cannot be without knowledge, but neither will the mere acquisition of knowledge confer on him these qualities; his moral, as well as his intellectual powers, must contribute to this great end, and the true fashioning of these to this purpose is right education. Such, Sir, is the acceptation which I attribute to the term education... . .

. . . The business of Government is not, and can no longer be, the affair of a few. Within these few years a new element has arisen, which now ought to enter into all political calculations. The multitude—the hitherto inert and submissive multitude—are filled with a new spirit— their attention is intently directed towards the affairs of the State—they take an active part in their own social concerns, and however unwilling persons may be to contemplate the fact, any one who will calmly and carefully watch the signs of the times, will discover, and if he be really honest and wise, will at once allow, that the hitherto subject many are about to become paramount in the State. I speak not now in the character of one desiring or fearing this consummation, but merely as one observing the passing events around me, and I mention the coming circumstance in the same spirit as that in which an astronomer would predict an eclipse; to me the result appears inevitable; and I therefore cast about me to learn in what way this new force may be made efficient to purposes of good, and how any of its probable mischievous results may be prevented. Although I be one who believe that no good Government can be attained without the concurrence of the people— to speak in still plainer terms—that the people will never be well governed until they govern themselves—still I am far from believing that the golden age will be attained merely by creating a Democratic Government. The people at present are far too ignorant to render themselves happy, even though they should possess supreme power to-morrow. Of the many evils even which they now suffer, the larger part arises from their own ignorance, and not immediately from the Government. The Government, indeed, does not inflict much direct and positive oppression, although it produces immense indirect mischief. Indeed the evils of bad Government in this country are, for the most part, not of a positive, but of a negative description. The Government does not often immediately inflict misery on the people by any brutal or bare-faced oppression—but by abstaining from its duty, by shrinking from doing the good that it ought to do, enormous misery is allowed to continue. By fostering and perpetuating ignorance among the people, it inflicts more injury than by any or all of its direct oppressions—all its immense taxation, considered as a burthen, is a feather in the scale when compared with the ills produced by the ignorance it has engendered. Could we enlighten the whole population —could we at one moment give all of them knowledge and fore-thought—a thorough understanding of the circumstances on which their happiness is dependent—and at the same time endow them with fortitude to resist present temptations to enjoyment—in a few short years they would laugh at the taxes, when called a burthen, and wonder at those who believed, that so long as they existed, no happiness for the people could ever be known.

22   Education: by its fruits?

From *Quarterly Journal of Education*, 1834. See note to 17 above.

NATIONAL EDUCATION
Appendix to the Report of the Poor Law Commissioners
It has been said, and, it must be allowed, with some plausibility, that where any degree of education has been tried in many parts of England, the result has not been of that beneficial character which was looked for; that those on whom the experiment has been made, have not become better workmen, better citizens, or better sons, husbands, or fathers. There is undoubtedly truth in some of these assertions—and if true, they throw some obstacle in the way of a diffusion of education. The present article is devoted to the purpose of showing, from the valuable evidence, collected by His Majesty's Poor Law Commissioners, what is the nature of these obstacles, and how they may be removed. It is believed that it can be most satisfactorily shown that

these difficulties are not necessarily connected with the subject of
education; but, that they mainly spring from the mal-administration
of the poor-laws in this country—and with that, but only with that,
will vanish. . . .

The question is very well stated and the objections answered in the
following evidence of the Rev. H. C. Curtis, Rector of Padworth,
Berks, which was ordered to be printed last Session of Parliament.

Having considered what I shall term the spiritual advantages to
be derived by the lower classes from the ability to read, let me
state, in the next place, what may be termed the temporal benefits
arising from the same qualification, to themselves and the
community at large.

Perhaps some may smile at this doctrine, and ask, how can this
form a better ploughman? Shall a man make a better hedge
because he is able to read? My answer is, most certainly; for if
the mind make the man, a labourer whose intelligence is improved,
by what means it may, will always be found to do his work with
more expedition, neatness, and durability; and this I uphold, will
be the case of the labouring man, abstractedly considered, without
reference to any particular information to be acquired from books
treating on agricultural subjects. But if the low-priced publications,
the penny and half penny weekly magazines, are continued, what
an ample supply of information will be offered to those who are
capable of profiting by them! I have one before me, which
contains a variety of instructive and entertaining matter, that a
labouring man of common understanding might read with
pleasure and advantage. One article treats on the management of
fir plantations. They who are unacquainted with agricultural
pursuits are apt to imagine that to hold the plough it is necessary
only to look out for the greatest dunces in the country. But an
intelligent ploughman is of the first consequence on the farm.
In short, there is as much (if not more) intelligence required in
the different employments of the agricultural classes as in those of
mechanics or tradesmen. Intelligence is requisite in all, and the
more this is increased and perfected throughout the kingdom, the
greater will be the quantity of agricultural produce.

I have heard some exclaim, Ah! thanks to this march of intellect,
we shall be soon without ploughmen! &c. My answer to this
foolish unmeaning cavil is this: It is not taught in the Scriptures,
nor is it to be inferred by any reasoning from analogy, that there

is a certain line of improvement beyond which the human race cannot advance. On the contrary, it might be shown by sound argument, and the most clear illustrations from the past history of man, that the human intellect is capable of making continual advances, and thereby inducing proportionate improvements in civilization and social happiness. Let not those, then, who are in the higher classes stand still, and be merely the *fruges consumere nati*. Rather let them march onward, and lead the way to the highest point of improvement which in the present dispensation is possible for man. For the natural (and in every state whose constitution is framed on sacred and liberal principles, the necessary) distinction of the higher from the lower classes consists in their intellectual attainments; and these must ever have the superiority over skill in handicraft work or manual labour of any kind; hence, as in the human so in the political body, the head must ever have the direction, and the hands the actual labour of cultivating the earth, whose productions are necessary to the support of both.

Again, I have heard some object to the instruction of the lower classes in reading, that they will neglect their work, and puzzle their heads needlessly about politics, eagerly catching at any of the seditious publications which may be thrown in their way. But this is merely arguing against the use of a thing from the abuse of it. Now, from what I have before said, the ability to read will enable them to search the Scriptures. These, from the zeal manifested by different societies in supplying them, may be obtained by every one at a cheap cost, and will serve as an antidote to any poison which may be offered to their minds through seditious or immoral publications.

Strange as it may seem, I have heard some object to teaching the lower classes to write, though they will allow them the privilege of learning to read: that common but unsound argument before mentioned is here made use of, but it is not worthy of a particular refutation. I shall merely state, that the same argument in favour of giving them this acquirement may be urged with the same force as in the case of that of reading, which is, that it will increase their intelligence, refine their manners, and improve their habits, as might be clearly shown by a regular train of consequences. And here, let us ask, have not the labouring classes the same wants and the same feelings as the higher? Why should they be debarred the facility of making notes, &c., and in general by the art of writing of assisting themselves in the business of life? Why should they not be enabled to communicate to one another at a distance their circumstances, desires, and affections? In fine, let us remember that the lower classes are no longer slaves, but freemen, and that the more refined their manners and habits are, and the more improved their intelligence is, the more useful members of society they will become. . . .

The statements of Mr Curtis are fully borne out by the following evidence from other quarters. It will be observed that none of these answers are from the counties most distinguished for poor-law mal-administration.

The labourers are industrious, and are good workmen; better taught, and therefore better workmen; good husbands, kind fathers, and loyal subjects, except when goaded by poverty into discontent—(Worcester.) King's Norton. P. M. James, late Overseer.

My labourers are better informed, more to be depended on, more regular and industrious in their habits, than formerly, and I think such is the character of labourers in this parish, with exceptions—(Salop.) Selattyn. George N. K. Lloyd, Rector and J.P.

The labourers, in general, more intelligent and consequently better workmen. I would instance particularly the workmen in the slate-quarries, of whom there are 1600 in one quarry— (Carnarvon.) Bangor. James Henry Cotton, Vicar.

We had no riots in this part of the country in 1830; and in 1831 one case of fire only, which might have been accidental. All classes here are tolerably well educated in the Endowed Schools of the Netherby Estate; and this is considered one great cause of the country remaining undisturbed—(Cumberland.) Kirkandrews upon Esk. Andrew Armstrong, Assistant Overseer. . . .

In Northumberland the mal-administration of the poor-laws which has reached such a height in some of the southern and midland counties has made no progress, or so little that its effects have scarcely become discernible: consequently, the improved system of education which has of late years come into operation in Northumberland for the poorer classes, has not met with any very material impediment.

It should be remarked that the general tenor of the answers to the questions from Northumberland shows that the labourers are more skilful, as well as more industrious, than formerly. The following answers are particularly worthy of attention, as distinctly and specially indicating the cause of that improvement:—

> Increasing and better workmen, because more intelligent, and not so much addicted as formerly to run after idle sports and games, such as cock fighting, horse races, &c.—(Northumberland.) Whelpington (not Kirkwhelpington), consisting of ten townships. John Hodgson, Vicar.
>
> Much as formerly. No change, except in becoming more skilful and intelligent.—(Northumberland.) Wooler. Robert Jobson, Matthew Culley, Overseers. . . .
>
> The industry of the multitude is neither more nor less than it used to be, though, in many individual instances, it is increased, and all are decidedly better workmen, owing to a greatly improved system of agriculture, and to a very slight pressure of numbers; for the spirit of independence being unbroken among the people, the competition tends to make them both more industrious and better workmen. Many are also looking forward to becoming proprietors of land in Canada, or tenants of farms at home; this stimulates them to save. It is also asserted that both masters and servants are more civilized—more 'polite' was one of the terms used to me; and certainly their language and address are decidedly superior to that of the same class in the south of England. The colliers also are very much improved; and the education of all, both male and female, is a much better description than this class can usually command, and it is moreover paid for by themselves—(Northumberland.) Ford. John Chalfont, Blackden.

23   If mankind are ever to be . . .

From *Quarterly Journal of Education*, 1835. See note to 17 above.

If mankind are ever to be rendered enlightened, virtuous, and happy, it must be by removing all the prejudices of ignorance, and not by confining the knowledge of truth to a small number of persons, which is nearly as bad as leaving her in her fabled well.

The only difficulty that now lies in the way of educating all classes, at least to some point of usefulness, and so far to the enjoyment of greater happiness, is the ambition that sects and parties have to govern and to lead the minds of those whom they undertake to educate; to implant fixed opinions, and enslave, instead of freeing the mind from prejudices. All would have their pupils become sectarians in religion and partisans in politics; they would have them educated only to this point: when they become unruly, and look for any knowledge out of their school, education must stop. The party who are open would-be destructives, aware of this, recruit their own forces from the poor, by publications adapted to their tastes and pockets. If the poor had been really educated, they would, in all probability, have attached themselves to a party more rational in their views, and less mischievous in their designs. In national education all differences of opinion in religion and politics should be laid aside; we should endeavour to fortify the mind against prejudices and error by inculcating principles of universal truth; and we should prepare all men for the duties of social life by that kind of discipline which shall render the passage from boyhood to manhood safe and easy, instead of being, as it now is, a sudden and often a dangerous transition.

A poor man in civilized life may in a considerable degree be looked on as a savage, who with difficulty procures his food and the other necessaries of life; he has no time to cultivate his understanding, or to listen to the voice of tender and generous affections. Such men should be especially encouraged to contemplate the surrounding objects of nature, and to study the most simple laws of mechanics and chemistry; and the better to enable them to do this, while as boys they are at the national schools, they should read books descriptive of the kind of labour and the processes by which, it is most probable, they will be called upon to obtain a living. They should read books, and receive oral instruction at the same time, which should tend to give them notions, sound as far as they go, of the most general laws of animal physiology, of the principles on which mainly depend the preservation of health, and the practical rules as to exercise, cleanliness, and sobriety, deducible from these principles: they should be taught the general laws which govern the production and distribution of wealth, and, in a word, their education should be directed towards making them profitable members of that society in which they must live. Idle hours will thus be provided for by directing the turn of thought when young; scenes of revelry and drunkenness would then lose their charm; an engaged mind seldom lapses into a state of irredeemable stupid, sottish animalization. The impulses of the appetite can only be restrained by reflection, the subjects for which should be well selected and simplified, and form the earliest reading lessons of the poor; and the best subjects for forming this habit of reflection in children are the phenomena of nature. The only effectual way of redeeming the mind of the lower classes is to begin with nature; turn their thoughts to her works, and every other good effect will follow.

24   The scanty opportunities of the poor

From J. Gilderdale's *Letter to Lord Brougham*, 10 March 1838.

The Rev. J. Gilderdale was born in 1802 in Essex and, after an early bent towards a seafaring life, he became ordained. This letter is his only published work on education.

Are then the advocates of a Christian Education enemies to the diffusion of knowledge? We answer emphatically, no. We know that ignorance is unfavourable to morality; we therefore rejoice in the spread of useful information, and in the expansion of the public mind. But we would not teach science to the exclusion of religion;—we would make that *primary* and *fundamental* which is *first* in importance;—we would not occupy the scanty opportunities of the poor with *human* learning, and leave them destitute of that which is *divine*;—we would not educate man for *time* only, but for *eternity* also.

25   Education and survival

From J. Phillips Kay's *Recent Measures for the Promotion of Education in England*, 1839. See note to 19 above.

The rapid progress of our physical civilisation has occasioned the growth of masses of manufacturing population, the instruction, and moral, and religious elevation of which have hitherto been neglected by the State. These communities exhibit alarming features; labouring classes, unmatched in the energy and hardihood with which they pursue their daily toil, yet thriftless, incapable of husbanding their means, or resisting sensual gratification; high wages and want under the same roof; while other portions of the same classes are struggling on the barest pittance with continual labour, abstinent by necessity. From opposite quarters misery and discontent are goading both. The Rev. Mr. Close, perpetual Curate of Cheltenham, says, in a sermon just published, 'It is a well-known fact that, in the manufacturing districts, where the highest wages are obtained, the greatest poverty often prevails; where money is easily acquired, it is as quickly spent, and often in feasting as well as drunkenness; persons in this rank of life will not unfrequently discover a degree of extravagance in the gratification of their appetites, which would astonish those who are much their superiors in station; expending a week's wages in one feast, heedless of the wants of their families to-morrow.' At the next door to the highly-paid artisan, who has squandered his week's earnings on the Sunday's feast, pines the hand-loom weaver, exhausted with continual penury and toil.

Physical prosperity stimulates all the animal appetites, and, if unaided by moral restraint, wastes her resources, and instead of connecting content and peace with plenty, continually rouses the population to feverish exertion. Notwithstanding the high wages of the artisan, the wife commits her infant to an hireling, and leaves her domestic duties to work in the manufactory. The parents, to enable ill-regulated means to satisfy increasing wants, lead their children of a tender age to the same scene of continual exertion. Domestic virtue and household piety have little opportunity to thrive in a population alternating between protracted labour and repose, or too frequent sensual gratification. When all the animal powers are thus continually called into action, adversity is met with sullen discontent, or with fierce outbreaks of passionate disquiet. Whoever will promise less toil and more money, is a prophet in the manufacturing districts; and . . . prophets will always be found ready to teach the population to seek a remedy for the evils they endure by violent attempts at social change. To the ignorant man, who has only the sense of the continual necessity to labour, in order to gratify his unappeased desires for sensual gratification, and to meet the wants created by wasted means, who can be more welcome than he who comes with the golden promise of high wages and ease, instead of leading him to an enlightened estimate of his domestic and social duties, and teaching him how much a resolute will, under the influence of morality and religion, may do, even in adverse circumstances, to render the lot of the poor man peaceful and happy? Less work and more means have always, therefore, been the promises of every impostor who has practised on the ignorance, discontent, and suffering of the manufacturing population.

We shall have to speak, in subsequent pages, of the political and social combinations which have of late prevailed in the manufacturing districts; the Trades' Unions, in which incendiarism, personal violence and even assassination, are practised for the unattainable object of sustaining the rate of wages above the level resulting from the natural laws of trade—and the more recent armed associations for political purposes, in which the working classes have been exhorted to obtain by force privileges withheld by the constitutional representatives of the people; results, which are all ascribable to the fact that the physical development of the population has been more rapid than the growth of our intellectual, moral, and religious institutions.

On the other hand, it is cheering to know, that the accumulation of the people in masses renders them more accessible to the beneficial influence of well-regulated social institutions. Having once encountered the necessity of supplying the intellectual and moral wants of the labouring classes, knowledge and virtue will, with adequate agencies make more rapid progress among a concentrated than a scattered population. So long as our artisans lived in cottages scattered over the moors of our northern, and the wolds of our southern counties, little danger might arise to the State from their universal ignorance, apathy, and want; but if the necessity for raising their moral and intellectual condition could, under such circumstances, have been as pressing as it now is, the difficulty of civilising them would have been almost insuperable. In the concentrated population of our towns, the dangers arising from the neglect of the intellectual and moral culture of the working class are already imminent; and the consequences of permitting another generation to rise, without bending the powers of the executive government and of society to the great work of civilisation and religion, for which the political and social events of every hour make a continual demand, must be social disquiet little short of revolution. But the same masses of population are equally open to all the beneficial influences derivable from a careful cultivation of their domestic and social habits; from the communication of knowledge enabling them to perceive their true relation to the other classes of society, and how dependent their interests are upon the stability of our institutions and the preservation of social order.

The law recognises the duty devolving on property, as respects the education of the factory children; and we rejoice to believe that, under the guidance of men of high intelligence and benevolence, such as many of the most wealthy manufacturers are, we shall soon realise what are the fruits of a well-devised system of intellectual, moral, and religious training, in rendering the communities, in whose well-being they have so deep a stake, examples of what may be effected by applying to the moral elevation of the population the same sagacity and perseverance which has occasioned its physical prosperity. A short time only will elapse before, in some of our great towns, the most influential inhabitants will combine for the erection and support of Model Schools. Such institutions will create and diffuse a more correct estimate of the value of Education, and will promote its spread.

For another neglected class also the State has interfered. Under the parochial system, the orphan, deserted, and illegitimate children—waifs of society—were scattered through the parochial workhouses of England, where they were promiscuously mingled with the idiots, the sick, the sturdy vagabond, and profligate women. From the parochial workhouses, the gaols and hulks recruited the ranks of crime. These children are now under the care of Boards of Guardians, separated from the adult paupers, and measures are in progress to educate them so as to render them efficient and virtuous members of society.

For the juvenile offenders the Government is carefully preparing a system of reformatory discipline and training, in which all the resources of the educator will be exhausted to redeem these outcasts from the depravity consequent on neglect and evil example.

Besides these signs of coming improvement, we hail, as a presage of no little importance, the fact that the subject of National Education has occupied the attention of the Houses of Parliament during five nights of anxious discussion. We never were so sanguine as to expect that the great embarrassments with which it is surrounded could be at once dispelled; but we have a confident belief that every hour increases the anxiety of all friends of our constitutional liberties and national institutions, to preserve both by the education of the people.

26 Education and property

From Dr Arnold's letter to *Hertford Reformer*, 20 July 1839.

Thomas Arnold was born in 1795 in the Isle of Wight, where his father was a collector of customs. In 1811, he was elected a scholar of Corpus Christi, Oxford, where his friends included Keble and Coleridge. In 1827, he was elected Headmaster of Rugby, which had expanded from its humble origins as a grammar school to become a prosperous public school, but was still nowhere near the leading schools in importance. Arnold treated the boys with confidence, as individuals, seeking to imbue them with reverence for learning and duty and to build their character towards the ideal of the Christian gentleman. His teaching was profoundly stimulating, though he had a sternness of appearance which formed the basis for Lytton Strachey's celebrated caricature in *Eminent Victorians*. In theology, Arnold was liberal and erastian, and an implacable opponent of the Oxford Movement. He died in 1842.

Lord Lansdowne, in the late debate in the House of Lords on the Government scheme of education, expressed a benevolent wish that education, if generally introduced amongst our manufacturing population, might greatly reduce the amount of crime. God forbid that I should speak or think slightingly of the blessings of education; but I greatly fear that we are expecting more from it in the actual state

of our society than it can alone by possibility accomplish. Most wisely
has Mr Laing said in his most instructive account of Norway, that 'a
man may read and write and yet have a totally uneducated mind; but
that he who possesses property, whether he can read and write or not,
has an educated mind; he has forethought, caution, and reflection
guiding every action; he knows the value of self-restraint and is in the
constant habitual practice of it.' What we commonly call education is
invaluable when it is given in time to a people possessing the education
of property;—when it opens to them intellectual enjoyments whilst
they are yet in a condition to taste them,—and so, by accustoming
them to raise their standard of happiness, it prevents them from
recklessly sinking to a lower condition. Education, in the common
sense of the word, is required by a people before poverty has made
havoc amongst them;—at that critical moment when civilization makes
its first burst,—and is accompanied by an immense commercial
activity. Then is the time for general education, to teach the man of
smaller means how to conduct himself in the coming fever of national
developement:—to make him understand the misery of sinking from
the condition of a proprietor to that of a mere labourer; and if this
cannot be avoided at home, then to dispose him to emigrate to a new
country, whilst he still retains the habits which will make him a
valuable element in a new society there. But can what is called education,—can book learning really educate beggars, or those whose
condition is so low that it cannot become lower? Our population
want book knowledge, and they also want the means in point of social
well-being to render this knowledge available. This is the difficulty of
the problem that we know not where to begin. And we shall have
gained something, if we are well convinced that no single measure,
whether of so called education, or of emigration, or of an improved
poor-law,—and far less any political privilege which when given to
men unfit to use it is an evil to themselves rather than a good,—will be
of real efficacy to better our condition. . . .

27   Infant education: the duty, the expediency, and the frustrations

From Lord Brougham's *Letter to the Duke of Bedford*, 1839. See note to 13 above.

The Lords have declared by a majority of one hundred and twelve . . . against any plan of Education in which the Established Church shall not be consulted, that is to say, shall not have some deference paid to its claims beyond those of the different sects—some superiority assigned to it above the level on which all sects are to be kept. This, and certainly nothing more than this, is the amount of that very important decision. All intolerance, all compulsion upon the Dissenters, all claim of the Church to exclude them directly or indirectly from the benefits of whatever Education shall be patronized by the State, all desire to force upon them any observances contrary to their consciences, was most explicitly, and, I believe, most sincerely disavowed by every speaker, lay or spiritual, who bore a part in that celebrated debate. But some recognition of the Establishment was regarded as its right. . . .

Then let us be well assured that no Government in this country ever can carry a plan of National Education in which a perfect absolute equality between all sects of religious professors shall be established, according to your principles and mine. . . . So far we must make up our minds, looking our position steadily in the face, to admit that we are completely defeated. . . . A controversy of thirty years, with all the reason and almost all the skill, and, until very lately, all the zeal on our side, has ended in an overthrow somewhat more complete than we should in all probability have sustained at the commencement of our long and well-fought campaign. Such is the force and effect of an Establishment, the growth of ages, pushing its roots into the hearts of the people, entwining its branches with all our other institutions,— let us in justice add, adorned with eminent gifts; let us in candour confess, bearing but seldom the harsher fruits of intolerance; for assuredly if the Church of England be a nursing mother to her own children, she is also, generally speaking, a quiet neighbour to those of other families. . . .

But suppose I am wrong in my predictions, and that there were any reasonable prospect of bringing over the public opinion to our side . . . every one must at once admit, that this change can only be the work of time, aye, and of a very long time. For it must be an almost universal change of opinion that can so far sway the Lords as to make them rescind their late resolution; so that we are to go on for this long course of years, suffering the people to be uneducated, and vice with ignorance to stalk through the land as over their own appointed and exclusive province. Are we prepared to embrace this alternative? Are we willing that not only you and I, but our children, and our children's children, shall flourish and fade, rising up and going down to the grave, while the plague of darkness still wraps the land in clouds, only broken occasionally by the glare of civil broils?

For do not let it be imagined that ignorance is as harmless now as it was before any men were well informed, or any were misled by half knowledge, and set on to mislead others; in times when, without any change, 'one generation passed away and another came up,' but the established order of things under which the earth was ruled, seemed as if it abode for ever; when 'France before the ark adored and slept.' Even in those peaceful days we were taught to believe 'that the soul be without knowledge, it is not good'. But in our own times, to leave the people uninformed, or half informed, is to leave the edifice of our social system resting upon a quicksand, if its foundation be not rather like the sides of a volcano. Should there, however, be any that deem such apprehensions chimerical, I will come to a very practical view of the matter. I am not inquiring how far the happiness of a rational creature can be secured even in this world, without drawing away his mind from the contemplation of sensual objects, winning over his affections from the taste for gross and grovelling indulgence. On that subject, indeed, I have no kind of doubt; but let us come to the more commonplace topic of the Gaol Roll, the Assize Calendar. I pretend to prove that, without waiting for the comparatively slow progress of general improvement by the operation of knowledge universally diffused, six or seven years would not elapse before every Prison, and every Circuit, and every Sessions in the country felt the blessed effects of Infant Schools, if the State did its duty, and took that effectual, that only effectual mode of preventing crime, instead of vainly trusting to the Gibbet, the Convict ship, and the Hulks, for deterring by the force of example,—that feeble, because misapplied force, which operates only on the mind at a moment when the passions are still, and has no more power to quell their tempest, than the rudder has to guide the ship through a hurricane which has torn every sail to rags. I pretend to prove that, as the malefactors who infest the country are not the growth of your class, your station in society, nor of mine, nor of the middle rank of life, nor even of the more respectable portion of the humbler classes, but of a lower class to be found scattered every where, but chiefly in the towns,—a class which always bears a certain calculable proportion to the whole numbers of the people;—so if Infant Schools were planted for the training of all children between three and seven years of age, so as to impress them with innocent and virtuous habits, their second natures thus super-induced, would make it as impossible to pervert them, as it is to make men and women of the upper classes rush into the highways each time they feel the want of money.

To this doctrine of mine I know that some have an answer; and one friend . . . has asked if any training can stifle the passions that grow up with age, or even prevent children while young from listening to the parents that would inculcate dishonest practices. I can only answer, that there is no other reason in the world for persons in the upper classes of society, such as my excellent and much loved friend himself, not giving way to temptation, than the habits which they have acquired from their earliest infancy, of regarding these things as altogether out of the question. That, in other matters, they are frail like their neighbours, and very far indeed from either the prudence which avoids a conflict with the passions, or the fortitude which carries us in safety through such struggles, every hour's experience fully proves. I place, therefore, the most absolute reliance on the certain effects of Infant Training to create such habits as, in the vast majority of instances, will be found proof against all seduction, and preserve the mind alike from being wrecked by the gusts of passion, and from being undermined and corrupted by the more debasing influence of sordid appetite. But it is by no means necessary that I should shew this to be certain. All reason is on my side to prove, that I am probably in the right; all experience is with me as far as the fact can be known by trial. Then, have we not a right to demand that the experiment shall be made upon an adequate scale? Or, has the supreme power in the State a right to delay any longer making the trial? But, above all, shall we delay, dare we delay, so very long as it would take to bring round either the Church to the views of the Dissenters, or the Dissenters to the views of the Church, upon the point which is alone in controversy between them, namely, How far there shall be clerical interference with the process of instruction?

It is certain, that as things now stand, the two great parties into which the community is unhappily split upon this mighty question, are resolved that we should have no system of Education at all,—no National Plan for Training Teachers, and thereby making the schools that stud the country all over, deserve the name they bear,—no national plan for training young children to virtuous habits, and thereby rooting out crimes from the land. And this interdict, under which both parties join in laying their country, is by each pronounced to be necessary for the sacred interests of religion. Of religion! Oh, gracious God! Was ever the name of thy holy ordinances so impiously profaned before? . . .

Once more let us view our present position, without shrinking from the sight. The question is, and the only question,—I repeat it again and again,—shall we have a system of National Education, or shall we not? Shall we meet our clerical adversaries half-way, that some plan of public instruction adequate to the wants of the community may be carried into execution? Or shall we churlishly stand on our own ground, and leave the people to thirst after knowledge, and to thirst in vain? Do we really wish for the improvement of our species, as our first object, or do we only desire the general good of our fellow-creatures, so far as the pursuit of it may afford the means of obtaining a victory for our sect? In a word, is contention, and triumph, and the humbling of our adversaries, our real purpose—our primary occupation; and the extirpation of vice, the diffusion of happiness, the promotion of true religion, only a secondary object; conveniently talked of—little cared for—the cover and cloak of our spiritual pride, our worldly contentiousness, not the end and aim of our endeavours—or at least a thing which we are willing enough to seek if we can gain it for nothing, but a thing for which we will make no sacrifice that wounds our vanity, or clashes with our self-seeking, or galls our self-importance? That is the real question on which it now behoves all friends of Education anxiously to search their hearts. . . .

'Oh, but we will go on planting schools as we have done, by the exertions of Private Beneficence.' That is the sound, the plausible sound, which I hear echoed from many respectable quarters. Far, very far from me, be the idea of underrating those admirable, I will say, those truly glorious efforts!—the more especially because I well know, that in the very parts of the country where ignorance most prevails, no little exertion is required to make the poor avail themselves of the means of instruction which are actually provided; and that consequently, the best plan we can devise must still lean a good deal upon voluntary and individual help for its successful working. My Bill has been expressly framed in great part upon the admission of this principle. But I also know full well, that the resources of private bounty are precarious, and are local; that in the great towns, where the want of Education is the greatest, they are the most inadequate; that they impose a burthen most unequal, most unfair in its pressure, taxing severely the worthy and generous poor, while the churlish rich oftentimes escape. I know full well that voluntary exertions are of necessity made at an enormous expense compared with the good they accomplish, because experience must be purchased by the costs of failure through ignorance or unskilfulness; and the expertness that has been acquired in one place cannot, for want of system, indeed for want of communication, be made available to any other. I know full well, that in many parts of the country, schools established twenty years ago are now gone to decay; that the death of an individual, the quarrel of two families, the splitting of a committee, a hundred other accidents, have extinguished many seminaries, and may every day destroy more. I know full well, that in hardly any schools are the best methods of teaching adopted, or the proper branches of knowledge taught; while in very many the incapacity of the instructors and the neglect of the pupils is such, as to leave no pretext for calling the operation which is carried on without their walls, by so respectable a name as Education. Above all, I know that nothing like a provision has been any where made for Infant Training, by far the most essential branch of tuition,— the one to provide which is the duty of our rulers, above every other duty imperative upon them, and which, if they discharge not, they forfeit their title to rule.

28   Rising Chartists

From a speech in the House of Lords by the Marquess of
Lansdowne, 5 July 1839.

The Third Marquess was born in 1780, and was a leading Whig in
the years of exile after Fox. Under Grey, he became President of
the Council by choice, rejecting higher office, and he remained so
under Melbourne. From the mid-1830s, he concentrated on
educational questions, and the speech from which this extract comes
was considered his most famous performance in the House. By
temperament a liberal, he strongly opposed the slave trade, and
all forms of religious discrimination, including that against Jews.
In the 1850s, he opposed the Reform Bills. Died 1863.

In the 80,000 uninstructed children now growing out of infancy, as it
appeared in three or four only of the great towns of the north without
any creed, if it were not a farce to talk of creeds in connexion with
persons so ignorant, your Lordships may see the rising Chartists of
the next age. I declare to this House and to the public of this country,
that if they neglect to supply that instruction which is so loudly called
for, and to supply it in a proportion increasing with the increase of
population, they may repress the excesses of untaught violence by
penal laws, but they will have no right to acquit themselves of the guilt
of having neglected to lead those misguided men into the way in which
they should go, and make them useful, respectable, and orderly
members of society.

29   An eternal duty: and the needs of the hour

From Thomas Carlyle's *Chartism*, 1840.

Thomas Carlyle was born in 1795 in Annandale. Precocious and eclectic from childhood, he gave up his early idea of ordination along with his Christian beliefs, and found the idea of 'school-mastering' intolerable. In the 1830s, he wrote his *French Revolution*, and later the prophetic aspects of his temperament were given further rein. He was neither Whig, Tory, nor ordinary radical— yet in the 1840s, some of the young said 'Carlyle is my religion', and many Victorians, including Dickens, came under his influence. His bent was strongly romantic, but with an emphasis on personal religion, strong willpower, and on saying 'Yes' to life. In these and other ways he anticipates a modern prophet like D. H. Lawrence, and also certain modern existentialists (and totalitarians). His commitment to education was matched by contempt for democracy; hence the special interest of his thought on Chartism. Died 1881.

Condition of England question. A feeling very generally exists that the condition and disposition of the Working Classes is a rather ominous matter at present; that something ought to be said, something ought to be done, in regard to it. And surely, at an epoch of history when the 'National Petition' carts itself in wagons along the streets, and is presented 'bound with iron hoops, four men bearing it,' to a Reformed House of Commons; and Chartism numbered by the million and half, taking nothing by its iron-hooped Petition, breaks out into brickbats, cheap pikes and even into sputterings of con-flagration, such very general feeling cannot be considered unnatural! To us individually this matter appears, and has for many years appeared, to be the most ominous of all practical matters whatever; a matter in regard to which if something be not done, something will *do* itself one day, and in a fashion that will please nobody. The time is verily come for acting in it; how much more for consultation about acting in it, for speech and articulate inquiry about it!

We are aware that, according to the newspapers, Chartism is extinct; that a Reform Ministry has 'put down the chimera of Chartism' in the most felicitous effectual manner. So say the newspapers;—and yet, alas, most readers of newspapers know withal that it is indeed the 'chimera' of Chartism, not the reality, which has been put down. The distracted incoherent embodiment of Chartism, whereby in late months it took shape and became visible, this has been put down; or rather has fallen down and gone asunder by gravitation and law of nature: but the living essence of Chartism has not been put down. Chartism means the bitter discontent grown fierce and mad, the wrong condition therefore or the wrong disposition, of the Working Classes of England. It is a new name for a thing which has had many names, which will yet have many. The matter of Chartism is weighty, deep-rooted, far-extending; did not begin yesterday; will by no means end this day or tomorrow. . . . What means this bitter discontent of the Working Classes? Whence comes it, whither goes it? Above all, at what price, on what terms, will it probably consent to depart from us and die into rest? These are questions.

. . . Delirious Chartism will not have raged entirely to no purpose, as indeed no earthly thing does so, if it have forced all thinking men of the community to think of this vital matter, too apt to be overlooked otherwise. Is the condition of the English working people wrong; so wrong that rational working men cannot, will not, and even should not rest quiet under it? A most grave case, complex beyond all others in the world; a case wherein Botany Bay, constabulary rural police, and such like, will avail but little. Or is the discontent itself mad, like the shape it took? Not the condition of the working people that is wrong; but their disposition, their own thoughts, beliefs and feelings that are wrong? This too were a most grave case, little less alarming, little less complex than the former one. In this case too, where constabulary police and mere rigour of coercion seems more at home, coercion will by no means do all, coercion by itself will not even do much. If there do exist general madness of discontent, then sanity and some measure of content must be brought about again,—not by constabulary police alone. When the thoughts of a people, in the great mass of it, have grown mad, the combined issue of that people's workings will be a madness, an incoherency and ruin! Sanity will have to be recovered for the general mass; coercion itself will otherwise cease to be able to coerce. . . .

Who would suppose that *Education* were a thing which had to be advocated on the ground of local expediency, or indeed on any ground? As if it stood not on the basis of everlasting duty, as a prime necessity of man. It is a thing that should need no advocating; much as it does actually need. To impart the gift of thinking to those who cannot think, and yet who could in that case think: this, one would imagine, was the first function a government had to set about discharging. Were it not a cruel thing to see, in any province of an empire, the inhabitants living all mutilated in their limbs, each strong man with his right arm lamed? How much crueller to find the strong soul, with its eyes still scaled, its eyes extinct so that it sees not! Light has come into the world, but to this poor peasant it has come in vain. For six thousand years the Sons of Adam, in sleepless effort, have been devising, doing, discovering; in mysterious infinite indissoluble communion, warring, a little band of brothers, against the great black empire of Necessity and Night; they have accomplished such a conquest and conquests: and to this man it is all as if it had not been. The four-and-twenty letters of the Alphabet are still Runic enigmas to him. He passes by on the other side; and that great Spiritual Kingdom, the toilwon conquest of his own brothers, all that his brothers have conquered, is a thing non-extant for him. An invisible empire; he knows it not, suspects it not. And is it not his withal; the conquest of his own brothers, the lawfully acquired possession of all men? Baleful enchantment lies over him, from generation to generation; he knows not that such an empire is his, that such an empire is at all. O, what are bills of rights, emancipations of black slaves into black apprentices, lawsuits in chancery for some short usufruct of a bit of land? The grand 'seedfield of Time' is this man's, and you give it him not. Time's seedfield, which includes the Earth and all her seedfields and pearl-oceans, nay her sowers too and pearl-divers, all that was wise and heroic and victorious here below; of which the Earth's centuries are but as furrows, for it stretches forth from the beginning onward even into this Day!

> 'My inheritance, how lordly wide and fair;
> Time is my fair seedfield, to Time I'm heir!'

Heavier wrong is not done under the sun. It lasts from year to year, from century to century; the blinded sire slaves himself out, and leaves a blinded son; and men, made in the image of God, continue as two-legged beasts of labour;—and in the largest empire of the world, it is a debate whether a small fraction of the Revenue of one Day (30,000*l.* is but that) shall, after Thirteen Centuries, be laid out on it, or not laid out on it. Have we Governors, have we Teachers; have we had a Church these thirteen hundred years? What is an Overseer of souls, an Archoverseer, Archiepiscopus? Is he something? If so, let him lay his hand on his heart, and say what thing!

But quitting all that, of which the human soul cannot well speak in terms of civility, let us observe now that Education is not only an eternal duty, but has at length become even a temporary and ephemeral one, which the necessities of the hour will oblige us to look after. These Twenty-four million labouring men, if their affairs remain unregulated, chaotic, will burn ricks and mills; reduce us, themselves and the world into ashes and ruin. Simply their affairs cannot remain unregulated, chaotic; but must be regulated, brought into some kind of order. What intellect were able to regulate them? The intellect of a Bacon, the energy of a Luther, if left to their own strength, might pause in dismay before such a task; a Bacon and Luther added together, to be perpetual prime minister over us, could not do it. No one great and greatest intellect can do it. What can? Only Twenty-four million ordinary intellects, once awakened into action; these, well presided over, may. Intellect, insight, is the discernment of order in disorder; it is the discovery of the will of Nature, of God's will; the beginning of the capability to walk according to that. With perfect intellect, were such possible without perfect morality, the world would be perfect; its efforts unerringly correct, its results continually successful, its condition faultless. Intellect is like light; the Chaos becomes a World under it: *fiat lux*. These Twenty-four million intellects are but common intellects; but they are intellects; in earnest about the matter, instructed each about his own province of it; labouring each perpetually, with what partial light can be attained, to bring such province into rationality. From the partial determinations and their conflict, springs the universal. Precisely what quantity of intellect was in the Twenty-four millions will be exhibited by the result they arrive at; that quantity and no more. According as there was intellect or no intellect in the individuals, will the general conclusion they make out embody itself as a world-healing Truth and Wisdom, or as a baseless fateful Hallucination, a Chimaera breathing *not* fabulous fire!

30 Education and the vote

From William Lovett's *Chartism; A New Organisation of the People*, 1840.

William Lovett was born in 1800 in Cornwall. His father died before he was born, and his mother sold fish in Penzance. He became apprenticed to a rope-maker, and in 1821 went to London. Self-taught, he joined a discussion society, the 'Liberal' in Soho, and a Mechanics' Institute. In 1826 he married, and in the same year joined the first London Co-operative Society. He became a friend of Owen, Cobbett and other reformers, and in 1831 joined the 'National Union of the Working Classes'. In 1832 he was tried, and acquitted, on charges of political agitation. In 1836 he helped to form the London Working Men's Association, and in this way became a leader among the Chartists, and one of the authors of the Charter of 1838. He was tried and imprisoned in 1839. His *Chartism*, from which this extract is taken, was denounced by O'Connor and the militant wing of Chartism as 'middle-class', yet Lovett failed—as he fully expected—to engage the active sympathies of the middle class for his cause. After 1849 he disengaged himself from politics, but continued to labour hard in radical causes. An idio-syncratic, honest man; died 1877.

We have said that good education embraces the cultivation of *all* the mental and bodily faculties; for be it remembered, *that all individuals* (unless they are malformed or diseased) possess the same kind of faculties, though they may materially differ in size and power, just as men and women differ in size and strength from each other. All men are not gifted with great strength of body or powers of intellect, but all are so wisely and wonderfully endowed, that all have capacities for becoming intelligent, moral, and happy members of society; and if they are not, it is *for want of their capacities being so properly cultivated*, as to cause them to live in accordance with the physical laws of their nature, the social institutions of man, and the moral laws of God. Education will cause every latent seed of the mind to germinate and spring up into useful life, which otherwise might have lain buried in ignorance, and died in the corruptions of its own nature; thousands of our countrymen, endowed with all the capabilities for becoming the *guides* and *lights* of society, from want of this glorious blessing, are doomed to grovel in vice and ignorance, to pine in obscurity and want. Give to a man knowledge, and you give him a light to perceive and enjoy beauty, variety, surpassing ingenuity, and majestic grandeur which his mental darkness previously concealed from him—enrich his mind and strengthen his understanding, and you give him powers to render all art and nature subservient to his purposes—call forth his moral excellence in union with his intellect, and he will apply every power of thought and force of action to enlighten ignorance, alleviate misfortune, remove misery, and banish vice; and, as far as his abilities permit, to prepare a highway to the world's happiness.

There is every reason, however, for supposing that many persons have been led to doubt the great benefits of education, from what they have witnessed of the dissipated and improper conduct of those who have had great wealth expended on their education; and that others, observing the jealousies, contentions, and ambition of men *professedly* learned, have been led to inquire 'whether *educated men* are happier than those who are *ignorant*.' But from want of moral training in unison with intellectual acquirements, such characters cannot be said to be 'educated,' in the proper sense of the term; they have knowledge without wisdom, and power without the motive to goodness. But as regards '*happiness*', (which may be defined to mean the highest degree of pleasurable sensations,) we think we may safely aver that *the ignorant man can never be truly happy*. He cannot even enjoy the same *animal* happiness in eating, drinking, and sleeping as the brute; for the demands society requires from him in return for these enjoyments give him anxieties, cares, and toil which the brute does not experience. The instinct, too, which nature has bestowed on the lower animals to guide their appetites, seems to give them superior advantages over a man destitute of knowledge. For, ignorant of his own nature, and needing the control of reason, he is continually marring his own happiness by his follies or his vices. Wanting *moral perceptions*, the temptations that surround him frequently seduce him to evil, and the penalties society inflict on him *punish him without reclamation*. Ignorant of the phenomena of nature, he becomes credulous, superstitious, and bigoted—an easy prey to the cunning and deceitful; and, bewildered by the phantoms of his own ignorant imaginings, he is miserable while living, and afraid of dying.

But, it may be asked, what proofs can be adduced to show that *the truly educated man is the happier for being so?* We will anticipate such a question, and endeavour to afford such proofs as, to us, appear clear and conclusive. In the first place, nature has given to most of her children a *faculty* for acquiring knowledge, which, once *quickened and directed by education*, is continually gratified with its acquisitions, and ever deriving fresh pleasures in new pursuits and accumulation of knowledge. To give the greatest delight to those who wisely exercise this faculty, nature has provided a multitudinous variety to be investigated and enjoyed; she has spread out her wonders around them, and unfolded her beauties to their gaze. By giving them the power to transmit their acquirements to posterity, she has opened to their mental view the whole arcana of science and range of art, to afford them unlimited sources of enjoyment.—In the next place, nature has in her bounty conferred on them all the *powers* of moral superiority and social gratification, which, if *wisely cultivated*, afford them pleasures inexhaustible. Those noble attributes of man's nature, ever stimulating him to great deeds and good actions, cast a continual sunshine over the mind of him who obeys their dictates; they render his life useful, and give him peace and hope in the hour of death. Nor can any *cultivated man* for a moment doubt these positions; he has the proof and evidence in his own feelings, and his righteous actions will afford the best testimony to the rest of mankind.

From what we have said on the *nature* and *intention of education*, we think its importance must begin to be evident; for what man is there who, in inquiring into the laws of his nature, finds that his own *individual happiness* is a condition dependent on the cultivation of his mental and moral powers, but will readily admit the importance and necessity of *proper education?* . . .

. . . Can any man of reflection fail in perceiving that most social evils have their origin in ignorance? *What but the want of information to perceive their true interest, and the want of moral motives to pursue it,* can induce the *wealthier* classes of society to perpetuate a system of oppression and injustice which in its reaction fills our gaols with criminals, our land with paupers, and our streets with prostitution and intemperance? What but the want of intellectual and moral culture occasion our *middle-class population* to spend their careworn lives in pursuing *wealth* or *rank* through all the soul-debasing avenues of *wrong;* and, after all their anxiety to secure the objects of their ambition, find they have neglected *the substantial realities of happiness* in the pursuit of its phantom? And what shall we say of that large portion of our population who have been born in evil and trained in vice?—nay, whose very organization, in many instances, has been physically and mentally injured by the criminality of their parents? Their perceptions continually directed to evil, their notions of right and wrong perverted by pernicious example, and thereby taught that the gratification of their animal appetites is the end and object of their existence, can we wonder that they become the hardened pests of society, or, rather, the *victims of social and political neglect*—beings whom punishments fail to deter from evil, and for whom prisons, penitentiaries, laws, precepts, and sermons are made in vain? What man, then, perceiving these lamentable results of ignorance, and possessing the least spark of benevolence, is not prepared at once to admit the necessity for beginning our social reformation *at the root of the evil*, by establishing a wise and just system of education? . . .

. . . Convinced of the *importance* of an improved system of education, we think there needs little to convince any one of the necessity of its being made as *general* as possible; for, if the effects of ignorance are so generally detrimental to happiness, the remedy must be sought for in the general dissemination of knowledge;—we see and feel enough of the effects of partial knowledge, to warn us against the evil of instructing one portion of society, and suffering the other to remain in ignorance. What, but the superior cunning and ingenuity of the few, and the ignorance of the many, have led to the establishment of our landed monopoly in its present state—our trading and commercial monopolies—our legislative and municipal monopolies—our church and college monopolies—and, in short, all the extremes of wealth and wretchedness which characterize our fraudulent system? In fact, the cunning and trickery which uphold this system have become so evident, that all those who seek to profit by it, are not so much induced to send their children to schools and universities to acquire knowledge for its own sake, or to make them *better* or more *useful* members of society, as they are to qualify them *to rise in it;* in other words, to enable them to live in idleness and extravagance on the industry of other people. . . .

. . . If our government were based upon *Universal Suffrage* tomorrow, we should be equally opposed to the giving it any such powers in education, as some persons propose to invest it; its power should be of an *assisting* and not an *enforcing* character. Public education ought to be *a right*—a right derivable from society itself, as society implies *a union for mutual benefit*, and, consequently, *to provide publicly security and proper training of all its members.* The public should also endeavour *to instruct the country*, through a board of instructors, (popularly chosen), on *the best plans of education or modes of training;* and should induce, by prizes or otherwise, men of genius and intelligence to aid them in devising the best. After their plans have been matured, and the greatest publicity given to them, the people should be called upon to choose (by universal suffrage), two members from each county, to form a special body, *to consider such plans,* and to amend, adopt, or reject them, as they may think proper; leaving those in the *minority* to adopt such plans as their constituents may approve of, till the merits of the plans selected by the majority became obvious to all. Such a mode as this would be more in accordance with liberty and justice than the legal enforcement of any particular plans of education, as of all other subjects it involves greater consequences of good or evil. Government, then, should provide the means for erecting schools of every description, wherever they may be deemed necessary; and empower the inhabitants of the respective districts to elect their own superintendents and teachers, (if qualified in normal schools,) and to raise *a district rate* for the support of the school and remuneration of the teachers. If we had a liberal government to do this for education— *if the whole people were to be interested in the subject, through popular election,* instead of a select clique, we might safely trust to the progress of knowledge and power of truth to render it popular, as well as to cause the best plans, ere long, to be universally adopted. But from our government no such liberality is to be expected—we have every thing to fear from it, but nothing to hope for; hence, we have addressed ourselves to you, working men of Britain, and you of the middle classes who feel yourselves identified with them, as you are the most interested in the establishment of a wise and just system of education. And we think we have said sufficient to convince you of the necessity of guarding against those *state* and *party* schemes some persons are intent on establishing, as well as to induce you to commence the great work of education yourselves, *on the most liberal and just plan you can devise,* and by every exertion to render it *as general* as possible; hoping that the day is not distant *when your political franchise will give you the power to extend it with rapidity throughout the whole empire.*

31   Education of the young

From Samuel Wilderspin's *A System for the Education of the Young,
Applied to All the Faculties*, 1840.

Samuel Wilderspin was born in 1792 (?) in Hornsey. He began life
as a clerk, but left to devote himself to education, and became
joint-founder of the infant school system in England. In 1820, he
opened a school in Spitalfields, influenced by a plan of Brougham's;
afterwards, he helped to spread this system through the UK, and
for two years (1839–41) was headmaster of the central model school
in Dublin. He published many books, starting with *On the
Importance of Educating the Infant Poor* in 1824, and described himself
as 'Inventor of the System of Infant Training'. Died 1866.

Thousands are carried away by mere phantasies, for the want of having
had a proper basis laid in childhood. The most unphilosophical, the
most irrational, the most ignorant, and the most bigoted men, will
gain a hearing from the multitude, just in proportion as they go into
opposite extremes. If such men as Mr Owen address them under the
specious pretext of making them all happy, by merely uniting them
together, like a flock of sheep, to eat and drink together, to sleep
together, if they think fit, and to enjoy all the propensities of the
natural man just as *mere animals* would do, they will listen to him, set
him down as a wonderful philosopher, and collect money to build
what they call 'a Hall of Science', in such a thickly populated place as
Manchester, look upon him as little less than a god, and give him credit
for things which he himself would never claim; and, in short, go so far
as to say that all men are irrational, and *never did know how to live*, nor
ever will know how to live, until they can swallow all down as gospel
which he chooses to assert. We are to have the most wonderful changes
in the shortest time; the population of whole towns are to be changed
in a few months; the greatest wonders are to be accomplished by the
mighty genius and unwearied philanthropy of this individual and his
followers, and woe be to those who dare stand up and call any of

these nostrums in question; they settle the matter at once by calling him an ignorant fool. . . .

Once more let us view our present position, without shrinking from the sight. The question is, and the only question,—I repeat it again and again,—shall we have a system of national education, or shall we not? . . .

The infant school languishes; but Newgate flourishes—Newgate, with her thousand cells to corrupt their youthful inmates; seducing the guiltless, confirming the depraved. The infant school is closed, but the Penitentiary day and night yawns to engulph the victims of our stepmother system,—the Penitentiary, where repentance and penance should rather be performed by the real authors of their fall. The infant school receives no innocents whom it might train or might hold fast to natural virtue; but the utterly execrable, the altogether abominable hulk, lies moored in the face of the day which it darkens, within sight of the land which it insults, riding on the waters which it stains with every unnatural excess of infernal pollution, triumphant over all morals!—And shall civilized, shall free, shall Christian rulers, any longer pause, any more hesitate, before they amend their ways, and attempt, though late, yet seriously, to discharge the first of their duties? . . . Lawgivers of England! I charge ye, have a care!

32   The just portion of freemen

From Thomas Arnold's letter to the *Hertford Reformer*, 1 February 1840. See note to 26 above.

This is the real problem;—it is how to keep more than twenty millions of human beings in such a state, as that, speaking in the mass, they shall have sufficient physical comforts, and a share of political rights, and some degree at least of intellectual and spiritual cultivation. All these are the just portion of freemen,—and if we do not think it possible to provide these for our people, then let us cease to revile the Greeks and Romans and Americans, and confess that we too have slavery amongst us, and confess it to be an inevitable evil.

No, Sir,—by God's blessing it is not inevitable, if we look steadily at it, and will pay the price of removing it. We do not scruple to pay twenty millions to get rid of it in the West Indies;—would we and ought we not to pay twice as much if needful to remove it at home? . . .

33   A call to hatred

From Friedrich Engels's *The Condition of the Working Class in England*, 1844.

Engels, like Marx, was born in the Rhineland (in 1820), of substantial middle-class parents. Engels was sent to England to manage a family mill near Manchester. He was an active Chartist, and was at work on the famous book from which this extract is taken before he first met Marx in 1844. The rhetoric of revolution was not new, but in this work, the analysis of class war moves towards its distinctively communist form. Died 1895.

We turn now to consider the cultural and educational state of the workers, as distinct from their physical condition. Since the middle classes allow the workers only a bare minimum standard of living, it is not surprising that they receive only as much education as will serve the interests of their masters, which in fact amounts to very little. In relation to the size of the population the educational facilities in England are negligible. There are a very limited number of day schools available to working-class children; they are of a poor standard and attract only a very few scholars. The teachers are retired workers or other unsuitable persons who, unable to earn a living in any other way, have turned to teaching as a last resort. The vast majority of these 'teachers' are themselves virtually uneducated and lack the moral qualities essential in a teacher. Moreover, they are under no sort of public control. In education, as in everything else, free competition is the rule, and as usual the wealthy derive all the advantages from this arrangement. . . . There is no compulsory education in England. In the factories, as we shall see, compulsory education exists only in name. During the parliamentary session of 1843, the Government proposed to enforce compulsory education for factory children. The factory owners resisted this proposal vigorously, although it was supported by the workers themselves. Large numbers of children work throughout the week in factories or at home and consequently have no time to attend school. There are evening institutes which are intended to serve the needs of such children and young workers, who are fully employed during the day-time. These institutes have very few scholars and those who do attend derive no profit from the instruction given. It is really too much to expect a young person who has been at work for twelve hours to go to school between 9 p.m. and 10 p.m. Most of those who do attend fall asleep, as is proved by hundreds of statements by witnesses before the Children's Employment Commissioners. It is true that there are also Sunday schools in existence, but they are quite inadequately staffed and are of value only to pupils who have already learnt something in a day school. The interval between one Sunday and another is too long for an ignorant child to remember on the second attendance what he has learnt on the first a week before. On the basis of thousands of proofs contained in the statements of witnesses examined on behalf of the Children's Employment Commission, the Report of this Commission emphatically declares that the existing provision of day schools and Sunday schools is wholly inadequate for the present needs of the country.

This Report gives a picture of the abysmal ignorance of the English working classes which one might expect to find in such countries as Spain and Italy. What else is to be expected? The middle classes have little to hope and much to fear from the education of the workers. In an enormous budget of £55,000,000 a mere £40,000 is devoted to public education. If it were not for the fanaticism of the religious sects—which does at least as much harm as good—the amount of education available would be even less. . . . The working classes have often enough demanded from Parliament the introduction of a purely secular system of public education, which would make religious instruction solely the responsibility of the ministers of the various churches. They have not been able to obtain anything approaching a sympathetic hearing from any Government. . . . In Wolverhampton R. H. Horne found among others the following examples: A girl of eleven years who had attended both day and Sunday school, but had 'Never learnt of another world, nor of heaven, nor of another life. . . .' Another young person, 17 years of age, 'did not know how many two and two made, nor how many farthings there were in two-pence, even when the money was placed in his hand'. '. . . You will find boys who have never heard of such a place as London, nor of Willenhall (which is only three miles distant, and in constant communication with Wolverhampton)'. '. . . Some [of the children] have never heard the name of Her Majesty, nor such names as Wellington, Nelson, Buonaparte, etc. But it is to be especially remarked, that among all those who had never even heard such names as St Paul, Moses, Solomon, etc., there was a general knowledge of the character and course of life of Dick Turpin, the highwayman, and more particularly, of Jack Shepherd, the robber and prison-breaker.' A youth of 16 did not know 'how many twice two make', nor 'how much money six farthings make, nor four farthings'. A youth of seventeen asserted that '10 farthings make 10 halfpence', a third, sixteen years old, answered several very simple questions with the brief statement 'He be'nt no judge o' nothin' '.

These children, who are crammed with religious doctrines for four or five years at a stretch, know as little at the end as at the beginning. One child has 'attended a Sunday school regularly for five years. . . . Does not know who Jesus Christ was, but has heard the name of it. Never heard of the twelve apostles. Never heard of Samson, nor of Moses, nor Aaron, etc.' . . . This shows what the middle classes have done for the education and improvement of the working classes. Fortunately the circumstances in which the workers live are such as to give them a practical training which is not only a substitute for mere book-learning, but also renders harmless the confused religious instruction which is associated with the knowledge gained at school. The workers are actually in the vanguard of the national movement in England. Necessity is the mother of invention, and what is even more important, is also the mother of thought and action. Although the average English worker can hardly read, let alone write, he nevertheless has a shrewd notion of where his own interest and that of his country lie. He knows, too, where the selfish interest of the bourgeoisie lies, and what he may expect from the middle classes. He may not be able to write, but he can at least speak and he can speak in public. He may not be very good at arithmetic but he knows enough about the facts and figures of political economy to see through and to defeat the attempts of the middle classes to foist Corn Law repeal on him. He may still be somewhat uncertain concerning spiritual affairs—in spite of all the preachings of the parsons—but he is no fool when it comes to dealing with secular, political, and social problems. . . .

From a moral point of view, as in the physical and intellectual spheres, the workers are neglected and spurned by the possessing classes. The middle classes control the worker not by inculcating moral principles but simply by means of the shackles imposed on them by the legal system. The workers are treated like dumb beasts who can only be taught by means of the whip. If the workers threaten the interests of their superiors even to the slightest extent, the middle classes do not reason with them but use the brutal discipline of legal repression. In the circumstances it is not surprising that workers who are treated like beasts either behave like beasts or are able to maintain their self-respect as human beings only by continually harbouring hatred of the powerful oppressors. The workers retain their humanity only so long as they cherish a burning fury against the property-owning classes. They become animals as soon as they submit patiently to their yoke, and try to drag out a bearable existence under it without attempting to break free. . . .

34   If every child had the opportunity . . .

From Sir James Kay-Shuttleworth's *Explanation of the Minutes of 1846*, 1847.

See note to 19 above. J. Phillips Kay became Sir James Kay-Shuttleworth on his marriage in 1842.

There is little or nothing in the profession of an elementary school-master, in this country, to tempt a man having a respectable acquaintance with the elements of even humble learning to exchange the certainty of a respectable livelihood in a subordinate condition in trade or commerce, for the mean drudgery of instructing the rude children of the poor in an elementary school, as it is now conducted.

For what is the condition of the master of such a school? He has often an income very little greater than that of an agricultural labourer, and very rarely equal to that of a moderately skilful mechanic. Even this income is to a great degree contingent on the weekly pittances paid from the earnings of his poor neighbours, and liable to be reduced by bad harvests, want of employment, strikes, sickness among the children, or, worst of all, by the calamity of his own ill-health.

Of late years he may more frequently have a small cottage rent-free, but seldom a garden or fuel.

Some portion of his income may be derived from the voluntary subscriptions of the promoters of the school—a precarious source, liable to be dried up by the removal or death of patrons, and the fickleness of friends.

Amidst these uncertainties, with the increase of his family his struggles are greater. He tries to eke out his subsistence by keeping accounts, and writing letters for his neighbours. He strives to be elected parish clerk, or registrar, or clerk to some benefit club. These additions to his income, if he be successful, barely keep him out of debt, and in old age he has no prospect but hopeless indigence and dependence.

To intrust the education of the labouring classes of this country to men involved in such straits, is to condemn the poor to ignorance and its fatal train of evils. To build spacious and well-ventilated schools, without attempting to provide a position of honour and emolument for the masters, is to cheat the poor with a cruel illusion. Even the very small number of masters now well trained in Normal and Model Schools, will find no situation in which their emoluments and prospects will be equal to those which their new acquirements and skill might insure if they should desert the profession of an elementary school-master. Whilst their condition remains without improvement, a religious motive alone can induce the young men, who are now trained in Normal Schools, to sacrifice all prospects of personal advancement for the self-denying and arduous duties of a teacher of the children of the poor. . . .

It may be well that the poor should give proof of the value they attach to the education of their children, by making some sacrifice from their earnings to promote the comfort of the schoolmaster, and should thus preserve a consciousness of their right to choose the school in which their children are to be trained, and to exercise some vigilance over the conduct of their master; but the social condition of the poor must be greatly superior to what the most sanguine can expect it will become in the next half-century, before they can afford to provide an adequate subsistence for the schoolmaster; and their moral and intellectual state must be at least equally improved, before they are prepared by the value they attach to the education of their children, to make sacrifices adequate to the remuneration of the teacher.

From the contributions of the poor, therefore, little more can be expected in aid of the master's income, and that increase, if procurable, must be derived both from a more lively appreciation of the benefits of education to a labouring man, and from an improvement in his own means of subsistence. . . .

While the condition of the master is one of such privation and uncertainty, he has by the existing system of school instruction been placed in a situation, the difficulties of which are insuperable, even by the highest talent and skill, much less by men struggling with penury, exhausted with care, often ill-instructed, and sometimes assuming the duties of a most responsible office, only because deemed incompetent to strive for a livelihood in the open field of competition. Men so circumstanced, have been placed, without other assistants than monitors, in charge of schools containing from 150 to 300 scholars and upwards. The monitors usually employed are under twelve years of age, some of them being as young as eight or nine, and they are in general very ignorant, rude, and unskilful. The system of monitorial instruction has practically failed in this country because of the early period at which children are required for manufacturing and agricultural labour. It has been generally abandoned on the Continent on account of its comparative imperfection under any circumstances, but it was probably never exhibited under greater disadvantages than in England.

The earliest efforts of recent promoters of the education of the labouring classes were made in towns. The schools of towns are commonly large—the children are sent to work at a very early age—the population is migratory, and the school attendance short, irregular, and uncertain. One master was placed over a school containing for the most part from 200 to 400 children, and he was not supplied with any assistance, expecting what he could derive from the scholars committed to his charge. His own efforts to create an instructed class, which might render him this service, were constantly thwarted by the migration of the parents, by the removal of the child to work, and the extreme difficulty of combining the instruction and training of the monitorial class with such an attention to the whole school as would preserve order and discipline, and secure so much progress in the several classes as to furnish a proper succession in the first class of ripe scholars from whom to select the monitors. . . .

If this be the condition of the master, and if this be the character of the only assistance afforded him in the discipline and instruction of his school, is it a legitimate subject of surprise, that a very large proportion of the children attending elementary schools in this country should not even acquire the art of reading accurately, much less with ease and expression, and that all the higher aims of education should appear, notwithstanding constant school extension, to be unattainable? Can we wonder that the working classes should attach no value to an education so meager and worthless, and consequently that the school attendance of their children should not exceed a year and a half on the average throughout entire districts? Is it surprising that juvenile delinquency should be on the increase?

. . . In the denser parts of great cities, a large and possibly an increasing number of children have no training in any handicraft, but seek a precarious livelihood by coster-mongering; by casual employment in errands; and in small services to persons whom they encounter in the streets. Such habits naturally tend to mendicancy, vagrancy, petty thefts, and the criminal career and vagabond life of a juvenile delinquent. Such children have often no home; the father is dead, or has absconded; the mother may be a prostitute, or may have married and deserted her offspring; or the child has fled from the drunken violence or loathsome selfishness of his parents. Many sleep under the open arches of the markets, or of the areas of the houses of ancient construction; in deserted buildings, out-houses, and cellars, and rise in the morning not knowing where or how to obtain a meal. Others are driven forth by their parents to beg or to steal, and not allowed to eat until they have brought home the produce of their knavery or cunning. Some live in the haunts of professed thieves, are trained in all the arts of pilfering, instructed how to elude the police, and to evade the law. They are reared to regard society as their enemy, and property as a monstrous institution on which they may justly prey. The majority of this class of children are practically heathens. They probably never heard the name of Christ. Christianity has done nothing for them.

The most obvious advantage to be offered to such children is the means of earning a livelihood by training them in some handicraft requiring skill. If every such child had the opportunity of entering a workshop in which he could acquire the art of a smith, or a carpenter, or a cooper, or other similar trade, and after some hours of application was provided with a coarse but wholesome meal, it is not to be doubted that many, attracted not less by the sympathy which such arrangements would prove to exist for their forlorn condition, than by the opportunity of escaping from the misery of a life of crime and privation, would become assiduous scholars in such schools of industry. If also an hour or two daily were set apart for instruction in the general outline of Christian faith and duty, and in the rudiments of humble learning, how many children might we not hope would be saved

from ruin. To promote such arrangements, their Lordships have
offered assistance towards the erection of the requisite buildings,
towards the purchase of tools, and for the encouragement of the master
workmen by granting gratuities for every boy who, in consequence
of skill acquired in the workshop, shall have become a workman or
assistant in any trade or craft whereby he is earning a livelihood.

35   The iniquity of taxes

From B. Parsons's *The Unconstitutional Character of the Government
Plan of Education proposed by the Marquis of Lansdowne*, 1847.

The Rev. Benjamin Parsons was born in 1797 in Gloucestershire.
He was ordained a congregational minister in 1826, and took a
living near Stroud, where he remained for the rest of his life.
He took a vigorous interest in education, opening a day school in
1840, and lecturing to men in the evenings. His three main concerns
were the voluntary principle, temperance, and strict sabbath
observance; he was an enthusiastic exponent always of *laissez-faire*.
Died 1855.

Our dearest interests are at stake. Many of those who once approved
of government grants for the erection of school houses, had they ever
dreamt that this little horn was to become so despotic, would never
have taken a single penny. They confided in the patriotism of the
whigs, and now have to pay dearly for their simplicity. . . .

   It is grievous to see how, by this measure, the working classes are
to be misled. It comes to them in the form of a boon, and yet there is
no doubt that this education will actually cost them twice as much as
it would if the privy council had nothing to do with it. The government will first take the money from them in the shape of a tax, and
afterwards will profess to return a portion in the form of a charity.
Then as only one *twenty-fifth* child is to be apprenticed, the remaining
twenty-four will have to support him. What would be said if the privy
council undertook to tax every twenty-four families, to apprentice the
children of every twenty-fifth family to be weavers or carpenters, or

any thing else, and to provide for them for life? Would this be just, or would it be borne? No government has any right to practice such gross injustice, that such a thing should even be mentioned in a free country is a striking proof of the opinion that the concoctors of it have of the perfect degradation of the nation.

36   Knowledge, freedom, and the world league tables

From Thomas King's *National Education Conducive to the Liberties and Essential to the Happiness of the People*, 1847.

This 'Letter Addressed to the Inhabitants of England' was written by Thomas King, who described himself as 'Surgeon, Chelmsford'.

Your freedom and independence as a people, your religious rights and privileges, which *you are bound to cherish and maintain*, can never be injured by the universal diffusion of useful and religious knowledge. Search diligently the history of past ages—look attentively to the passing events of the present time; and then say in what part of the habitable globe despotism and misrule are co-existent with science and the *free communication* of knowledge to all classes of society—the enquiry will be in vain, so undeviatingly do the records of past times confirm the assertion of our enlightened statesman Lord Brougham, in his address at the Manchester Mechanics' Institution. 'I am quite confident,' says his lordship, 'that with the knowledge of men, the rights of men, I mean their indefeasible rights of every kind—the rights which they have to civil liberty, and to religious liberty, the greatest of earthly and social blessings—*are sure to be infinitely promoted*; nor do I know of any more certain mode of reforming a country, any better way of redressing her grievances, than by *giving education to her people.*' ...

... It remains now to be seen, whether, as inhabitants of this highly favoured country, living under a free and enlightened Government, and possessing inexhaustible resources, you will consent that, whilst every other civilized part of the globe is making rapid strides in the acquirement of knowledge, England shall remain stationary, and relinquish her once proud and distinguished pre-eminence among the nations. In France, in Prussia, in Germany, in Denmark, in Bavaria, in Belgium, in America, nay, even in Russia, (which, though a gigantic empire, stands lowest in the scale of civilization,) in all these countries they have organized a complete society and system of national education. Shall the British Isles only be excepted?

37 Education and the Russell Cabinet

From *The Labourer*, 1847.

The Labourer, a monthly magazine of politics, literature, poetry, etc. ran from 1847 to 1848. It was edited by Feargus O'Connor and Ernest Jones, two of the most militant and radical of the Chartist leaders.

The object of teaching should not be so much a desire to plant in as to draw out; not to teach certain theories as true, but to so train or exercise the mental faculties to distinguish between truth and falsehood in all things, as will enable children, when arriving at maturity, to depend more upon their powers of discrimination than upon the discrimination and advice of others. Self-educated men, who have risen to an eminence in society, are distinguished for their keenness of perception and power of reflection, which properties heighten their value as thinkers, and give them a marked advantage over our men of merely school and college training. This superiority we attribute to habits of self-reliance, of free and natural exercise of the reasoning faculties; and the so-called uneducated peasant who speaks truth as by inspiration, is indeed an educated man. Some may be disposed to attribute the superiority to the force of genius, and we admit that in most cases it is a natural force of superior intellect to break through the conventionalities of habit, and to claim among men individuality and distinctness of position; but there is a training necessary before this position is acquired, and if we turn over the biographies of great men, springing from all ranks, we discover that the training of all is nearly

similar; that their mental greatness is more attributable to their private
and individual training than to their school or public instruction; and
that their distinctness of mental vision has begot a consciousness of
power which has enabled them to give manners and forms to society,
to disseminate opinions, and forced the wondering many to say of
them as Wordsworth hath of Milton, 'Thy soul was like a star, and
dwelt apart.'

We think it would be advisable, on the part of teachers and parents,
to endeavour to reduce the system of training practised by the self-
educated great minds, into their forms of domestic and school discipline. Our public schools are lamentably deficient in their process of
mental exercise. Children are taught to read and write, and in too
many cases the learning by rote of a page of English grammar, or
running glibly over the age of kings, is mistaken for a sound education;
the pupil being disgusted by long hours and dull application, instead
of a cultivation of that curiosity that made him but a few years ago
desire to know all things, you have a so-called clever boy, who may
perhaps tell you the names of the planets, work a question in the rule
of three, and is extremely pleased when your inquiries cease. But has
he been taught to reason and investigate? to distinguish and resolve?
No, the husk has been mistaken for the kernel, and the naming of words
for an exercise of thought. . . .

. . . The government plan of education is now causing considerable
controversy, and the question of whether or no the government should
educate the people, is warmly discussed. We submit, that society makes
government, and in the present case the government measure is an
effect resulting from the spread of intelligence, and general tendency
of the present age for change. A few years ago the squirearchy and
nobility generally declared the people knew too much, and that they
were growing insolent and lazy demagogues, and objecting to obey
their masters; whilst the millocracy refused to lessen the hours of toil,
and spoke of their mill hands as a part of their estate. They also were
too wise—they wanted to be gentlefolks, and had too much spare
time already. Appearances have changed, and now dissenters and
churchmen are resolved that the people shall know more than ever.
Who has produced the change? The demagogues, and the public press,
that great inculcator of knowledge, that powerful teacher of the
nation; and the government is now discovering that the laws and
institutions that suited and became the old mind of England, do not
suit the growing mind of England; the swaddling clothes of infancy
grace not the limbs of manhood. We have never yet heard a really

valuable argument against government interference on questions of education, and, so far as the right of government is concerned, we opine that it is not only the right, but the duty of governments to do as the majority of the male adult population will they should do, and above all, that measures purporting to be for a nation's interest should be carefully constructed both for the immediate good and lasting benefit of the entire population, sound in principle, wise and efficient in execution. Neither have we any fault to find with the interested or benevolent acts of private individuals, provided such acts be not injurious to the best interests of the community, and not in opposition to laws framed by the majority for the government of all. And, under existing circumstances, we would encourage all men to aid by every laudable means the education of the people, and if the friends of voluntary education could by private subscription establish and support a school with efficient teachers in every street, our words would be, 'Go on and prosper.' . . .

We affirm that the right of every child to be educated is as binding as is its right to be fed when hungry. The appetite of the youthful mind is not less keen than the appetite of the youthful man, and the good or evil services rendered to the state depend as assuredly on a well-regulated mind as they do on a healthy and well-trained body. If the low wages and inadequate means of parents be such as prevent them from educating their children, it is the duty of those parties who profit by their labour to provide the necessary education: they are debtors, and if they possess the means to pay and will not, they must be summoned, brought into court, and forced to discharge their debts, provided the claim of the creditor be fairly and truthfully established; and this, in our case, will be an easy task. The claim of the pauper is acknowledged, and to some extent provided for; the debt due to the mental pauper is not less just, and the necessity for payment not less urgent. . . .

. . . The government scheme of education seems to us to be partial and unjust—it is no scheme of national education. . . . Such are politics —mean trafficking to prejudice, sordid love of place—a fair specimen of genuine Whiggism. The Catholics must be insulted . . . their faith sneered at, their privileges of citizenship denied, on purpose to be kindly treated hereafter; the Wesleyans must be deceived and hood-winked into a belief of government distrust of Catholicism, their love of purity and Protestantism courted for ministerial advantage. The man who, in private life, would be guilty of so base and crafty a scheme of organised hypocrisy, would be denounced and mistrusted; but, in this age of strange morals, that which is private disgrace is patronised as public worth. . . . The details of the government scheme indicate not only ignorance of the means of carrying their scheme of education into effect, but prove to us the inability of the Whig administration to legislate for the present and future happiness and greatness of this country. . . .

The education of the people is a great and glorious theme, embracing within itself the germ of future intelligence and power, and the ministry which would give to England a truly national education, would confer on the world a blessing. The Russell Cabinet are not the men possessing the requisite knowledge and firmness for such a measure; they are too desirous to be liberal in appearance to please the fanatics in religion, and too imbecile in action to hoist the standard of equality and right, and abide by the issue, calmly waiting the result and relying on the power of the intelligent and truly liberal—secure in the affections of the people, because of the people's confidence in their honesty of intention and boldness of action. The Whigs are not the men for the many; they crucify progression by a conflict of opinions in the cabinet, and disturb the public mind without having the means of satisfying the people's demand; they aim at leading the band without a knowledge of their instrument; they blow a cracked whistle, but cannot sound a full trumpet. . . .

38   Education cures: but what is it?

From David Stow's *National Education*, 1847.

David Stow was Hon. Sec. to the Glasgow Normal Seminary in 1847.

We have always advocated large Government grants for the mora and intellectual training of the young, knowing that otherwise the people would never educate themselves, and that the private subscrip-tions of the wealthy would fail in providing the requisite funds for that purpose. Let all good men of every truly christian sect and party now heartily unite in the effort of rendering the people of this nation, not merely the greatest but the best—the most moral—the most intelligent —the most pious in the world. Let our strength lie not only in our fleets and armies and mechanical power, but in an intelligent, a moral, a religious and therefore a prosperous and happy people. Let us shew to Government that we can realise all the money it requires of us; and by the prudence of the expenditure lay claim to further and much larger sums.

My object is to shew that while great improvements have been made in Education of late years, still the wants and condition of the people are not yet met by a system fitted to elevate them morally and intellectually, and more particularly to meet the condition of the youth of large towns.

All seem to agree in prescribing EDUCATION as a cure for the evils of society, and yet we scarcely meet with two persons who agree as to what education actually is. . . . A child is said by some to be *educated* when he can read words of two or three syllables—better no doubt when he can pronounce every word of a sentence, although he may not understand the meaning of one half of its terms, and repeats sounds from memory without attaching any idea to them. He is no more than *educated*, say others, when he can write, cast accounts, repeat the rules of English grammar and knows a little geography; and is simply *educated*, others still declare, when he has passed the whole curriculum of the highest University. . . . In these days *the most important of all the questions we can determine is*, WHAT IS POPULAR EDUCATION? WHAT OUGHT IT TO BE? The wealthy may choose for themselves; they may be satisfied at any step, from the 'ab-eb-ib-ob-ub' of the old rote system of the English school, to that which embraces the most finished education. The idea however is now becoming more and more prevalent that, in the true sense of the word, we are never educated— that Education progresses or ought to progress through life—and that, although Methusaleh himself had lived to complete 970 instead of 969 years his education would only then have been finished.

What the education is that will best enable a man to educate himself ought surely to be the sovereign question. Is it *Instruction*, or is it *Training?*—Is it the amount of elementary knowledge communicated, or is it the exercise of mind required by which the pupil may educate himself? Till lately the term used to define Education was INSTRUCTION. Give religious instruction, it was and is still said, and this will be sufficient.—Teach the poor to read the Bible, and forthwith you will make them holy, happy, and good citizens,—good parents,—obedient children,—kind and compassionate,—honorable in their dealings,—

and crime will diminish. Hundreds of thousands have received such an education—are such the results? We trow not. Have we hit upon the right kind of education, *or the proper mode of communication*? Will all the instruction it is possible to give produce the results which are so fondly anticipated? Will all the *telling* or teaching or instruction in the world enable a person to make a shoe, construct a machine, ride, write or paint, without *training*—that is without *doing*? Will the *knowledge* of religious truth make a good man without the practice of it? The boy may repeat most correctly and even understand in a general way the precepts, 'Avenge not yourselves but rather give place unto wrath,' 'Render not evil for evil,' 'Be courteous;' but see him at play among his companions, neither better nor perhaps worse than himself, unsuperintended and his conduct unreviewed by parent or school-master, and what do these scriptural injunctions avail him when engaged in a quarrel?—Reason is dormant, passion reigns for the time, and the repeated exercise of such propensities strengthens the disposition, and eventually forms evil *habits*. . . .

After closely remarking the deep moral degradation of great masses of the population in the city and suburbs of Glasgow, and in other large towns in Great Britain, and the effects which education, such as it was, had on their moral and intellectual condition. . . . I became fully convinced that our parochial and private English schools elevated the mass of the population but slightly in an intellectual point of view, and their moral improvement under such *Teaching* was scarcely perceptible.

39   No education outside the church

From A. P. Perceval's *Letter to Lord John Russell*, 1847.

The Hon. and Rev. A. P. Perceval was born in 1799, son of the 2nd Baron Arden. From 1826, he was royal chaplain to George IV, William IV and Queen Victoria. A fervent tractarian. Died 1853.

On the Unitarian tendency imputed in the public mind to one member of your Lordship's cabinet, and the supposed Presbyterian predilections of three or four, I will say no more, than that I trust no misrepresentations from any quarter will induce your Lordship for one moment to believe, that the English people will allow the Education of the nation to be subjected to their influence; least of all, that the Universities, which the history of our country in successive centuries has shown to be the strongholds of loyalty and liberty, whether menaced by the Crown, the people, or a popular minister, should be molested by the forced intrusion of those who have, with too few exceptions, been found enemies to both; the absurd project for whose compulsory admission into Oxford and Cambridge, has again been brought under the notice of the Imperial Parliament. It cost King James his throne, and the nation a change of dynasty, when these seats of learning were tampered with in favour of those who believe *too much:* I fear, my Lord, that in the present temper of the nation, a similar attempt in favour of those who believe *too little*, will COST MORE.

'But,' perhaps your Lordship will say or think, 'can we do nothing to improve the social, moral, intellectual, and religious welfare of the people?' Yes, my Lord, *every thing:* provided you will set about it *according to the laws of the nation*, and the spirit of its *ancient constitution*; and not in violation of these.

40 Boarding school accounts

An account from George Pocock's Academy, Bristol, 1847.

January 18th, 1847:
An account paid by Mr John James of Dyffryn, Clynderwen [Pembrokeshire], for his son's education at
'Mr George Pocock's Academy, Bristol:
Half-year's Board and Education £13-2-6; Washing £1-2-6; Pens, Ink and paper 2/6; Library 2/6; Writing Book 6/-; Ciphers Book 1/6; Spelling Book 1/6; Pencils 6d.; half Quire letter paper 5d.; Cap 5/-; Gloves 1/6; Shoemakers 5/9; Tailor 2/6; Weekly money 2/8; Cash 12/6; £16-9-10.
Mr James provided the School with butter, £12-3-9½; and paid the balance of £4-6-0½.'

41   Tenthly and lastly

From Karl Marx and Friedrich Engels, *The Manifesto of the Communist Party*, 1848.

Marx was born in 1818 in the Rhineland and studied philosophy at Bonn and at the University of Berlin, where his political views brought him into trouble. In 1843, he fled to Paris, then to Brussels and eventually to London, where he met Engels in 1844. One of the early fruits of their partnership was the pamphlet from which this extract is taken. Marx spent most of his life after this working in the British Museum on *Das Kapital*. Died 1883. For note on Engels, see 33 above.

(*Editor's note*: the tenth and last point of the 'measures' that would mark the communist revolution):
10. Free education of all children in public schools. Abolition of children's factory labour in its present form. Combination of education with industrial production, etc.

42   Nurture versus nature

From Emily Brontë's *Wuthering Heights*, 1848.

Emily Brontë was born in 1818 at Haworth, Yorkshire. Her fame is as a novelist, along with her sisters Charlotte and Anne, all too well known to need notes. Died 1848.

'I have tied his tongue,' observed Heathcliff. 'He'll not venture a single syllable, all the time! Nelly, you recollect me at his age—nay, some years younger. Did I ever look so stupid, so "gaumless", as Joseph calls it?'

'Worse,' I replied, 'because more sullen with it.'

'I've a pleasure in him,' he continued, reflecting aloud. 'He has satisfied my expectations. If he were born a fool I should not enjoy it half so much. But he's no fool; and I can sympathise with all his feelings, having felt them myself. I know what he suffers now, for instance, exactly; it is merely a beginning of what he shall suffer, though. And he'll never be able to emerge from his bathos of coarseness and ignorance. I've got him faster than his scoundrel of a father secured me, and lower; for he takes a pride in his brutishness. I've taught him to scorn everything extra-animal as silly and weak. Don't you think Hindley would be proud of his son, if he could see him— almost as proud as I am of mine? But there's this difference: one is gold put to the use of paving-stones, and the other is tin polished to ape a service of silver. *Mine* has nothing valuable about it; yet I shall have the merit of making it go as far as such poor stuff can go. *His* had first-rate qualities, and they are lost—rendered worse than unavailing. *I* have nothing to regret; *he* will have more than any but I are aware of. And the best of it is, Hareton is damnably fond of me! You'll own that I've outmatched Hindley there. If the dead villain could rise from his grave to abuse me for his offspring's wrongs, I should have the fun of seeing the said offspring fight him back again, indignant that he should dare to rail at the one friend he has in the world!'

Heathcliff chuckled a fiendish laugh at the idea. I made no reply, because I saw that he expected none.

43   Cobden out-Cobdened

From B. Parsons's *Letter to Richard Cobden on the Impolicy and Tyranny of Any System of State Education*, 1852. See note on 35 above.

But it is not more evident that voluntaryism in trade is the great secret of our wealth, than it is that voluntary education has placed the working classes of this country at the head of all nations, for intelligence and morality; and, therefore, I speak most advisedly, when I say, that you could not perform a more cruel or injurious act, than to put down the voluntary efforts of a nation in respect of public schools.

Nothing more strikingly shows the determination of the masses to educate themselves, than that so much has been done, notwithstanding the opposition that has been encountered. Why, Sir, it was only a little time ago, and long since my remembrance, that the gentry, clergy, and masters and mistresses generally, were averse to the education of the people. They reviled it, laughed at it, caricatured it, wrote against it, spoke against it, and preached against it. I have known a clergyman in the greatest dismay, lest his poor neighbours should be able to read, and should have the Bible put into their hands. Within the last twenty years, it has been said by many, that if you educated the masses, they would not work; but would read newspapers, their masters' and mistresses' letters, &c. &c.; and, in fact, that neither the Throne, the Church, the Constitution, nor Christianity, would be safe. And even now, it is pretty evident that many want the whole affair to be made a Government job, as on the Continent, that our day-schools for the masses may become as stationary as Oxford and Cambridge. But if, notwithstanding this powerful opposition, there has been such an unheard-of progress in the number of schools, what but the grossest legislative meddlesomeness, trickery, jobbing, or ignorance, could induce any man who loves intelligence, morality, and liberty, to interfere with a principle which has worked so effectually and vigorously, even in the face of the most virulent adversaries? If, with a thousand voices protesting against popular instruction, and ten thousand authoritative tongues assuring the people that 'ignorance was bliss,' that 'learning' for them, whether 'little' or much, 'was a dangerous thing;' yet so many myriads of our operatives have esteemed knowledge, and have determined to educate themselves and their offspring; then, why destroy a power which has done so much, and introduce another which, though it might provide funds, would have no influence to increase the number of scholars, and, if past experience may be taken as a test, would rather diminish than multiply the attendance?

For, after all, what are your schools supported by a rate to be, but mere parish or pauper schools? There will be something just as low and degrading in them, as in the pauperism of the workhouse. You are going to send all our children to the parish. To create charity-schools for the whole nation, and send all our offspring to this Educational Union. This New Poor Law of yours will be a thousand times more degrading and despotic, than the present Poor Law has been. Charity under very few circumstances works well for the character of the recipient. There is a sense of poverty and degradation about it; and it often engenders indolence, and completely destroys that independence, activity, and industry, which are so important to the intellectual and moral progress of a nation. One thing that many of us have been labouring at for years has been to restore that noble independence which was felt fifty years ago, and which caused the poor to dread nothing so much as to come to the parish, and be supported by the poor-rate. Why, at that time a charity-school was considered a disgrace. And I am happy to say, that this old-fashioned English feeling is fast growing up among us again. In the hundreds of lectures that I have delivered to the masses, on the Corn Laws, Temperance, &c., &c., I have always found a hearty response to the sentiment, that the working classes of this country do not ask for *'charity bread,' 'charity clothing,' 'charity coals,'* or *'charity education.'* Their language is, 'Unfetter trade,' 'Reduce taxation,' 'Diminish your standing army,' 'Abolish your pensions, and your other jobbing in inspectorships, commissioners, placemen, and sinecures; take the taxes from knowledge; repeal all unjust laws; give us our natural and constitutional share of liberty; and then,' with one voice they exclaim, 'we shall have a fair day's wage for a fair day's work, and we will buy our own bread, coals, candles, and clothing; worship where we please; and educate our children in what schools we like best.' Were I to say that I have heard these principles responded to from thousands upon thousands of voices, I should not exaggerate; and am equally proud to know that this Old English independence is not yet dead among the operatives and peasants of the country generally. . . .

. . . If you will read 'The Reports of the National School Society,' you will find the Inspectors stating that charity education does not succeed. I might quote largely, but the declaration of the Rev. Mr Field, afterward Bishop of Newfoundland, is sufficient. In the Report of 1841, he remarks to the Bishop of Worcester, *'That a charge as large as the children can reasonably be expected to pay, is in all cases desirable.* INSTRUCTION THAT COSTS NOTHING IS GENERALLY VALUED AT WHAT IT COSTS. *It is really better that even the poorest should pay for instruction, that they may learn to value it.'* Man was never created, Sir, to be a pauper or a beggar, and in proportion as he feels this truth, he spurns the idea of being educated *'in formâ pauperis.'* There are few charity-schools that work well. A minister, anxious to improve the neighbourhood in which he lived, said to me not long since, 'This parish is cursed with charities. Between charity-bread and charity-schools, I can do nothing to raise the working classes.' . . . Generally speaking, the system demoralizes the master and the scholars. The children that attend worst in our schools, are those which are paid for by charity. I went into a British school some time ago, and saw sixteen boys standing on a form for coming in late. The master told me they were paid for by charity, and were hardly ever in proper time. The English people, when they pay for anything, like to have their penny's-worth for a penny; but there are few persons proof against the debasing influence of compulsion or charity. . . .

Every one is at a loss to account for it, that you, my dear Sir, should lend your voice to a system so degrading as compulsory education must of necessity be; and the only conclusion to which they can come is, that either you have not given it proper thought, or are still under the influence of habits engendered by your belonging to a church which rests for support on compulsion, and, for want of faith in its creed and its ministers, cannot intrust itself to the benevolence of its members; forgetting that this expressed deficiency of confidence is the hardest thing that was ever said against it. If you had only looked at the matter, you would not only have seen that the majority of your own ecclesiastical edifices and property have sprung from voluntary benevolence, but that the Dissenters, notwithstanding their poverty, have built places of worship equal in number to those of the Establishment; and that they support their own ministers, and give them on an average a salary quite as large as that which is received by the *working* Episcopal clergy. That, in addition to these, they have established colleges for the education of their ministers and members, which are well sustained. That they have erected numbers of school-houses, and conduct them at their own cost; and are now making greater sacrifices than ever to advance the education of the country. The effort and money expended on Sunday-schools, are a noble monument of their energy, liberality, patriotism, and Christianity. And their power, their means, their desire, and their zeal for the cause of voluntary religion and education, were never more active than now; and yet this is the time when you wish that their most benevolent efforts for the elevation of the masses should be terminated by a most superfluous, unjust, irreligious, and tyrannous act of legislation.

Were it necessary to say more on this subject, I might refer to 'Mechanics' Institutes,' 'Reading-rooms,' &c., &c., supported by voluntary effort, as a proof that the thirst for knowledge among the masses is rapidly increasing. What an immense circulation there is at the present time of cheap and valuable literature; and what an anxiety for night-schools, and Mutual Improvement Societies, exists among those whose education has been formerly neglected! Our very best educated citizens are those who have educated themselves. I might here mention a fact not generally known. In prospect of the opening of the Crystal Palace, I wrote an article in '*The Working Man's Friend*,' recommending our operatives to study French; and the consequence was, that the Editor's table was, within a few days, loaded with letters, asking which was the best way to begin. Lessons were immediately supplied them, and about six months after, when a prize was offered for the best Essay in French from the working men who had thus been induced to commence the study, not less than TWO HUNDRED ESSAYS were sent in at the time appointed! Why, there is not a town or village in the country, where the young people and the parents are not thirsting for mental improvement, and willing to pay and, unless the Government compelled us to teach them, and took the money by main force out of our pockets, we should actually allow them to grow up in 'brutal ignorance?' In this supposition, there is a gross insult offered to the people of these realms, and especially to the benevolent spirit of the pure and philanthropic religion which they profess. We might add that what has been done has been effected by comparatively a few of our countrymen; and therefore, if a handful of persons have cheerfully effected so much, what may not be anticipated, when the sympathies of the nation shall be fully awakened to engage in this patriotic work? . . .

. . . If I were to give you the history of some of the working people who have kept their children in Ebley School for *six* or *eight* years, there would be a fine example of what parents with a very small income could do towards the instruction of their offspring. Some of these poor persons have been widows, have been afflicted, have often from illness been off their work, and at best have had very low wages; and yet the sense of duty, and a noble principle of independence, have induced them to keep their children at the day-school for periods varying from six to ten years. And this feeling you may create every-where, if philanthropists and ministers of religion will only exert themselves, associate more with the masses, and give them that encouragement and advice which they need. And the calling forth of this virtuous independence is education of the highest order; because it not only elevates the children, but improves the parent. And yet this sense of duty and patriotic self-reliance is the very thing which your compulsory rate and Government grants would completely destroy; and no one in the country is more convinced of this than our friend Richard Cobden. In your better moments, you would exclaim, '*Nothing will so effectually degrade and pauperize a people as to pauperize their education.*'

A little investigation, also, would show, that numbers of those who call out so loudly for these Parish rates and Government grants, have the most ample means of carrying on the cause of education, without having any resort to such degrading and enslaving expedients. . . .

. . . Thousands of our operatives and labourers also have it in their power, by a very little exertion, economy, and self-denial, to supply all the funds requisite for the schooling of their offspring. Wages are now as high, if not higher, than they were when bread was double its present price; and, if they could live then, of course they can now furnish the very small sums required to obtain a thorough education for their sons and daughters. And further, there is every reason to believe that, both in the agricultural and manufacturing districts, the remuneration for labour will considerably increase. 'There is a good time coming,' both for the fields and the factories. No one has a greater faith in this sentiment than yourself. In your speeches you have held out glorious prospects to the artisan, the peasant, the farmer, the tradesman, and the merchant. You believe that the Golden Age is advancing, and that it is even now on the threshhold; and yet, in this period of cheap bread, cheap clothing, and high wages, you propose to destroy all moral and voluntary exertion in education, and to make tuition a piece of legislative machinery, to degrade and pauperize the population! . . .

. . . Thus, my dear Sir, there is no view that can be taken of these exertions in favour of compulsory education, which does not either insult or disgrace the empire. To say the people of England, who cheerfully spend their tens of thousands annually to instruct other nations, will not educate their own brothers and sisters unless compelled to do so, is not only an insult, but a fouler charge on Christianity than Voltaire or Tom Paine ever dared to prefer against it. To declare that the rich will not give sufficient wages to enable the poor to spare a few pence per week for the instruction of their children, is to represent them as avaricious task-masters; or, if you shudder at this charge, and tell us that the people are well paid, but care nothing for their offspring, then you insult and condemn those very masses, whom yourself and Messrs. Bright, Fox, &c., &c., have been accustomed to address as the very *élite* of English intelligence, justice and morality. . . .

. . . It is not the duty of the Government to educate the country. Government was not created for any such purpose. It betrays no small amount of political ignorance, to say that the State has no right to punish crime, if it has neglected to educate the criminals. Secular education cannot make the people moral, and therefore cannot prevent crime. And then the Government cannot be a religious teacher without being a persecutor, on the one hand; or, indifferent to all religion, on the other. To tax all the people to pay for one religion, is political and spiritual tyranny and persecution; and to tax the people to teach all religions, even the most contradictory, is to destroy the foundation of morality, by proclaiming that religion is a mass of contradictions and falsehoods. To this source may be traced the latitudinarianism and infidelity of the Continent. . . .

. . . Many of the men who are loudest in their demands for State interference are either aristocratic despots, or democratic tyrants, who have not learnt the A. B. C. of sound political economy, or rational liberty. It is a striking fact, and a most ominous one for freedom, that Tory and Radical, Conservative and Socialist, are beginning to shake hands. The most perfect system of despotism ever propounded to the world was, the community-plan of Robert Owen. It proposed, not merely to make a voluntary slave, but a perfect machine of every human being. It is rather edifying to see in our day, how cozily despots and certain *soi-disant* democrats move together, and, like Herod and Pontius Pilate, lay aside their former antipathies, in the hope of bringing all rational liberty to the Cross. . . .

44   Education in the best sense

From a letter of John Stuart Mill to the Rev. H. W. Carr, 7 January 1852. See note on 20 above.

Sir,. . . The question you ask me is one of the most difficult which any one can put either to others or to himself, namely, how to teach social science to the uneducated, when those who are called the educated have not learnt it; and nearly all the teaching given from authority is opposed to genuine morality.

What the poor as well as the rich require is not to be indoctrinated, is not to be taught other people's opinions, but to be induced and enabled to think for themselves. It is not physical science that will do this, even if they could learn it much more thoroughly than they are able to do. After reading, writing, and arithmetic (the last a most important discipline in habits of accuracy and precision, in which they are extremely deficient), the desirable thing for them seems to be the most miscellaneous information, and the most varied exercise of their faculties. They cannot read too much. Quantity is of more importance than quality, especially all reading which relates to human life and the ways of mankind; geography, voyages and travels, manners and customs, and romances, which must tend to awaken their imagination and give them some of the meaning of self-devotion and heroism, in short, to unbrutalise them. By such reading they would become, to a certain extent, cultivated beings, which they would not become by following out, even to the greatest length, physical science. As for education in the best sense of the term, I fear they have a long time to wait for it. The higher and middle classes cannot educate the working classes unless they are first educated themselves. The miserable pretence of education, which those classes now receive, does not form minds fit to undertake the guidance of other minds, or to exercise a beneficent influence over them by personal contact. Still, any person who sincerely desires whatever is for the good of all, however it may affect himself or his own class, and who regards the great social questions as matters of reason and discussion and not as settled long ago, may, I believe, do a certain amount of good by merely saying to the working classes whatever he sincerely thinks on the subjects on which they are interested. Free discussion with them as equals, in speech and in writing, seems the best instruction that can be given them, specially on social subjects.

With regard to the social questions now before the public, and in which, as I gather from your letter, the working classes of your town have begun to take an interest, it seems to me chiefly important to impress on them—first, that they are quite right in aiming at a more equal distribution of wealth and social advantages; secondly, that this more equal distribution can only be permanently affected (for merely taking from Peter to give to Paul would leave things worse than even at present) by means of their own public spirit and self-devotion as regards others, and prudence and self-restraint in relation to themselves. At present their idea of social reform appears to be simply higher wages, and less work, for the sake of more sensual indulgence. To be independent of master manufacturers, to work for themselves and divide the whole produce of their labour is a worthy object of ambition, but it is only fit for, and can only succeed with people who can labour for the community of which they are a part with the same energy and zeal as if labouring for their own private and separate interest (the opposite is now the case), and who, instead of expecting immediately more pay and less work, are willing to submit to any privation until they have effected their emancipation. The French working men and women contended for a principle, for an idea of justice, and they lived on bread and water till they gained their purpose. It was not more and costlier eating and drinking that was their object, as it seems to be the sole object of most of the well-paid English artisans. . . .

45   University training: individual and society

From John Henry Newman's *The Idea of a University*, 1852.

Newman was born in 1801, in the City of London. He was a leading figure in the Oxford Movement until his conversion to Rome in 1845, and one of the great theologians of the century. In 1854 he went to Dublin as rector of the Catholic university. This university failed, as a practical project; but Newman's famous thesis on university education—and on education itself—was one of the fruits of his preparation for the experiment. He became a Cardinal, and died in 1890.

The Philosopher has the same command of matters of thought, which the true citizen and gentleman has of matters of business and conduct. If then a practical end must be assigned to a University course, I say it is that of training good members of society. Its art is the art of social life, and its end is fitness for the world. It neither confines its views to particular professions on the one hand, nor creates heroes or inspires genius on the other. Works indeed of genius fall under no art; heroic minds come under no rule; a University is not a birthplace of poets or of immortal authors, of founders of schools, leaders of colonies, or conquerors of nations. It does not promise a generation of Aristotles or Newtons, of Napoleons or Washingtons, of Raphaels or Shakespeares, though such miracles of nature it has before now contained within its

precincts. Nor is it content on the other hand with forming the critic
or the experimentalist, the economist or the engineer, though such too
it includes within its scope. But a University training is the great
ordinary means to a great but ordinary end; it aims at raising the
intellectual tone of society, at cultivating the public mind, at purifying
the national taste, at supplying true principles to popular enthusiasm
and fixed aims to popular aspiration, at giving enlargement and
sobriety to the ideas of the age, at facilitating the exercise of political
power, and refining the intercourse of private life. It is the education
which gives a man a clear conscious view of his own opinions and
judgments, a truth in developing them, an eloquence in expressing
them, and a force in urging them. It teaches him to see things as they
are, to go right to the point, to disentangle a skein of thought, to
detect what is sophistical, and to discard what is irrelevant. It prepares
him to fill any post with credit, and to master any subject with facility.
It shows him how to accommodate himself to others, how to throw
himself into their state of mind, how to bring before them his own,
how to influence them, how to come to an understanding with them,
how to bear with them. He is at home in any society, he has common
ground with every class; he knows when to speak and when to be
silent; he is able to converse, he is able to listen; he can ask a question
pertinently, and gain a lesson seasonably, when he has nothing to
impart himself; he is ever ready, yet never in the way; he is a pleasant
companion, and a comrade you can depend upon; he knows when to
be serious and when to trifle, and he has a sure tact which enables him
to trifle with gracefulness and to be serious with effect. He has the
repose of a mind which lives in itself, while it lives in the world, and
which has resources for its happiness at home when it cannot go
abroad. He has a gift which serves him in public, and supports him in
retirement, without which good fortune is but vulgar, and with which
failure and disappointment have a charm. The art which tends to make
a man all this, is in the object which it pursues as useful as the art of
wealth or the art of health, though it is less susceptible of method, and
less tangible, less certain, less complete in its result.

46   Strange state

From Charles Dickens's *Bleak House*, 1852.

Dickens was born in Portsea in 1812. He became famous with
Pickwick Papers in 1836, and afterwards was one of the most
celebrated Victorian novelists, journalists and social reformers. His
thinking on education is the subject of Philip Collins's fine study,
Dickens and Education.

It is well known that Dickens was one of the most powerfully
subversive critics of his society, but his own political ideals remain
elusive. He feared revolution, and had too little trust in human
nature to be one of nature's democrats. No doubt he would recognise
the fulfilment of many of his hopes in the later welfare state. The
two brief extracts in this volume both demonstrate his characteristic
genius for dramatising a particular social ill with unforgettable
force. Died 1870.

It must be a strange state to be like Jo! To shuffle through the streets,
unfamiliar with the shapes, and in utter darkness as to the meaning, of
those mysterious symbols, so abundant over the shops, and at the
corners of streets, and on the doors, and in the windows! To see
people read, and to see people write, . . . and not to have the least idea
of all that language—to be, to every scrap of it, stone blind and
dumb! . . . To be hustled, and jostled, and moved on; and really to
feel that it would appear to be perfectly true that I have no business,
here, or there, or anywhere; and yet to be perplexed by the consideration that I *am* here somehow, too, and everybody overlooked me until
I became the creature that I am! . . .

Jo . . . sits down to breakfast on the door-step of the Society for the
Propagation of the Gospel in Foreign Parts, and gives it a brush when
he has finished, as an acknowledgment of the accommodation. He
admires the size of the edifice, and wonders what it's all about. He
has no idea, poor wretch, of the spiritual destitution of a coral reef in
the Pacific, or what it costs to look up the precious souls among the
cocoa-nuts and bread-fruit.

47   The tyranny of the commonplace

From Walter Bagehot's 'The Character of Sir Robert Peel', in *National Review*, July 1856.

Bagehot was born in Somersetshire in 1826. He was economist, journalist and critic—and, during the last seventeen years of his life, edited the *Economist* newspaper, which had been established during the anti-corn law agitation to present free trade principles. His most important work was on the English Constitution, where views on democracy and education coloured much of his thought. He believed (for instance) that the throne and the Lords have their proper function not so much in *checking* the Commons, as in inducing people to look above themselves in education and social rank when choosing leaders, and in this way to safeguard their own best interests. Died 1877.

It might be said that this is only one of the results of that tyranny of commonplace which seems to accompany civilisation. You may talk of the tyranny of Nero and Tiberius; but the real tyranny is the tyranny of your next-door neighbour. What law is so cruel as the law of doing what he does? What yoke is so galling as the necessity of being like him? What *espionage* of despotism comes to your door so effectually as the eye of the man who lives at your door? Public opinion is a permeating influence, and it exacts obedience to itself; it requires us to think other men's thoughts, to speak other men's words, to follow other men's habits. Of course, if we do not, no formal ban issues, no corporeal pain, the coarse penalty of a barbarous society, is inflicted on the offender; but we are called 'eccentric'; there is a gentle murmur of 'most unfortunate ideas', 'singular young man', 'well-intentioned, I dare say; but unsafe, sir, quite unsafe.' The prudent, of course, conform. The place of nearly every body depends on the opinion of every one else. There is nothing like Swift's precept to attain the repute of a sensible man: 'Be of the opinion of the person with whom at the time you are conversing.' This world is given to those whom this world can trust. Our very conversation is infected.

Where is now the bold humour, the explicit statement, the grasping
dogmatism of former days? They have departed; and you read in the
orthodox works dreary regrets that the *art* of conversation has passed
away.

48   The same flesh and blood?

From Thomas Hughes's *Tom Brown's Schooldays*, 1857.

Thomas Hughes was born in 1822 in Berkshire. He claimed that
Tom Brown was not autobiographical, but a picture of a
representative of 'the commonest type of English boy of the upper
middle classes'; none the less, it drew heavily on his own
experience as a pupil under Dr Thomas Arnold at Rugby. In January
1854, at a meeting of the promoters of associations, a motion by
Hughes in favour of a people's college led to the foundation of the
Working Men's College in Great Ormond Street, which then
became one of his chief interests in life. This is one of the many
instances, remarked on often here (see especially 50 below), of
strong links between the public school ideals of Dr Arnold and
working-class ideals of self-help.

What village feasts have come to, I fear, in many cases, may be read
in the pages of *Yeast* (though I never saw one so bad—thank God!).
  Do you want to know why? It is because, as I said before, gentlefolk
and farmers have left off joining or taking an interest in them. They
don't either subscribe to the prizes, or go down and enjoy the fun.
  Is this a good or a bad sign? I hardly know. Bad, sure enough, if it
only arises from the further separation of classes consequent on twenty
years of buying cheap and selling dear, and its accompanying over-
work; or because our sons and daughters have their hearts in London
Club-life, or so-called Society, instead of in the old English home
duties; because farmers' sons are apeing fine gentlemen, and farmers'
daughters caring more to make bad foreign music than good English
cheeses. Good perhaps, if it be that the time for the old 'veast' has gone
by, that it is no longer the healthy sound expression of English country

holiday-making; that in fact we as a nation have got beyond it, and are in a transition state, feeling for and soon likely to find some better substitute.

Only I have just got this to say before I quit the text. Don't let reformers of any sort think that they are going really to lay hold of the working boys and young men of England by any educational grapnel whatever, which hasn't some bona fide equivalent for the games of the old country 'veast' in it; something to put in the place of the back-swording and wrestling and racing; something to try the muscles of men's bodies, and the endurance of their hearts, to make them rejoice in their strength. In all the new-fangled comprehensive plans I see this is all left out: and the consequence is, that your great Mechanics' Institutes end in intellectual priggism, and your Christian Young Men's Societies in religious Pharisaism.

Well, well, we must bide our time. Life isn't all beer and skittles—but beer and skittles, or something better of the same sort, must form a good part of every Englishman's education. If I could only drive this into the heads of you rising Parliamentary Lords, and young swells who 'have your ways made for you', as the saying is—you, who frequent palaver houses and West-end clubs, waiting always ready to strap yourselves on to the back of poor dear old John, as soon as the present used-up lot (your fathers and uncles) who sit there on the great Parliamentary-majorities' pack-saddle, and make believe they're guiding him with their red-tape bridle, tumble, or have to be lifted off!

I don't think much of you yet—I wish I could; though you do go talking and lecturing up and down the country to crowded audiences, and are busy with all sorts of philanthropic intellectualism, and circulating libraries and museums, and Heaven only knows what besides; and try to make us think, through newspaper reports, that you are even as we of the working classes. But, bless your hearts, we 'ain't so green', though lots of us of all sorts toady you enough certainly, and try to make you think so.

I'll tell you what to do now: instead of all this trumpeting and fuss, which is only the old Parliamentary-majority dodge over again—just you go each of you (you've plenty of time for it, if you'll only give up t'other line) and quietly make three or four friends, real friends, among us. You'll find a little trouble in getting at the right sort, because such birds don't come lightly to your lure—but found they may be. Take, say, two out of the professions, lawyer, parson, doctor, which you will; one out of trade, and three or four out of the working classes, tailors, engineers, carpenters, engravers,—there's plenty of choice. Let them be men of your own ages, mind, and ask them to your homes; introduce them to your wives and sisters, and get introduced to theirs: give them good dinners, and talk to them about what is really at the bottom of your hearts, and box, and run, and row with them, when you have a chance. Do all this honestly as man to man, and by the time you come to ride old John, you'll be able to do something more than sit on his back, and may feel his mouth with some stronger bridle than a red-tape one.

Ah, if you only would! But you have got too far out of the right rut, I fear. Too much over-civilisation, and the deceitfulness of riches. It is easier for a camel to go through the eye of a needle. More's the pity. I never came across but two of you, who could value a man wholly and solely for what was in him, who thought themselves verily and indeed of the same flesh and blood as John Jones the attorney's clerk, and Bill Smith the costermonger, and could act as if they thought so.

49   Danger of brainwashing?

From John Stuart Mill's *On Liberty*, 1859.

For note on Mill, see 20 above. *On Liberty* was one of his most important, and most carefully written, works.

Consider . . . the case of education. Is it not almost a self-evident axiom, that the State should require and compel the education, up to a certain standard, of every human being who is born its citizen? Yet who is there that is not afraid to recognise and assert this truth? Hardly any one indeed will deny that it is one of the most sacred duties of the parents (or, as law and usage now stand, the father), after summoning a human being into the world, to give to that being an education fitting him to perform his part well in life towards others and towards himself. But while this is unanimously declared to be the father's duty, scarcely anybody, in this country, will bear to hear of obliging him to perform it. Instead of his being required to make any exertion or sacrifice for securing education to his child, it is left to his choice to accept it or not when it is provided gratis! It still remains unrecognised, that to bring a child into existence without a fair prospect of being able, not only to provide food for its body, but instruction and training for its mind, is a moral crime, both against the unfortunate offspring and against society; and that if the parent does not fulfil this obligation, the State ought to see it fulfilled, at the charge, as far as possible, of the parent.

Were the duty of enforcing universal education once admitted there would be an end to the difficulties about what the State should teach, and how it should teach, which now convert the subject into a mere battlefield for sects and parties, causing the time and labour which should have been spent in educating to be wasted in quarrelling about education. If the government would make up its mind to require for every child a good education, it might save itself the trouble of providing one. It might leave to parents to obtain the education where and how they pleased, and content itself with helping to pay the school fees of the poorer classes of children, and defraying the entire school expenses of those who have no one else to pay for them. The objections which are urged with reason against State education do not apply to the enforcement of education by the State, but to the State's taking upon itself to direct that education; which is a totally different thing. That the whole or any large part of the education of the people should be in State hands, I go as far as any one in deprecating. All that has been said of the importance of individuality of character, and diversity in opinions and modes of conduct, involves, as of the same unspeakable importance, diversity of education. A general State education is a mere contrivance for moulding people to be exactly like one another: and as the mould in which it casts them is that which pleases the predominant power in the government, whether this be a monarch, a priesthood, an aristocracy, or the majority of the existing generation; in proportion as it is efficient and successful, it establishes a despotism over the mind, leading by natural tendency to one over the body. An education established and controlled by the State should only exist, if it exists at all, as one among many competing experiments, carried on for the purpose of example and stimulus, to keep the others up to a certain standard of excellence. Unless, indeed, when society in general is in so backward a state that it could not or would not provide for itself any proper institutions of education unless the government undertook the task: then, indeed, the government may, as the less of two great evils, take upon itself the business of schools and universities, as it may that of joint stock companies, when private enterprise, in a shape fitted for undertaking great works of industry, does not exist in the country. But in general, if the country contains a sufficient number of persons qualified to provide education under government auspices, the same persons would be able and willing to give an equally good education on the voluntary principle, under the assurance of remuneration afforded by a law rendering education compulsory, combined with State aid to those unable to defray the expense. . . .

50 Self-culture and power

From Samuel Smiles's *Self-Help*, 1859.

Samuel Smiles was born in 1812 at Haddington, one of the eleven children of Samuel Smiles, a paper maker and later general merchant, who died of cholera in 1832. He was educated at Haddington grammar school, and then became a medical apprentice. Later, he took a medical diploma at Edinburgh, and became a GP.

He is best known as an educationist, and an advocate of various radical causes (he was the first secretary of the Leeds 'Household Suffrage Association' for instance, though he opposed Chartism). His greatest success was *Self-Help*, which was immensely influential in its own time, running into many editions. It remains an important book, a classic statement of the importance of dedicated hard work in any scheme for education. Died 1904.

'The best part of every man's education', said Sir Walter Scott, 'is that which he gives to himself.' The late Sir Benjamin Brodie delighted to remember this saying, and he used to congratulate himself on the fact that professionally he was self-taught. But this is necessarily the case with all men who have acquired distinction in letters, science, or art. The education received at school or college is but a beginning, and is valuable mainly inasmuch as it trains the mind and habituates it to continuous application and study. That which is put into us by others is always far less ours than that which we acquire by our own diligent and persevering effort. Knowledge conquered by labour

F

becomes a possession—a property entirely our own. A greater vividness and permanency of impression is secured; and facts thus acquired become registered in the mind in a way that mere imparted information can never effect. This kind of self-culture also calls forth power and cultivates strength. The solution of one problem helps the mastery of another; and thus knowledge is carried into faculty. Our own active effort is the essential thing; and no facilities, no books, no teachers, no amount of lessons learnt by rote will enable us to dispense with it.

The best teachers have been the readiest to recognise the importance of self-culture, and of stimulating the student to acquire knowledge by the active exercise of his own faculties. They have relied more upon *training* than upon *telling*, and sought to make their pupils themselves active parties to the work in which they were engaged; thus making teaching something far higher than the mere passive reception of the scraps and details of knowledge. This was the spirit in which the great Dr Arnold worked; he strove to teach his pupils to rely upon themselves, and develop their powers by their own active efforts, himself merely guiding, directing, stimulating, and encouraging them. 'I would far rather', he said, 'send a boy to Van Diemen's Land, where he must work for his bread, than send him to Oxford to live in luxury, without any desire in his mind to avail himself of his advantages.' 'If there be one thing on earth', he observed on another occasion, 'which is truly admirable, it is to see God's wisdom blessing an inferiority of natural powers, when they have been honestly, truly, and zealously cultivated.' Speaking of a pupil of this character, he said, 'I would stand to that man hat in hand.' Once at Laleham, when teaching a rather dull boy, Arnold spoke somewhat sharply to him, on which the pupil looked up in his face and said, 'Why do you speak angrily, sir? *indeed*, I am doing the best I can.' Years afterwards, Arnold used to tell the story to his children, and added, 'I never felt so much in my life—that look and that speech I have never forgotten.'

From the numerous instances . . . of men of humble station who have risen to distinction in science and literature, it will be obvious that labour is by no means incompatible with the highest intellectual culture. Work in moderation is healthy, as well as agreeable to the human constitution. Work educates the body, as study educates the mind; and that is the best state of society in which there is some work for every man's leisure, and some leisure for every man's work. . . .

. . . The use of early labour in self-imposed mechanical employments may be illustrated by the boyhood of Sir Isaac Newton. Though a comparatively dull scholar, he was very assiduous in the use of his saw, hammer, and hatchet—'knocking and hammering in his lodging-room'—making models of windmills, carriages, and machines of all sorts; and as he grew older, he took delight in making little tables and cupboards for his friends. Smeaton, Watt, and Stephenson were equally handy with tools when mere boys; and but for such kind of self-culture in their youth it is doubtful whether they would have accomplished so much in their manhood. . . . Elihu Burritt says he found hard labour *necessary* to enable him to study with effect; and more than once he gave up school-teaching and study, and, taking to his leather apron again, went back to his blacksmith's forge and anvil for his health of body and mind's sake. . . .

. . . The crown and glory of life is Character. It is the noblest posses-sion of a man, constituting a rank in itself, and an estate in the general goodwill; dignifying every station, and exalting every position in society. It exercises a greater power than wealth, and secures all the honour without the jealousies of fame. It carries with it an influence which always tells; for it is the result of proved honour, rectitude, and consistency—qualities which, perhaps more than any other, command the general confidence and respect of mankind.

Character is human nature in its best form. It is moral order embodied in the individual. Men of character are not only the conscience of society, but in every well-governed State they are its best motive power; for it is moral qualities in the main which rule the world. . . .

. . . Though a man have comparatively little culture, slender abilities, and but small wealth, yet, if his character be of sterling worth, he will always command an influence, whether it be in the workshop, the counting-house, the mart, or the senate. Canning wisely wrote in 1801, 'My road must be through Character to power; I will try no other course; and I am sanguine enough to believe that this course, though not perhaps the quickest, is the surest.' You may admire men of intellect; but something more is necessary before you will trust them. Hence Lord John Russell once observed in a sentence full of truth, 'It is the nature of party in England to ask the assistance of men of genius, but to follow the guidance of men of character.'

. . . That character is power, is true in a much higher sense than that knowledge is power. Mind without heart, intelligence without conduct, cleverness without goodness, are powers in their way, but they may be powers only for mischief. We may be instructed or amused by them; but it is sometimes as difficult to admire them as it would be to admire the dexterity of a pick-pocket or the horsemanship of a highwayman.

Truthfulness, integrity, and goodness—qualities that hang not on any man's breath—form the essence of manly character, or, as one of our old writers has it, 'that inbred loyalty unto Virtue which can serve her without a livery'. He who possesses these qualities, united with strength of purpose, carries with him a power which is irresistible. . . .

51   The qualified teacher

From Dr W. B. Hodgson's evidence to the Newcastle Commission, 1859.

Dr Hodgson was one of two metropolitan Assistant Commissioners, who reported on St George's Southwark, Newington, Wandsworth, St Olave's Southwark, and St Saviour's Southwark. His evidence is printed in the Report of the Newcastle Commission (see 60 below) and is a fascinating insight into the state of education in South London at this period.

. . . None are too old, too poor, too ignorant, too feeble, too sickly, too unqualified in any or every way to regard themselves, and to be regarded by others, as unfit for school-keeping. Nay, there are few, if any, occupations regarded as incompatible with school-keeping, if not as simultaneous, at least as preparatory, employments. Domestic servants out of place; discharged barmaids; vendors of toys or lollipops; . . . cripples almost bedridden; . . . men and women of seventy and even eighty years of age; persons who spell badly . . . , who can scarcely write, and who cannot cipher at all.

52   Mr Wopsle's great-aunt's school

From Charles Dickens's *Great Expectations*, 1860.

For note on Dickens, see 46 above.

Mr Wopsle's great-aunt kept an evening-school in the village; that is to say, she was a ridiculous old woman of limited means and unlimited infirmity, who used to go to sleep from six to seven every evening, in the society of youth who paid twopence per week each, for the improving opportunity of seeing her do it. . . .

The Educational Scheme or Course established by Mr Wopsle's great-aunt may be resolved into the following synopsis. The pupils ate apples and put straws down one another's backs, until Mr Wopsle's great-aunt collected her energies, and made an indiscriminate totter at them with a birch-rod. After receiving the charge with every mark of derision, the pupils formed in line and buzzingly passed a ragged book from hand to hand. The book had an alphabet in it, some figures and tables, and a little spelling—that is to say, it had had once. As soon as this volume began to circulate, Mr Wopsle's great-aunt fell into a state of coma; arising either from sleep or a rheumatic paroxysm. The pupils then entered among themselves upon a competitive examination on the subject of Boots, with the view of ascertaining who could tread the hardest upon whose toes. This mental exercise lasted until Biddy made a rush at them and distributed three defaced Bibles (shaped as if they had been unskilfully cut off the chump-end of something), more illegibly printed at the best than any curiosities of literature I have since met with, speckled all over with ironmould, and having various specimens of the insect world smashed between their leaves. This part of the Course was usually lightened by several single combats between Biddy and refractory students. When the fights were over, Biddy gave out the number of a page, and then we all read aloud what we could— or what we couldn't—in a frightful chorus; Biddy leading with a high shrill monotonous voice, and none of us having the least notion of, or reverence for, what we were reading about. When this horrible din had lasted a certain time, it mechanically awoke Mr Wopsle's great-aunt, who staggered at a boy fortuitously, and pulled his ears. This was understood to terminate the Course for the evening, and we emerged into the air with shrieks of intellectual victory. It is fair to remark that there was no prohibition against any pupil's entertaining himself with a slate or even with the ink (when there was any), but that it was not easy to pursue that branch of study in the winter season, on account of the little general shop in which the classes were holden—and which was also Mr Wopsle's great-aunt's sitting-room and bed-chamber— being but faintly illuminated through the agency of one low-spirited dip-candle and no snuffers.

Three 1860–1870: Democracy and education: the decisive years

In 1867, the extension of the franchise in the second great Reform Act pointed towards full adult suffrage, and made its eventual coming seem inevitable. In 1870, Forster's Education Act, following the logic of democracy, endorsed this view that the destination was now clearly visible though still very far off. Robert Lowe described these events as a second and greater English revolution, a moment of decisive and irreversible change. Others hoped that it would prove to be a power adjustment that averted revolution, smoothing a path to further gradual and orderly adjustments in a developing world.

Harry Chester (53), assured that National Education is now inevitable, sets out in 1860 some basic ideals. Education should train us for work, but also for leisure; it should be planned for all social classes and unfolded in a variety of schools. Ideally, men should not be crammed with learning, but stimulated; the educational means are as important as the ends. Elementary education must be seen for what it is, a mere beginning, and linked with further education at some later stage.

For the first time in these pages, women are considered (earlier instances, from Tennyson's 'Princess' and elsewhere, could of course be found). Though women are not yet seriously in the running for democracy, or indeed for much in the way of education, their claims will one day have to be heard. Chester's piece is of interest chiefly, perhaps, because it combines an exalted view of the importance and potential of education with prose attuned to practical rather than to visionary ideals.

Matthew Arnold's graceful essay (54) was part of his evidence prepared for the Newcastle Committee, and lifts the debate far above merely provincial concerns. He reminds us that the two ruling parties since 1689 have both been aristocratic, and that this has prescribed a certain tone in English affairs. The gradual erosion of this ascendancy has been inevitable, and wise men will accept it as such, with whatever regrets. For the lower orders this change is a blessing, though not an unmixed one, since there is a risk now of losing touch with the past. In guarding and passing on culture, the aristocrats perhaps transcended themselves; will the new democrats do nearly as well? The educational challenge will be to civilise the new rulers and, more particularly, that influential sector, the energetic middle classes.

George Moberly, headmaster of Winchester (55), ponders the history and inner nature of the public schools, and the peculiar qualities of character which they confer. Their achievements can be more easily recognised than itemised, and are admired by many people who have been excluded from the benefits themselves. Moberly points out that two marks of such schools are a structure, well understood by both teachers and taught and generally accepted, and, within this structure, a process of participation (akin to a democratic ideal?). His plea is that though these schools may be socially anomalous, they produce excellence; he hopes that the Clarendon Commission, now sitting, will do nothing to bring them harm. In the event, his fears proved ungrounded; but this is an early instance of the egalitarian threat to quality being clearly perceived.

Moberly's reflections criss-cross with those of Arnold in the previous extract (54), and suggest one of the major problems to be faced for the next hundred years. Are the great established schools models, which the new education can hope to emulate; or are they citadels of privilege in their inner soul? Do they guard a heritage towards which the whole democracy can be lifted, or do they presuppose a moneyed and powerful élite? Are the admired qualities of character peculiar to born rulers; and, if in the fullness of time we are all born to rule equally, can the appropriate graces be passed on to all?

Charles Ratcliff (56) and Dr Guthrie (57) provide an immediate contrast, returning us to the crisis in the ragged schools. Far in the future, these Birmingham children, or their children, or their children's children may become equal in excellence, but the immediate needs are of a humbler kind. Dr Guthrie accepts that most of the parents are an unmitigated hindrance, and that the children need first to be rescued from their homes. (In *Great Expectations* (1860–1) Dickens depicts the anger of Mrs Joe when her husband and the young Pip try to become literate, and so threaten to slip from her power. In *Our Mutual Friend* (1864–5) he shows Gaffer Hexam's violent opposition to his son's education, and to anything which might make a father feel inferior to his own flesh and blood.)

In counterpoint again, Kay-Shuttleworth (58) rehearses some of the prevalent political hopes and fears. People are being scared away from further extension of the franchise by trade union behaviour, and by the danger of giving agitators a vote. Perhaps the right to vote would be more safely linked to educational than to property qualifications? Good education must prove to be good economics in the end.

Two more contrasts: George Rumsey (59) wafts education to a new peak of mistiness; the Newcastle Commission delivers its report (60). With Newcastle—the first of the five great educational Reports of the century—national education really comes into its own. The volumes of statistics, evidence, recommendations and appendices stretch out imposingly, too heavy for most men to lift, let alone to read. To hear this tramp of bureaucratic feet towards a new Valhalla is to be assured that education is serious business at last.

Next, Thomas Crampton, headmaster of Brentford (61), gives evidence that by mixing social classes in one school you level them up, and help everyone. This argument was destined to a great future, though not in his time. Harry Chester (62) writes of the levelling-up of ability, keeping closer to educational than to political ideals. While he agrees with Samuel Smiles (50) that exceptional men *can* rise from social obscurity to the highest eminence, he sees the more normal pattern as a gradual levelling-up inside the prescribed context of social class. His notion seems to be that each class will be slowly raised, both in its ideals and in its attainments, but that the distinction between classes will always remain. Individuals will benefit, and so will the nation, but there will be no radical social change.

The second of the great reports, Clarendon (63), is on the leading public schools, and comes out in their favour, despite George Moberly's fears (55). It pays tribute to the unique character and achievement of the famous schools, and records that they have for the most part purged themselves of 'roughness, tyranny and licence', the older defects. It commends the degree of participation enjoyed by the masters in some of the schools, including Harrow, and offers this as a model for Eton, where less democracy prevails. Undoubtedly, the reform of the public schools associated chiefly with Dr Arnold of Rugby has done much to rescue them, and to

F*

set them on the course of resilient survival for many years to come.

In 1865, we come to the serious debates in Parliament, and to the brief and fascinating ascendancy of Robert Lowe. Morley quotes, without giving any reference, a note on this written much later by Gladstone: Lowe 'pursued the modest Reform Bill of 1866 with an implacable hostility, and readily supplied the whole brains of the opposition. So effective were his speeches that, during this year, and this year only, he had such a command of the House as has never in my recollection been surpassed. . . .' First, Lowe challenges the idea that democracy is a 'right' (64), and finds the notion that it is 'inevitable' a cowardly and unEnglish collapse. His key objection is educational and eminently concrete: is an 'educated and refined Englishman' to be equated with Australian savages and with Hottentots of the Cape? Lowe's comment is, of course, confined to the qualities of intelligence and judiciousness, and to the problem of giving educated and uneducated opinion equal weight. In intention, it is neither a racial nor a moral observation, though its tone has an unfortunate edge.

In 1866, Lowe's most famous speech in Parliament goes further (65). He asserts that 'war against all superiority' is 'the strictest democratic principle', and brings this home with instances of trade union power.

During 1866, Lowe's arguments were victorious, but 1867 brought the change. When it came, the *Quarterly Review* (66) appraised it in the guise of a book review; and whose voice but Lowe's could this be? The 1867 Act is described as a revolution, and, with grim irony, its advocates are given their due. Their work is marked by 'a systematic depreciation of culture and its effects', a 'preference for what is mean and vulgar', and 'a scarcely disguised hostility to our institutions', but they and their like *are* the masters now. One of Lowe's claims is that democracy came in against all the superior arguments and for 'ignoble' reasons, some of which he lists. There was the myth of 'inevitability'; there was the almost total failure of those who wielded power to defend themselves; and there was the defection of Disraeli and the Tories to a radicalism which left even the radicals aghast.

At this point, Disraeli's Memo (67) on the day-to-day pressures and calculations of the ruling party is a useful balance to Lowe's rhetorical mode. But Lowe too saw that democracy, now that it *had* arrived, required education, and that some kind of hope must be kept alive in the wreck. In an 1868 speech (68) he sets out his plans for the new situation. His aim now is to preserve and improve the existing best, to appease as many interests as possible, and to keep educational revolution at bay. Predictably, he draws at least one accusation of irresponsible treachery—from Mr Weir (69), whose main desire is to save Scotland's famous parish schools.

Our next document presents a catholic view. The real issue, says Vaughan (70), is Christianity versus secularism. He sees this not as a sectarian issue which divides Christians, but as a crisis in which all Christians should unite. One danger in democracy is shrewdly pinpointed: 'It too often happens, indeed, in communities and societies in which all have equal rights and powers, that the many are passive and otiose, while the energetic few rule and decide. Nothing can be more disastrous than such apathy.' Most of this extract is reactionary in tone but perceptive in content; it makes the two clerics following sound blinkered men. Vaughan saw, as too few Christians did, that Christians were fighting one another, for reasons rooted in the past and becoming rapidly irrelevant, at precisely the time when they should have been united together against a common enemy now gathering strength.

The Rev. W. Pound (71) accepts that the question for the future should be not 'shall we educate the masses?', but 'how shall we educate a great and moral people?' Perhaps this linguistic shift is idealism, perhaps it is prudence; a wise man doesn't insult his masters more than he need. The Rev. Alfred Dewes (72) asserts that the true equality of men is in their capacity for knowledge and in the joy which comes from it; but he evades, uneasily if understandably, the practical question hanging in the air. How *are* we to equalise our mental and spiritual treasures while ignoring the material ones; how *are* we to educate men to equality while the majority are poor? The Christian answer is and must be that the spiritual riches are greater, but a church allied to wealth risks turning its truth into cant. Besides, a man's choice of poverty, as of chastity, must be embraced freely, and has no meaning but a bitter one if enforced by the state.

Captain Maxse RN (73) accepts compulsory education as the 'Spirit of the Age and the wants of the country', and the influential Taunton Report (74) is another sign of the times. But Thomas Huxley (75) adds a sour note as he ponders the baseness lurking in a lot of the arguments we have been hearing, and confesses himself, amid the complexities, at a loss.

The next two pieces from George Eliot (76) and Matthew Arnold

(77) are seminal, and explore the basic choice of paths now confronting a democratic state. Will democracy prove the greatest friend possible to human culture and achievement, or will it let loose the destroyers and vandals? Will it open to all men the riches that were once exclusive, or will the riches themselves be disdained and despoiled? In Oxford, Arnold finds the ideal incarnate (78), but celebration and nostalgia merge in his tone.

And so to Forster (79) and to the arrival of national elementary education for the democracy, as a practical target if not yet as a fully fledged fact. Forster steers his way between the many and influential pressure groups and entrenched vested interests, selecting the arguments most politically ripe for the times. Education was not yet made compulsory—though local School Boards where they existed were allowed to do this—but the state took over the greater part of responsibility for the elementary education of the poor. We end this section of introduction with a quotation from Henry Craik's *The State in Relation to Education* (1884), where the position just before Forster's Act is summarised. It has been estimated that in 1869 about 1,300,000 children were being educated in state-aided schools, about 1,000,000 in schools that received no grant, were not inspected and were for the most part entirely inefficient; and that about 2,000,000 children were not at school at all. The main burden of national education fell on the 200,000 or so people whose voluntary subscriptions supported the schools. 'In other words,' Craik comments, 'the efforts of a handful out of the whole nation had accomplished the fairly efficient education of about one-third of the children, and had provided schools for about one-half; but the rest either went to inefficient schools, or to no school at all, and for them there was no room even had the power to compel their attendance existed.'

A problem of this magnitude would clearly not be solved immediately; nor would universal education beyond the elementary stage be easily achieved.

53   To the best . . . for all

From Harry Chester's *Schools for Children and Institutes for Adults*, 1860.

When Harry Chester gave evidence to the Newcastle Commission, he said that he had recently retired (in 1858) as assistant Secretary to the Committee of Privy Council on Education. He had been a leading official of this body since Queen Victoria set it up in 1839 to oversee the religious education of the young ('to superintend Parliamentary funds that should stimulate and assist, but never supersede, local efforts for the education of the poor'). Chester also described himself as Vice-President of the Society of Arts, Manufacture and Commerce, and (in 1863) as Chairman of the Metropolitan Association for Promoting the Education of Adults. The pamphlet from which this extract is taken was delivered as a paper to the Highgate Literary and Scientific Institution in January (an early version) and to the United Meeting of the Mechanics' Institutions of Hastings and St Leonards in May. These activities and organisations in many ways typify the mingling of small private, and official, initiatives from which the national system of education was later to grow.

Education is the development and training of the human being in all his capacities, spiritual, intellectual and physical; and in National Education we ought to have no less grand an object than to develop to the greatest possible extent, and to direct to the best possible aims, the spiritual, intellectual, and physical capacities of all the individuals who compose the nation. . . .

I shall waste no time in arguments to establish the importance of education. On all sides its importance, if not adequately appreciated, is at least loudly proclaimed. Great efforts have happily been made, in the last half century, by Parliament, by the Universities, by voluntary associations, by public companies, and by private persons, to provide increased and improved means of education. The mainspring of this great national advance has been undoubtedly the zeal of religious congregations led by their clergy. For the education of the highest classes the old public schools and grammar schools have been reformed; new schools and colleges have been created; the ancient universities have been improved; new universities have been created; the curriculum of studies has been every where reformed; and education has become more practical, more liberal, and more religious. For the children of that portion of the important middle classes of society, who take their education neither at the great public schools and grammar schools, nor at the National and British Schools, something has been already done; but an immense deal still remains for us to do. They get less in proportion to what they pay for education than any other class of the community. For the children of the poor the greatest efforts have been made, and on the whole with good results. With the aid of funds supplied by Parliament, and distributed by the Committee of Council on Education, since January, 1839, the zeal of the religious congregations has caused nearly 6000 elementary schools, and 46 training schools for Schoolmasters and Schoolmistresses, to be built; and almost all the incidents of elementary education to be strikingly improved. . . .

. . . There are better buildings on better sites; better furniture; better books and maps, and apparatus; better teaching; better discipline; a better appreciation of education; and, best of all, a better spirit of religion pervades the whole. If our best elementary schools were but a little more practical in their working, and more in harmony with the real wants of the after life of their scholars, they would not only be as good as any elementary schools in the world, but nearly as good as elementary schools for little children can be. We want, however, more schools; we want those that are inferior to be raised to the level of the best; we want them to be more practical, more preparatory to the real business of the life of the poor. We want more combination, less religious exclusiveness among the friends of education; not less zeal for 'the faith once for all delivered to the saints', but more charitable forbearance towards dissenters from our own views of that faith, and more clearness in distinguishing the limits where our responsibility in dealing with the children of poor parents becomes absorbed in the responsibility of the parents themselves. We greatly want more local authority in education, which we cannot have till we have more local combination in education; we want less running to Parliament, and to the Government, to help us to do that which, with more local combination, we could now do very well ourselves; less pauperising of schools by the fixing of school-fees—not at the market value of education, but—at the level of the semi-pauper's means. We want a more cordial co-operation between the managers of schools and the parents of their scholars. We want opportunities of fair competition between the children that have attended at our National, British, and other schools, that we may compare the results of the instruction imparted in them; and, above all, we want a far better provision of motives and means for the continuance of instruction after the children have left their elementary schools. While this last want, which represents the instruction of adults, and is intimately connected with the interests of mechanics' institutions, and similar bodies, remains unsupplied, we may talk and labour till we are tired, and every one is tired of us, about elementary education; but the people will not be educated; and their morality, their intelligence, their industry, their health and strength, their happiness and prosperity at home, and their estimation among the nations abroad, will remain below their proper level, below the level which God has given to them capacity to attain, and which He will hold us responsible for helping them to attain. I entreat, then, the friends of elementary education, the clerical and the lay promoters of schools for children, to consider whether, by the very motives which constrain them to their loving exertions for the education of the child, they ought not also to feel themselves constrained to further the instruction of adults, and to unite for that object with the promoters of mechanics' institutions.

Just reflect on the very early age at which the necessities of life compel our poor children to be removed from our National and British Schools. Under very favourable circumstances it is before twelve years of age, under less favourable circumstances it is even before ten years of age, that the bulk of our poor children are removed from school. Let us not undervalue what is there accomplished even in those brief periods of infancy: but, at best, is it more than the commencement of the education of babes? Does not by far the larger portion of the complete work of education remain to be subsequently effected? Does it not sadly sound like a mean mockery of a great idea when we apply the word 'education' to processes which terminate at those early ages? The rich man commonly sends his son for the first time from home to school at the age at which the poor man's child is commonly removed for the last time from school; and, when he is thus removed, he has too often to enter at once upon the tremendous struggle for bread and life. To the rich then especially I would say, 'Picture to yourselves your own children deprived of the blessings of education, and of systematic instruction, at that early age.' You revolt from the very thought of it. Surely then you will do all in your power to mitigate this vast evil to others. . . .

We have got rid (I hope) for ever of the fallacy that we may over-educate the people. We cannot over-educate the people. . . . Duties are well executed, generally, in proportion to the intelligence and fidelity of him who executes them; and even studies, which have no direct relation to a man's peculiar calling, may improve his performances in that calling, not only by the increase of his intelligence, of his mental power, which results from the exercise of his mind in study, but also by the disciplinal effect produced on his moral character by the patience, the perseverance, the self-restraint, which are inseparable from sustained study, and also by that loosening of prejudices which always follows the entrance of enlarged knowledge into the mind of a man. . . .

It is not, then, for the poor alone, that we need an improved and extended education. It is needed equally, if not in a greater degree, by the highest class, and by the classes intermediate between the two extremes of society. There is no kind of business in which a merchant, a manufacturer, a shopkeeper, a farmer, and those in their employment, can be engaged, that would not be better carried on by those who had a knowledge than by those who were ignorant of the science or sciences on which the processes of their business must ultimately rest; and there can be no one who would not be happier and better for having some definite object of favourite pursuit connected with literature, science, or art, by which to occupy his hours of leisure.

What I have said in reference to men is equally true in reference to women. There is just now among the benevolent an active movement, having for its object the more general and better remunerated employment of women. Now the root of this matter also lies in education— the education of women. The degree and value of the employment which they can obtain must be regulated by their qualifications; in other words, by the results of their education: and, if you wish to bring lucrative employment more generally than at present within their reach, you must enhance their qualifications by improving their education; and you may effect this improvement by providing for them, first, increased means of instruction of a better and more practical character, and, secondly, that which has long been found necessary in the education of men, a suitable tribunal which shall test and attest their attainments.

The foundation of all improvements in the education of either sex must be laid where systematic instruction commences, in the Elementary Schools. They must be conducted on a more natural and healthy system. They must lose much of their present character of forcing houses, which are dangerous alike to the spiritual and moral life, to the future intelligence, and to the physical health. When there is less hasty cramming, there will be a better digestion and assimilation of mental food. Fewer things will be taught to little children, but more things will be really learnt by them; and their powers of learning, understanding, and reasoning, will turn out to be far stronger in later years. . . .

You will see (I hope) that throughout this Address I am endeavouring to bring into view the relations, the perfectly natural and mutually beneficial relations, which ought to be felt to subsist between the promoters of elementary schools for children and the promoters of institutions for adults. The school is a necessary antecedent to the institution; and the institution is a necessary complement to the school. Neither can flourish if the other fails.

54   The coming of democracy

From an essay written by Matthew Arnold in 1860, in conjunction
with his evidence prepared for the Newcastle Commission.

Matthew Arnold was the son of Dr Arnold, born in 1822 near
Staines. After a brilliant academic career at Oxford, he became one
of the most celebrated of Victorian poets, critics and social prophets.
From 1857 to 1867 he was Professor of Poetry at Oxford, during
which period his distinctive cultural and social analysis matured.
Among the duties which he took most seriously were those of an
Inspector of Schools. He gained first-hand experience of education
in Britain and Europe, and wrote on educational topics from deep
professional commitment.

The evidence which he prepared for Newcastle took him on
extensive visits to the continent, and he decided to publish it
separately in an extended form. This Introduction, written in
February and March 1860 was, he said, 'one of the things I have
taken most pains with'. In 1879, it was published as a separate
essay, entitled 'Democracy'. Arnold died in 1888.

I propose to submit to those who have been accustomed to regard all
State-action with jealousy, some reasons for thinking that the circumstances which once made that jealousy prudent and natural have
undergone an essential change. . . .

The dissolution of the old political parties which have governed this
country since the Revolution of 1688 has long been remarked. It was
repeatedly declared to be happening long before it actually took place,
while the vital energy of these parties still subsisted in full vigour, and
was threatened only by some temporary obstruction. It has been
eagerly deprecated long after it had actually begun to take place, when
it was in full progress, and inevitable. These parties, differing in so
much else, were yet alike in this, that they were both, in a certain
broad sense, *aristocratical* parties. They were combinations of persons
considerable, either by great family and estate, or by Court favour, or
lastly, by eminent abilities and popularity; this last body, however,

attaining participation in public affairs only through a conjunction with one or other of the former. These connections, though they contained men of very various degrees of birth and property, were still wholly leavened with the feelings and habits of the upper class of the nation. They had the bond of a common culture; and, however their political opinions and acts might differ, what they said and did had the stamp and style imparted by this culture, and by a common and elevated social condition.

Aristocratical bodies have no taste for a very imposing executive, or for a very active and penetrating domestic administration. They have a sense of equality among themselves, and of constituting in themselves what is greatest and most dignified in the realm, which makes their pride revolt against the overshadowing greatness and dignity of a commanding executive. They have a temper of independence, and a habit of uncontrolled action, which makes them impatient of encountering, in the management of the interior concerns of the country, the machinery and regulations of a superior and peremptory power. The different parties amongst them, as they successively get possession of the government, respect this jealous disposition in their opponents, because they share it themselves. It is a disposition proper to them as great personages, not as ministers; and as they are great personages for their whole life, while they may probably be ministers but for a very short time, the instinct of their social condition avails more with them than the instinct of their official function. To administer as little as possible, to make its weight felt in foreign affairs rather than in domestic, to see in ministerial station rather the means of power and dignity than a means of searching and useful administrative activity, is the natural tendency of an aristocratic executive. It is a tendency which is creditable to the good sense of aristocracies, honourable to their moderation, and at the same time fortunate for their country, of whose internal development they are not fitted to have the full direction.

One strong and beneficial influence, however, the administration of a vigorous and high-minded aristocracy is calculated to exert upon a robust and sound people. . . . The Roman aristocracy did it; the English aristocracy has done it. They each fostered in the mass of the peoples they governed,—peoples of sturdy moral constitution and apt to learn such lessons,—a greatness of spirit, the natural growth of the condition of magnates and rulers, but not the natural growth of the condition of the common people. They made, the one of the Roman, the other of the English people, in spite of all the shortcomings of each, great peoples, peoples *in the grand style.* And this they did, while wielding the people according to their own notions, and in the direction which seemed good to them; not as servants and instruments of the people, but as its commanders and heads; solicitous for the good of their country, indeed, but taking for granted that of that good they themselves were the supreme judges, and were to fix the conditions.

The time has arrived, however, when it is becoming impossible for the aristocracy of England to conduct and wield the English nation any longer. It still, indeed, administers public affairs; and it is a great error to suppose, as many persons in England suppose, that it administers but does not govern. He who administers, governs* because he infixes his own mark and stamps his own character on all public affairs as they pass through his hands; and, therefore, so long as the English aristocracy administers the commonwealth, it still governs it. But signs not to be mistaken show that its headship and leadership of the nation, by virtue of the substantial acquiescence of the body of the nation in its predominance and right to lead, is nearly over. That acquiescence was the tenure by which it held its power; and it is fast giving way. The superiority of the upper class over all others is no longer so great; the willingness of the others to recognise that superiority is no longer so ready.

This change has been brought about by natural and inevitable causes, and neither the great nor the multitude are to be blamed for it. The growing demands and audaciousness of the latter, the encroaching spirit of democracy, are, indeed, matters of loud complaint with some persons. But these persons are complaining of human nature itself, when they thus complain of a manifestation of its native and ineradicable impulse. Life itself consists, say the philosophers, in the effort *to affirm one's own essence;* meaning by this, to develop one's own existence fully and freely, to have ample light and air, to be neither cramped nor overshadowed. Democracy is trying *to affirm its own essence*; to live, to enjoy, to possess the world, as aristocracy has tried, and successfully tried, before it. Ever since Europe emerged from barbarism, ever since the condition of the common people began a little to improve, ever since their minds began to stir, this effort of democracy has been gaining strength; and the more their condition improves, the more strength this effort gains. So potent is the charm of life and expansion upon the living; the moment men are aware of them, they begin to desire them, and the more they have of them, the more they crave.

* *Administrer, c'est gouverner,* says Mirabeau; *gouverner, c'est régner; tout se réduit là.*

This movement of democracy, like other operations of nature, merits properly neither blame nor praise. Its partisans are apt to give it credit which it does not deserve, while its enemies are apt to upbraid it unjustly. Its friends celebrate it as the author of all freedom. But political freedom may very well be established by aristocratic founders; and, certainly, the political freedom of England owes more to the grasping English barons than to democracy. Social freedom,— equality,—that is rather the field of the conquests of democracy. And here what I must call the injustice of its enemies comes in. For its seeking after equality, democracy is often, in this country above all, vehemently and scornfully blamed; its temper contrasted with that worthier temper which can magnanimously endure social distinctions; its operations all referred, as of course, to the stirrings of a base and malignant envy. No doubt there is a gross and vulgar spirit of envy, prompting the hearts of many of those who cry for equality. No doubt there are ignoble natures which prefer equality to liberty. But what we have to ask is, when the life of democracy is admitted as something natural and inevitable, whether this or that product of democracy is a necessary growth from its parent stock, or merely an excrescence upon it. If it be the latter, certainly it may be due to the meanest and most culpable passions. But if it be the former, then this product, however base and blameworthy the passions which it may sometimes be made to serve, can in itself be no more reprehensible than the vital impulse of democracy is in itself reprehensible; and this impulse is, as has been shown, identical with the ceaseless vital effort of human nature itself.

Now, can it be denied, that a certain approach to equality, at any rate a certain reduction of signal inequalities, is a natural, instinctive demand of that impulse which drives society as a whole,—no longer individuals and limited classes only, but the mass of a community,— to develop itself with the utmost possible fullness and freedom? Can it be denied, that to live in a society of equals tends in general to make a man's spirits expand, and his faculties work easily and actively; while, to live in a society of superiors, although it may occasionally be a very good discipline, yet in general tends to tame the spirits and to make the play of the faculties less secure and active? Can it be denied, that to be heavily overshadowed, to be profoundly insignificant, has, on the whole, a depressing and benumbing effect on the character? I know that some individuals react against the strongest impediments, and owe success and greatness to the efforts which they are thus forced to make. But the question is not about individuals. The question is about the common bulk of mankind, persons without extraordinary gifts or exceptional energy, and who will ever require, in order to make the best of themselves, encouragement and directly favouring circumstances. Can any one deny, that for these the spectacle, when they would rise, of a condition of splendour, grandeur, and culture, which they cannot possibly reach, has the effect of making them flag in spirit, and of disposing them to sink despondingly back into their own condition? Can any one deny, that the knowledge how poor and insignificant the best condition of improvement and culture attainable by them must be esteemed by a class incomparably richer-endowed, tends to cheapen this modest possible amelioration in the account of those classes also for whom it would be relatively a real progress, and to disenchant their imaginations with it? It seems to me impossible to deny this. And therefore a philosophic observer,★ with no love for democracy, but rather with a terror of it, has been constrained to remark, that 'the common people is more uncivilised in aristocratic countries than in any others;' because there 'the lowly and the poor feel themselves, as it were, overwhelmed with the weight of their own inferiority'. He has been constrained to remark,† that 'there is such a thing as a manly and legitimate passion for equality, prompting men to desire to be, *all* of them, in the enjoyment of power and consideration'. And, in France, that very equality, which is by us so impetuously decried, while it has by no means improved (it is said) the upper classes of French society, has undoubtedly given to the lower classes, to the body of the common people, a self-respect, an enlargement of spirit, a consciousness of counting for something in their country's action, which has raised them in the scale of humanity. The common people, in France, seems to me the soundest part of the French nation. They seem to me more free from the two opposite degradations of multitudes, brutality and servility, to have a more developed human life, more of what distinguishes elsewhere the cultured classes from the vulgar, than the common people in any other country with which I am acquainted.

I do not say that grandeur and prosperity may not be attained by a nation divided into the most widely distinct classes, and presenting the most signal inequalities of rank and fortune. I do not say that great

---

★ M. [Alexis] de Tocqueville. See his *Démocratie en Amérique* (edit. of 1835), vol. i, p. 11. 'Le peuple est plus grossier dans les pays aristocratiques que partout ailleurs. Dans ces lieux, où se rencontrent des hommes si forts et si riches, les faibles et les pauvres se sentent comme accablés de leur bassesse; ne découvrant aucun point par lequel ils puissent regagner l'égalité, ils désespèrent entièrement d'eux-mêmes, et se laissent tomber au-dessous de la dignité humaine.'
† *Démocratie en Amérique*, vol. i, p. 60.

national virtues may not be developed in it. I do not even say that a popular order, accepting this demarcation of classes as an eternal providential arrangement, not questioning the natural right of a superior order to lead it, content within its own sphere, admiring the grandeur and highmindedness of its ruling class, and catching on its own spirit some reflex of what it thus admires, may not be a happier body, as to the eye of the imagination it is certainly a more beautiful body, than a popular order, pushing, excited, and presumptuous; a popular order, jealous of recognising fixed superiorities, petulantly claiming to be as good as its betters, and tastelessly attiring itself with the fashions and designations which have become unalterably associated with a wealthy and refined class, and which, tricking out those who have neither wealth nor refinement, are ridiculous. But a popular order of that old-fashioned stamp exists now only for the imagination. It is not the force with which modern society has to reckon. Such a body may be a sturdy, honest, and sound-hearted lower class; but it is not a democratic people. It is not that power, which at the present day in all nations is to be found existing; in some, has obtained the mastery; in others, is yet in a state of expectation and preparation. . . . It is because aristocracies almost inevitably fail to appreciate justly, or even to take into their mind, the instinct pushing the masses towards expansion and fuller life, that they lose their hold over them. It is the old story of the incapacity of aristocracies for ideas,—the secret of their want of success in modern epochs. . . . English democracy runs no risk of being over-mastered by the State; it is almost certain that it will throw off the tutelage of aristocracy. Its real danger is, that it will have far too much its own way, and be left far too much to itself. 'What harm will there be in that?' say some; 'are we not a self-governing people?' I answer: 'We have never yet been a *self-governing democracy*, or anything like it.' The difficulty for democracy is, how to find and keep high ideals. The individuals who compose it are, the bulk of them, persons who need to follow an ideal, not to set one; and one ideal of greatness, high feeling, and fine culture, which an aristocracy once supplied to them, they lose by the very fact of ceasing to be a lower order and becoming a democracy. Nations are not truly great solely because the individuals composing them are numerous, free, and active; but they are great when these numbers, this freedom, and this activity are employed in the service of an ideal higher than that of an ordinary man, taken by himself. Our society is probably destined to become much more democratic; who or what will give a high tone to the nation then? That is the grave question. . . . I am convinced that if the worst mischiefs of democracy ever happen in England, it will be, not because a new condition of things has come upon us unforeseen, but because, though we all foresaw it, our efforts to deal with it were in the wrong direction. At the present time, almost every one believes in the growth of democracy, almost every one talks of it, almost every one laments it; but the last thing people can be brought to do is to make timely preparation for it. Many of those who, if they would, could do most to forward this work of preparation, are made slack and hesitating by the belief that, after all, in England, things may probably never go very far; that it will be possible to keep much more of the past than speculators say. Others, with a more robust faith, think that all democracy wants is vigorous putting-down; and that, with a good will and strong hand, it is perfectly possible to retain or restore the whole system of the Middle Ages. Others, free from the prejudices of class and position which warp the judgement of these, and who would, I believe, be the first and greatest gainers by strengthening the hands of the State, are averse from doing so by reason of suspicions and fears, once perfectly well-grounded, but, in this age and in the present circumstances, well-grounded no longer. . . .

In all the remarks which I have been making, I have hitherto abstained from any attempt to suggest a positive application of them. I have limited myself to simply pointing out in how changed a world of ideas we are living; I have not sought to go further, and to discuss in what particular manner the world of facts is to adapt itself to this changed world of ideas. This has been my rule so far; but from this rule I shall here venture to depart, in order to dwell for a moment on a matter of practical institution, designed to meet new social exigencies: on the intervention of the State in public education.

The public secondary schools of France, decreed by the Revolution and established under the Consulate, are said by many good judges to be inferior to the old colleges. By means of the old colleges and of private tutors, the French aristocracy could procure for its children (so it is said, and very likely with truth) a better training than that which is now given in the lyceums. Yes; but the boon conferred by the State, when it founded the lyceums, was not for the aristocracy; it was for the vast middle class of Frenchmen. This class, certainly, had not already the means of a better training for its children, before the State interfered. This class, certainly, would not have succeeded in procuring by its own efforts a better training for its children, if the State had not interfered. Through the intervention of the State this class enjoys better schools for its children, not than the great and rich enjoy (that is not the question), but than the same class enjoys in any country where the State has not interfered to found them. The lyceums may not be so good as Eton or Harrow; but they are a great deal better than a *Classical and Commercial Academy*.

The aristocratic classes in England may, perhaps, be well content to rest satisfied with their Eton and Harrow. The State is not likely to do better for them. Nay, the superior confidence, spirit, and style, engendered by a training in the great public schools, constitute for these classes a real privilege, a real engine of command, which they might, if they were selfish, be sorry to lose by the establishment of schools great enough to beget a like spirit in the classes below them. But the middle classes in England have every reason not to rest content with their private schools; the State can do a great deal better for them. By giving to schools for these classes a public character, it can bring the instruction in them under a criticism which the stock of knowledge and judgement in our middle classes is not of itself at present able to supply. By giving to them a national character, it can confer on them a greatness and a noble spirit, which the tone of these classes is not of itself at present adequate to impart. Such schools would soon prove notable competitors with the existing public schools; they would do these a great service by stimulating them, and making them look into their own weak points more closely. Economical, because with charges uniform and under severe revision, they would do a great service to that large body of persons who, at present, seeing that on the whole the best secondary instruction to be found is that of the existing public schools, obtain it for their children from a sense of duty, although they can ill afford it, and although its cost is certainly exorbitant. Thus the middle classes might, by the aid of the State, better their instruction, while still keeping its cost moderate. This in itself would be a gain; but this gain would be slight in comparison with that of acquiring the sense of belonging to great and honourable seats of learning, and of breathing in their youth the air of the best culture of their nation. This sense would be an educational influence for them of the highest value. It would really augment their self-respect and moral force; it would truly fuse them with the class above, and tend to bring about for them the equality which they are entitled to desire.

So it is not State-action in itself which the middle and lower classes of a nation ought to deprecate; it is State-action exercised by a hostile class, and for their oppression. From a State-action reasonably, equitably, and nationally exercised, they may derive great benefit; greater, by the very nature and necessity of things, than can be derived from this source by the class above them. For the middle or lower classes to obstruct such a State-action, to repel its benefits, is to play the game of their enemies, and to prolong for themselves a condition of real inferiority.

This, I know, is rather dangerous ground to tread upon. The great middle classes of this country are conscious of no weakness, no inferiority; they do not want any one to provide anything for them. Such as they are, they believe that the freedom and prosperity of England are their work, and that the future belongs to them. No one esteems them more than I do; but those who esteem them most, and who most believe in their capabilities, can render them no better service than by pointing out in what they underrate their deficiencies, and how their deficiencies, if unremedied, may impair their future. They want culture and dignity; they want ideas.

55   Public schools: model or citadel?

From George Moberly's *Five Short Letters to Sir William Heathcote*, 1861.

George Moberly was born in 1803. He had a brilliant academic career at Oxford, and from 1826 was one of the young tutors at Balliol whose reputation raised the college to pre-eminence. In 1835, he became headmaster of Winchester, a post he held for thirty years. In 1869, he became Bishop of Salisbury. Died 1885.

The system of Public School Education in England seems to me to be most strikingly characteristic of the nation in which it has sprung up and become matured. I say 'sprung up and become matured' because there is, so far as I know, no indication of its having been devised or planned, in any considerable degree, by any legislator or founder. It is the genuine growth of English character and English feelings, shaping, directing, and modifying a scheme, which in its first design and plan exhibited but few of those features which have become by degrees the most conspicuous and most characteristic in it. It has grown up, like the political constitution of the country, gradually, steadily, and beneficially; and if it presents some traits which seem difficult of explanation and defence in the presence of judges who have not had experimental acquaintance with it, it does but the more faithfully represent the likeness to that well-founded and self-developed polity with which I venture to compare it.

If any single person may be mentioned as more the author of it than any other, unquestionably that person is William of Wykeham, the great Bishop, Architect, and Chancellor, the Founder of Winchester College;—the one man to whom Education, both of boys and young men, owes more of the direction and course which it has taken in later ages than to any other single person who ever lived in England. His School at Winchester, and his 'New' College in Oxford,—the immediate models of Eton and King's,—not only gave a vast stimulus and a particular character to the Collegiate Education of boys and young men at the time, but also afforded a pattern, followed more or less closely by all the various Founders of Schools and Colleges who flourished in later ages than his own. . . .

What is a Public School, and what are the essential points in which it differs from a private one?

This is a question, as I think, more easily asked than answered. . . .

Must a Public School be an Endowed School? Yes, I think so. Not because the endowment has any direct connexion with the system of education and instruction itself, but because no system can be such as we mean unless it have a stability greater than any which depends on the character, genius, skill, or pecuniary solvency of any man or set of men. Precedent, history, established rights, well-understood and well-respected privileges (capable, no doubt, of legitimate abrogation or change, but sacred against caprice or ill-temper), seem essential to the full character of a Public School. Boys and masters alike must feel themselves part of an established system, knowing their places and knowing their duties; the one teaching and the other taught; the one punishing when need arises, and the other submitting to punishment, with a full sense of a traditional code, understood and respected, which includes them all.

Must a Public School be a Classical School? Perhaps, theoretically, no, not of necessity. . . . It is conceivable, for instance, that much of the benefit of the Public School training might be won, if the system of lessons were framed upon the knowledge of abstract science, other things remaining as they are. . . . While I earnestly hope that the time may never come when the classical languages and literature shall cease to be the main subjects of instruction in our Public Schools in England,

I am constrained to admit that they are not so inherently and absolutely necessary to the idea of a Public School as that, if they were to be changed for something else, a School would be 'Public' no longer. . . .

Must a Public School be one in which some part of the detail of government is entrusted to some of the boys themselves, or is it compatible with a Public School that the whole of it should be exercised by the minute and continual supervision of Masters? Here, I think, we have reached the 'jugulum causæ', the heart of the particular institution, known only to England, which makes the Public School boy a man different from his differently trained neighbours, whose mere attainments or powers may be not less great than his, and gives him that peculiar freeness and facility of mind and habit which, valuable as it is in itself, none value so highly as those who are without it. It is this which, penetrating the inner life of a School much more deeply, thoroughly, and constantly, than is possible in any other way, causes the consciousness of government and obedience to be felt down to the secret ways and more intimate communications of boys among themselves. Moreover, it penetrates thus not in a magisterial but in a boyish way: that is to say, it is directed by feelings and notions which are shared alike by those who are the holders of authority, and those who are set under it. Thus it pervades the whole school acceptably and intelligibly, not in the 'official' (whether 'donnish' or 'condescending') style of a master, but in the simple way of a schoolfellow, who 'knows all about it', and is known to do so. Above all, it is ruled by well-understood laws, exercised by a body of boys who are in many ways a check upon one another, exercised in the midst of a very free and intelligent public opinion, so that even if one boy exercises it ill, or tyrannically, public opinion brands him as a bully, and points him out as the mark of a deep dislike, mingled with contempt, which he feels painfully at the time, and which is apt to adhere to him longer than he expects. . . .

It has often appeared to me to be a very remarkable thing that our English Public Schools and Universities exercise so very great an influence as they do upon life and manners in this country. The two Universities together hardly have so many as three thousand Undergraduates at a time under tuition. The six most recognised Public Schools contain not many more than two thousand. Taking the average residence at the University at three years, and the average stay at School at four years, this gives but one thousand young men a year receiving University education, and five hundred boys a year receiving education at the chief Public Schools. . . . Yet, small as the number comparatively is, the Public School man, or the University man (and much more the Public School man than the University man), is easily to be recognised in every department of life,—in the regiment, in the counting-house, in the professions, may I add, in Parliament? He has got that, whatever it be, and whencesoever it arises, which his neighbours, who are without it, feel to be of very great value indeed. However many may be the exceptions to the rule, yet the rule is undeniable. The Public School man is felt to have an undoubted superiority,—not necessarily in learning, or attainment,—but in qualities which are beyond price, facility in using his powers, facility in his behaviour to others, facility in ascertaining and keeping his own position, the elements of command over other minds. These are qualities which no private system will give, and no system of competitive examination will test.

This, however, our Public Schools, anomalous as their system may seem to many, and little as it may approve itself to theorising Educationists, do, to a great extent, succeed in giving.

This system is now to be officially searched into, and reported upon. Most earnestly do I hope that no crude or bold legislation following on such report may ever so far interfere with it, as to do away in any degree with the great advantages which it has been the means of bestowing upon this country for many ages past.

56   Ragged schools described

From Charles Ratcliff's introduction to *Ragged Schools in Relation to the Government Grant for Education*, 1861.

The ragged schools for children of the very poor represented the efforts of a handful of idealists to cope with the educational challenge at its most apparently hopeless point. Charles Ratcliff was Honorary Secretary of an association which held a Conference at Birmingham on 23 January 1861. This and the following extract are from its Authorised Report.

The sympathy of the public has been great with the efforts which are made in Ragged and Industrial Schools to reach the outcasts of society, and to restore them by suitable educational help to a true position in it. The approbation of such efforts, by persons in high and influential positions in Government, has been general;—but it appeared not to be generally known, either, how little aid the Schools can receive under existing Minutes, or how necessary increased aid is to render the Schools efficient, or sufficiently numerous to meet the wants of the population. For the Pay Schools there is an ample educational staff provided by Government, as Pupil Teachers, who are entirely paid by the Government; many of whom receive, afterwards, excellent training as Queens' Scholars in Normal Schools. There is augmentation of the Certificated Teachers' salary, with gratuities of £5 per annum for the training of each Pupil Teacher, and additional gratuities for teaching drawing; the teachers are also eligible to pensions equal to two-thirds of their salaries when superannuated, under certain conditions; and there is also a capitation of £5 for each scholar who has attended a certain number of days in the year. In 1859, there was paid in augmentation to Teachers' Salaries, £86,328; to Assistants', £6,244; to Pupil Teachers', £252,550, besides the capitation for attendance. To none of these large grants are Ragged Schools eligible; nor are they, by the Minute of December, 1857, enabled to obtain any equivalent aid for teaching, that which is offered being solely directed to the Industrial Training; £5,000 being the entire sum devoted to Ragged Schools.

57   Education for crisis

From a speech by the Rev. Dr Thomas Guthrie of Edinburgh at a
Conference in Birmingham, 1861. See note to 56 above.

I believe that the present and the eternal welfare of thousands of help-
less children turn upon the decision of this day; and I shall regard it,
and I trust you will do the same, as an honour to the town of Birmingham, that it has been the scene where a most important step has been
taken—one that will tell for generations on the well-being of the lowest
classes of the community (hear, hear). The first resolution proposed
this morning. . . . runs thus: 'That obedience to the laws of God and
man is powerfully promoted by the diffusion of sound knowledge, and
the training up of the young in the exercise of the great duties of life;
therefore it is incumbent upon the State to insure education for all
children for whom their parents are through poverty unable, or
through ignorance unwilling, to provide it.' You will observe, ladies
and gentlemen, that this does not at all propose that we should educate
the upper classes of society. Let them educate themselves, as they are
well able and are bound to do. Neither do we propose by this resolution to take in charge the education of the middle classes of society;
they are equally well able to educate themselves; and if they don't do
it they will soon cease to be middle classes, and come down to the
bottom of the scale, as they deserve to do in that case (laughter and
applause). Nor do we propose to take the charge of educating the
industrious, honest, vigorous, and well-doing among tradesmen and
the working classes. They would count it an insult if we were to go and
educate them in the way of charity (hear, hear). The working men of
Great Britain—the working men of my own country—would think it
a poor compliment to you if I told them that the artisans of Birmingham were not able and willing to educate themselves (cheers). On the
other hand, there is a class at the bottom of the social scale; and the
question is, what is to be done with that class? There are persons who
go and spend . . . their money on unnecessary luxuries and ruinous
intoxicants—the money which should go to feed and educate the
children whom they are bound to support. Some say to me, 'What

have you to do with these children?' I reply that I have to do with every suffering object of humanity. Am I to allow a child to perish because its parent does not do a parent's duty? (Hear, hear.) I am bound to do the parent's part so far as I can, and save that child from perishing (hear, hear). Now the grand object ragged schools have in view is this—to rescue from vice, and misery, and crime in this world, and from ruin in the world to come, those who have no parents, and those who are worse than them that have none (cheers). It is both the interest and the duty of society to see that these children do not perish. Society not only does them, but does itself a wrong in allowing uneducated children to grow up within its bounds. No man or woman is a fit member of a civilised community if they are bred in all the ignorance of a savage (hear, hear). . . .

I say that the first resolution stands on ground impregnable—that it is the duty of society to see every child within its bounds is educated. I don't enter into the question of State education—here I have nothing to do with that; but I maintain that it is the duty of society to see that every child in the country is educated. . . . The second resolution of this morning. . . . 'That neglected and morally destitute children constitute a very large class of the community, yet that no educational aid is given for their education from the Parliamentary grant comparable to such as is given to such classes of schools as already receive Government assistance.' Now, ladies and gentlemen, this is the head and front of the offence committed against us. I go to Edinburgh. . . . In Edinburgh, fourteen years ago, our city was swarming with juvenile beggars—our prison cells were filled, not a few of them with juveniles. I recollect going, some fifteen years ago, to visit the gaol; and looking through the eyelet of a cell door, I saw a poor infant immured within those four walls—a little boy who ought to have been catching trout in a sunny stream, or making necklaces of daisies, or amid the hum of the busy school, or sitting at his mother's fireside; but there was this young creature buried alive, in a stone coffin—withering like a delicate flower—pining from morn to noon, from noon to night, in weary, weary solitude. . . .

And what is the state of matters now? Why, we haven't a boy, nor a girl, begging in our streets (cheers). You may live there for twelve months running, and you don't see a juvenile mendicant. There were hundreds, there were thousands before; there are none now. . . . Our 'great strength' lies in the Christian kindness we bring to bear on these infants. Only we say, 'Aid us—if you don't help to educate these children outside the prison, you must educate them within it' (hear,

hear). Is it a better thing to let disease rage and ravage in a community, and to attempt to cure it, than to prevent its entering, and check its growth? (hear, hear). But the first has been the Government way. They seem to think it is a grand thing to give a man the fever and then cure him; that it is not best to drain and cleanse the town and prevent the fever coming (applause). Think of Government refusing money to save a man's leg, but giving him liberally to buy a wooden leg when the limb is cut off (laughter and cheers). See what they do—they give much more to reformatory schools than to ragged schools; much more to those who try to reform one who has become bad, than to those who try to prevent him from becoming bad. . . . Now, as regards voluntary aid, we have done much by it—in Edinburgh a very great deal—yet this is our position, that large numbers of children are living there who should be in ragged schools; and who would be there, only we haven't the money to pay for them. Look at the case of a poor, wretched, widowed woman, who is neither a criminal nor a pauper! She has been, and she is struggling hard for existence; how is she to educate her children? Some people talk sheer nonsense—they say if you go on feeding as well as teaching, you will soon have all the poor children in the town in your schools. Why, it is often with the greatest difficulty that we get them into our ragged feeding school. The mother doesn't care a straw for education; the father cares for nothing but that cursed bottle—he has sunk his soul in drink. We have had the case over and over again. 'We want you to send this poor child to school.' 'Oh,' say the parents, 'we can't afford it.' And the child is kept at home to steal or to beg, that the idle father or drunken mother may live on its gains (hear, hear). The consequence is, that we have sometimes the greatest difficulty in getting these children to school; and unless we bridged over the gulf by a loaf of bread, nothing could be done. Accordingly we set up feeding as well as industrial schools. The children come at half-past seven in the morning—and come in rags, not in the decent clothes they wear in school—that wouldn't do; the parents would soon have them in the pawn or whiskey shop. The first thing they do is to strip—not to be thrashed, but washed. We have a bath, as long as this gallery, and they march along it as slow as if they were attending a funeral; and the consequence is that they get what many people are fools not to take—a delightful bath (hear, hear). What comes next? Some of you are, I dare say, Scotchmen, and will understand me. They get a grand breakfast of porridge and milk (laughter and applause). Then comes prayer; then a portion of Scripture is read; then the work of the school begins; so many hours of the day given to this thing, and so many to that, till seven o'clock in the evening. They learn to read, and to write, and to cipher; and they learn carpentering, and boxmaking, and shoemaking. Why, all our girls wash their own clothes and mend them, and clean up the house, and cook their own food—what many girls in Birmingham could not do. The fact is, I believe they would make better wives for honest workmen than many women with braw ribbons in their bonnets (cheers). Then a part of the boys make the clothes for our school, and mend them; and a large number employ their time in making various other useful articles. Then we have so many hours for play. In fact, the children were the pictures of misery before they came to the school; now there are no children happier (cheers). At half-past seven at night we take off their school dress, and give them back their rags; and they go home —and as the rags are not worth the pawning, they are allowed to keep them (applause). We never keep a child from home unless it is an infamous den of iniquity, or the parents are cruel. In the bosom of the child, worthless as the parents may be, God has planted a link of affection, and what we wish to do is to improve and strengthen that tie (hear, hear); and, besides, we have known instances where these poor children have carried salvation to their wretched homes (cheers). But this, ladies and gentlemen, requires much money—we must feed and we must clothe them—we must meet the expenses of teaching all, and of housing not a few of them; and surely schools such as ours are deserve the fostering protection and help of the Government (cheers).

58   Sifting out the best for franchise

From Sir James Kay-Shuttleworth's *Letter to Earl Granville*, 1861. See notes on 19 and 34 above.

Recently proposals have been submitted to successive Parliaments for a reduction of the county franchise to a rating occupation of £10, and of the borough franchise to one of £6. Nothing tended to defeat these measures so much as the alarm excited in the middle classes by the proceedings of the Trades' Unions. These combinations often attempted to regulate labour so as to interfere with the freedom of workmen, and dictated to capital so as to usurp the authority necessary to successful enterprise. The domination of the Unions was generally without the violence and vindictiveness of former times. But it was arbitrary—was often directed to objects so mischievous or impracticable, as to inspire a deep-seated aversion to the extension of the franchise by the reduction of the property qualification. That proposal for including a larger number of the most intelligent and morally deserving portion of the working classes within the pale of the constitution is indefinitely postponed. But all parties agreed in the importance of devising the means of sifting out the best representatives of the classes supported by manual labour from the mass, and conferring the franchise on them. The effect of a steady perseverance in a system of national education, such as is at present in operation, would be to raise such men within the pale of the constitution. The 23,000 teachers and pupil teachers will certainly all possess the franchise. They are nearly all children of parents supported by manual labour, or of persons not possessing the franchise. Their elevation is a type of the true and certain influence of the same kind of training on the mass. The fifty-eight millions annually expended on beer, spirits, and tobacco will be reduced. The money thus saved will be devoted to the rent of more comfortable houses, to better household management, to the education of the children. A better-housed population will soon have many heads of families within the pale of the present franchise.

To give the people a worse education from motives of short-sighted economy, would be, in these respects, utterly inconsistent with all preceding national policy. The idea that an ignorant, brutish people is either more subordinate or more easily controlled than a people loyal by conviction and contented from experience and reason, is exploded. The notion that the mass of the people are the sources of national wealth merely as beasts of burthen—that the nation has no interest in their intelligence, inventive capacity, morality, and fitness for the duties of freemen and citizens,—is a doctrine which would find no advocates. No Chancellor of the Exchequer would dare to avow that their sensuality was a prolific source of revenue which he could not afford to check. Why, then, is education to be discouraged by regulations which cut off all aid to children under seven and after eleven years of age? Why are the annual grants to be reduced two-fifths at one blow? Why are the stipends, training, and qualifications of schoolmasters to be lowered? Why is instruction in the school to be mainly concentrated on the three lower elements?

59   Education for paradise

From George Rumsey's *Thoughts and Hints on Education*, 1861.

George Rumsey describes himself as Principal of Pembroke College, Fortescue House, Twickenham.

Thanks be to the progress of civilisation and to the working of higher powers in the domain of thought;—thanks and gratitude be ours for the opening of the eyes to the blind, and the restoring of sight to those who would see,—for the rapid advance in the right direction of juvenile instruction.

Much has been done, much still remains to be done; and as we grow in years and in experience, we may now hope that the infirmities of human systems and human thoughts must continue to be felt and rectified until we arrive at something near perfection. This is a cheering consolation, because a certain one.

The future man lies in embryo in the school-room, and as each individual is a part of one universal whole, the importance—the vast concern of this subject—cannot be too earnestly felt and acknowledged.

The sobered mind, the intellectual soul is fraught with happiness to the world at large, and, apart from religious creeds or sectarian dogma, claims the tenderest care and solicitude from every wise and good man. One well-disciplined character ennobles a thousand. Like oils on the troubled waters, it smoothes the asperities of life; like the sun in the firmament of his power, it warms and resuscitates to existence by a genial influence all that is lovely to sight, to taste, to touch; like the air which breathes freshness around our dwellings, it sheds a grateful perfume through every habitation of our pilgrimage; like the earth we tread, fallowed and softened by snows and frosts, and worked with assiduous and judicious care, without which we may expect naught but briars and thorns and thistles, so the mind thus trained under good discipline, thus sown with good seed, must in due time, in the harvest of life, distribute far and wide its innumerable, never-dying, and ever-delightful fruits.

60   The voice of the bureaucrats

From the Newcastle Report, 1861.

This is the first of the five major reports on education in the nineteenth century (the others are Clarendon, 1864, Taunton, 1868, Cross, 1888 and Bryce, 1895). It was signed on 18 March 1861 by Newcastle and others, who record: 'On the 30th June 1858 we received Your Majesty's commands to inquire into the State of popular education in England, and to consider and report what measures, if any, are required for the extension of sound and cheap elementary instruction to all classes of the people.'

It is only within comparatively modern times, that the importance of providing elementary instruction for all classes of the population has been recognised. In the early periods of our history, the only education which the poor, as a general rule, received was, instruction in the art—agricultural or mechanical—by which they were in after-life to earn their living. This rule, however, was modified by important exceptions. From the very earliest times schools were established for the purpose of giving instruction to poor children. In these foundations they were often provided with food and clothing, besides gratuitous instruction, and were occasionally supplied by exhibitions with the means of support at one of the Universities. Before the Reformation these schools were in many cases connnected with monasteries. Such as were founded after the Reformation were, for the most part, independent bodies; but the general character of the objects which the founders proposed to themselves was the same; that of giving special advantages to poor children who were either distinguished for special aptitude, or were the natives of particular districts, or related to the founders. Many of these schools still exist in different parts of the country, and constitute one large class of institutions intended for the education of the children of the independent poor.

During the last century, the beneficial effects of education, even upon those who were destined to pass their lives in the humblest social positions, began to be more generally recognised; and various bodies made some efforts towards the establishment of schools for the poor; but these efforts were isolated and produced very slight results. Towards the end of the century, Mr Raikes, of Gloucester, first established Sunday schools, in which poor children were taught to read, and these schools, which attained great popularity, were, for a considerable time, the principal means of affording general elementary instruction to the class for which they were intended.

At the beginning of the present century, the first efforts were made for establishing a general system of popular education. They resulted in the foundation of the British and Foreign School Society, and the National Society, by which a considerable number of elementary schools were established between 1808 and 1839.

In 1832 the Government began to take part in the promotion of education. In 1839, and afterwards in 1846, it extended its operations, and it has continued to do so upon an increasing scale to the present day.

61   Levelling up by example

An extract from Thomas Crampton's evidence, printed in *Communications Relative to Education from Edwin Chadwick Esq.*, 1862.

Thomas Crampton, headmaster of Brentford school, was being questioned by an Education Commission.

Question: What effects, so far as you have observed, are obtainable by bringing classes of scholars of different social position under the same roof?

TC: Most beneficial ones. The superior manners and *tone* of conduct common to children whose parents are in easy circumstances, raises by imitation and example those inferior to them in these respects. Good communications here improve imperfect manners, while there are few, if any, opportunities for the operation of objectionable influences that might be supposed to emanate from the poorest. A well-dressed boy is disposed to value more highly his good clothing by seeing a poorly-clad schoolfellow, upon whom also the examples of neatness and carefulness of the richer boys act most beneficially. Feelings of mutual respect between various classes are also developed. A *respectable* boy also sees that his advance depends on his work, in which he is so frequently beaten by his indigent friend, as to cease priding himself on advantages of social position. The vestiges of *caste*, which tend to induce pride and idleness on part of the rich, and lead to servility and want of self-respect on part of the poor, are practically obliterated in our good public schools, where 'the rich and poor meet together'. The advantage to the school funds from the richer boys is also very considerable. In my own school *all pay what they please*. Those who cannot pay anything have their schooling paid for them when their necessities have been simply investigated. The majority pay 3d. weekly; many pay 10s. per quarter; and several make higher payments, besides subscribing liberally to the school funds. We have no trouble in getting money from parents; and since we opened the doors to the children of shopkeepers and tradesmen, our school fees have trebled in amount. Let me remark, that the small tradesman is often more in need of and benefited by the education offered in our good National or British Schools than his poorer neighbours. The latter can have their children well taught for a few pence per week, but the former would have to pay at the rate of 3s. per week to obtain as good an education for each of his children, irrespective of board.

Question: In the neighbourhood of Brentford, have you a population having children of the class which may be described as of the *ragged school* class?

TC: Yes; a large portion of the people of Brentford are very poor; many are professional *cadgers*; and one of the strongest pleas urged by Her Majesty's Inspector on behalf of our new schools was, that they largely aided the education of 'the poorest population of a very poor place'. . . . I believe that very superior advantages would accrue to 'ragged' scholars from being sent to mix with and be taught along with better class children than by being collected in 'ragged schools'. The coarse habits, untidiness, and want of cleanliness on the part of the poor 'ragged' boys is doubtless an obstacle to their partaking, at present, as much as they might do, of the educational advantages of our British and National Schools; but by a separate class-room or two, used as introductory rooms, in which this pariah class might be kept till made clean, neat, and orderly enough to be drafted off into the main school, these objections would be obviated. I regard the establishment of separate 'ragged' schools as much inferior to well-directed efforts for bringing the 'ragged' children into good public schools. These so-called 'ragged' schools will soon work upward—must indeed do so, if they are successful—into National or British schools, which latter were indeed formerly mostly filled with this class of scholars. Much greater scope is, I believe, open to effective visiting and personal effort in individuals of the 'ragged' class, than by the establishing of separate schools for them.

62   Levelling up by ability

From Harry Chester's *Education and Advancement for the Working Classes*, a speech delivered to Hackney Working Men's Institute on 20 January 1863. See note on 53 above.

I think it very right and useful that advancement in life, valuable appointments, higher wages, more power and influence, should be looked for, in a moderate spirit, as direct results of superior education. Among the wealthier classes, there is generally a desire to 'get on', to turn acquirements to account in the great struggles of life. If this were not so, we should lose a great natural motive—not the highest, but a natural and honest motive—to self-improvement, and we should have stagnation where there ought to be a constant advance. This being true of the wealthy classes, I think it is even more true of the poor; and I should be very sorry to see you too dull and indifferent to be thus moved. But, 'What about contentment?' I think I hear some one ask. Well, it is right, and our duty to be contented in our station. I advise you to make the best of your lot, to put away gloominess and grumbling, and to cultivate a cheerful, happy spirit. But no law, human or divine, bids us to be so contented with our station as to make no attempts to improve it by the use of such talents as we have received from God. His gifts may safely be used, and cultivated to the best of our power; and if, using all honesty and no mean practices, and not being over anxious to rise, we see before us natural opportunities of rising, we may use them with a good conscience, and hope to do more good to the world than we could have done in a lower station.

In this country, happily, a man with good abilities and character may rise from the lowest to the highest class, and leave behind him memories which his countrymen will not willingly let die. You all know the cases of the Stephensons, George and Robert—of the Peels and Arkwrights. Do you know that his Grace the Lord Archbishop of York, who is the third person in the kingdom after the Royal family, was once a little boy in a National school? Lord Tenterden (the eminent judge), and Turner (the great painter, whose grand pictures you see at South Kensington) were the sons of barbers; Telford (the famous engineer), Ben Jonson (the rare poet, whose epitaph, 'Oh, rare Ben Jonson', you see in Westminster Abbey), and Hugh Miller were masons; Inigo Jones (the architect of Whitehall Chapel) and John Hunter (who discovered the circulation of the blood in our veins) were carpenters; Cardinal Wolsey and Defoe were sons of butchers; John Bunyan (who wrote 'The Pilgrim's Progress') was a tinker; Herschel was a bandsman; Etty (the painter) was a printer; Sir Thomas Lawrence (who painted portraits of kings, queens, emperors, statesmen, generals, and other bigwigs) was the son of a tavern-keeper; the illustrious James Watt was the son of an instrument maker; Michael Farraday is the son of a blacksmith; Sir Isaac Newton's father was a yeoman, having a small farm, worth about 11s. 6½d. a week; Milton was the son of a scrivener; Pope and Southey were sons of linen-drapers; Sir Humphry Davy was apprentice to a country apothecary; Shakespeare was the son of a butcher and grazier; Lord Eldon (the celebrated Lord Chancellor) was the son of a Newcastle coalfitter; Lord St. Leonards (who was Lord Chancellor ten years ago) is the son of a barber, and began life as an errand boy. Honour to all these worthies! Double honour to them, say I, because of the difficulties of their origin. You will find all this, and much more, in Smiles's 'Self Help'. But all these were remarkable men; and few can hope to become as great as they. You cannot all rise out of your own natural class to become archbishops and lords chancellor, and to leave behind you famous memories, of which our country shall be always proud. True; but some of you may do even this; and if in times past, when there existed no special system for the discovery of talent in poor boys, so many of them made their way up to high places, what may you not expect in future, now that such a system does exist; now that in every corner of the kingdom a lad may undergo examination and make his talent to be known? Every one of you, by training his mind, acquiring knowledge, and having a good character, may raise himself, if not above his class, very notably in his class; and by so raising himself may help to raise the level of his whole class. These are worthy objects of ambition; but, after all, the grandest object is the reward which a man finds in himself, viz., increased powers of understanding and doing. We think it a great folly and a great sin for a man to starve his body, that body which His Creator gave him to nourish, develop, and train to its various wonderful uses. Is it less a folly and a sin to starve the mind, which was given to him by his Creator to be nourished with knowledge, developed by exercise, and trained to its still more wonderful uses? . . .

Nor is this all:—Think of other countries—Paris is now within ten hours and a half from London; and Paris swarms with evening schools for the working classes. If the French artisan, or the Belgian artisan, is to be better educated than his rival in England, the latter will be beaten in the markets of the world. Don't let us delude ourselves. There is no branch of industry whatever in which well-educated workmen will not surpass ignorant workmen. If we neglect to place within the reach of the people the best possible education, or if the people neglect to use it to the greatest possible extent, we shall certainly drift behind other nations in the world-wide competitions of manufactures, and—when this happens—you know what follows:—Selling at a loss, diminution of manufacture, half-time, lowering of wages, discharge of hands, want of wages, pawning and selling of goods, insufficiency of food, warmth, and clothing, premature removal of children from school, loss of health, and strength, and energy, national decay, and wretchedness of all kinds. . . .

63 Public schools: their distinctive achievements

From the Clarendon Report, 1864.

The Clarendon Report was signed on 16 February 1864 by Clarendon and others. It had been set up on 18 July 1861 to enquire into 'the Revenues and Management of Certain Colleges and Schools': i.e., Eton, Winchester, Westminster, Charterhouse, St Paul's, Merchant Taylors', Harrow, Rugby and Shrewsbury.

Origin of the schools
The schools to which this inquiry relates were founded within a period ranging from the close of the fourteenth century to the beginning of the seventeenth, from the reign of Richard II to that of James I. Winchester, the earliest, is older by several generations than the Reformation, and the revival of classical literature in England. Eton, half a century later, was modelled after Winchester. Each was an integral part of a great collegiate establishment, in which the promotion of learning was not the founder's sole purpose, though it seems to have been his principal aim. Westminster is one of the many grammar-schools attached to cathedral and collegiate churches, for which provision was made after the dissolution of the monasteries; but it acquired, or perhaps inherited from the ancient school of the great monastery of St Peter, an importance peculiarly its own. Harrow, Rugby, Shrewsbury, Merchant Taylors', and St Paul's, were among the multitude of schools founded in the sixteenth century, either by grants of church lands from the Crown, or by private persons (generally of the middle class), with endowments sufficient to afford the best education known at that day to so many day-scholars as the neighbourhood was likely to supply, or the reputation of a competent teacher to attract.

The endowments of the schools bear no proportion to their magnitude. The revenues of Eton College amount to about 20,000*l.* a year, but of this sum rather more than one-third is distributed among the

Provost and Fellows, and the residue is strictly appropriated to the benefit of the foundation scholars and the expenses of the College establishment. Those of Harrow which are appropriated to the school do not exceed 1,000*l.*, and are not likely to increase. In some cases the rise of a school has been either caused or greatly assisted by an exceptional rise in the value of its property. Of this Rugby furnishes a remarkable instance. To a large and popular school, so long as it is large and popular, a permanent endowment is not of essential importance; but there can be no doubt that such an endowment is of great service in enabling any school to provide and maintain suitable buildings, to attract to itself by exhibitions and other substantial rewards its due share of clever and hardworking boys, to keep up by these means its standard of industry and attainment, and run an equal race with others which possess this advantage, and to bear, without a ruinous diminution of its teaching staff, those fluctuations of prosperity to which all schools are liable. . . .

Head Master and Assistants

If it is important that a thorough understanding and opportunities for unreserved consultation should subsist between the Governing Body and the Head Master, it is even more so that the Head Master should be on similar terms with his assistants. That there should be friendly intercourse between them, and that an assistant should be at liberty to make suggestions to his chief, is not enough. Valuable suggestions and useful information, which individual masters, and they only, are qualified to afford, may often be lost for want of a recognised opportunity of communicating them; and private interviews, however readily granted, are not an adequate substitute for free and general discussion.

The practice introduced by Dr Arnold at Rugby, of meeting all his assistants for consultation at frequent intervals—a practice which has been continued, with some interruptions, by his successors, and is at present maintained by Dr Temple—appears to have had the happiest results. 'It is attributable to that', says one of the senior assistants, 'that we have so very harmonious a working of the school'. The same practice exists at Harrow; and it is impossible to read the evidence which has been furnished to us from those schools and from Eton respectively, without perceiving that in the former the assistants have a thorough sense of co-operation with the Head Master and with each other, which is wanting in the latter.

We think that where this practice exists it should receive some definite sanction and some regular shape, and that, where it does not exist, it should be established, the principle of representation being introduced wherever, on account of numbers or otherwise, it is thought expedient. We shall recommend, therefore, as a general rule, that in every school the assistants, or a certain number of them, should meet on fixed days, with the title of a 'School Council', and under the presidency of the Head Master if he be present; that they should consider any matters which may be brought before them by the Head Master or any member affecting the instruction or discipline of the school; that they should be entitled to advise the Head Master, but not to bind or control him in any way, and that they should have the right of addressing the Governing Body whenever a majority of the whole Council may think fit. . . .

Achievement of the Schools

It remains for us to discharge the pleasantest part of our task, by re-capitulating in a few words the advances which these schools have made during the last quarter of a century, and in the second place by noticing briefly the obligations which England owes to them,— obligations which, were their defects far greater than they are, would entitle them to be treated with the utmost tenderness and respect.

. . . important progress has been made even in those particulars in which the schools are still deficient, . . . The course of study has been enlarged; the methods of teaching have been improved; the proportion of masters to boys has been increased; the quantity of work exacted is greater than it was, though still in too many cases less than it ought to be. At the same time the advance in moral and religious training has more than kept pace with that which has been made in intellectual discipline. The old roughness of manners has in a great measure disappeared, and with it the petty tyranny and thoughtless cruelty which were formerly too common, and which used indeed to be thought inseparable from the life of a public school. The boys are better lodged and cared for, and more attention is paid to their health and comfort.

Among the services which they have rendered is undoubtedly to be reckoned the maintenance of classical literature as the staple of English education, a service which far outweighs the error of having clung to these studies too exclusively. A second, and a greater still, is the creation of a system of government and discipline for boys, the excellence of which has been universally recognised, and which is admitted to have been most important in its effects on national character and social life.

It is not easy to estimate the degree in which the English people are indebted to these schools for the qualities on which they pique themselves most—for their capacity to govern others and control themselves, their aptitude for combining freedom with order, their public spirit, their vigour and manliness of character, their strong, but not slavish respect for public opinion, their love of healthy sports and exercise. These schools have been the chief nurseries of our statesmen; in them, and in schools modelled after them, men of all the various classes that make up English society, destined for every profession and career, have been brought up on a footing of social equality, and have contracted the most enduring friendships, and some of the ruling habits, of their lives; and they have had perhaps the largest share in moulding the character of an English gentleman. The system, like other systems, has had its blots and imperfections; there have been times when it was at once too lax and too severe—severe in its punishments, but lax in superintendence and prevention; it has permitted, if not encouraged, some roughness, tyranny, and licence; but these defects have not seriously marred its wholesome operation, and it appears to have gradually purged itself from them in a remarkable degree. Its growth, no doubt, is largely due to those very qualities in our national character which it has itself contributed to form; but justice bids us add that it is due likewise to the wise munificence which founded the institutions under whose shelter it has been enabled to take root, and to the good sense, temper, and ability of the men by whom during successive generations they have been governed.

64 Democracy: a natural right, or a free choice?

From a speech by Robert Lowe on the Borough Franchise Bill, 1865.

Robert Lowe was born in 1811 in Nottinghamshire. His public career was distinguished and varied, but his fame rests chiefly on his contributions to debates on democracy and education in the mid-60s. In 1868, when his original seat at Calne was swept away under the 1867 Reform Act, he re-entered the Commons as first member for the University of London—a seat, Disraeli suggested later, 'created expressly for his benefit, and with the additional inducement that from it he might be able to destroy any liberal ministry in which he might take part'. He became Chancellor of the Exchequer under Gladstone, and in 1873 Home Secretary. In 1880 he was made Viscount Sherbrooke. Died 1892.

(1) When the Chancellor of the Exchequer said that the *onus probandi* lay with his adversary in this instance, he must have meant that anterior to the existence of society there was vested in every man some personal *a priori* right which nobody had authority to touch. When Mr Mill, in like manner, speaks of every citizen of a State having a perfect right to a share in its government, he appeals to some *a priori* considerations, in accordance with which every man would be entitled, not only to be well governed, but to take part in governing himself. But where are those *a priori* rights to be found? The answer to that question would lead me into a metaphysical inquiry which I shall not now pursue, contenting myself with saying that I see no proof of their existence, and that the use of the term arises from a bungling metaphor, by which a term appropriate to the rights arising under civil society is transferred to moral considerations antecedent to it. Can those alleged rights form a ground on which a practical deliberative assembly like the House of Commons can arrive at a practical conclusion? If they do in reality exist, they are as much the property of the Australian savage and the Hottentot of the Cape as of

the educated and refined Englishman. Those who uphold this doctrine must apply it to the lowest as well as to the highest grades of civilisation, claiming for it the same universal, absolute, and unbending force as an axiom of pure mathematics. A man, according to the theory of which I am speaking, derives the right of this kind from God, and if society infringe it, he is entitled to resist that infraction. He is judge without appeal in a cause over which no human tribunal has jurisdiction; he is executioner as well as judge, and so this seemingly harmless dream puts the dagger into the hand of the assassin. Those abstract rights are constantly invoked for the destruction of society and the overthrow of government, but they never can be successfully invoked as a foundation on which society and government may securely rest. . . .

(II) 'You must have it out', the hon. gentleman says, felicitously comparing the Constitution of this country to an unsound tooth; 'sooner or later you will have to give way',—using a line of argument which is at once the foundation and the blemish of the great work of De Tocqueville. M. de Tocqueville assumed that democracy was inevitable, and that the question to be considered was, not whether it was good or evil in itself, but how we could best adapt ourselves to it. This is, *ignava ratio*, the coward's argument, by which I hope this House will not be influenced. If this democracy be a good thing, let us clasp it to our bosoms; if not, there is, I am sure, spirit and feeling enough in this country to prevent us from allowing ourselves to be overawed by any vague presage of this kind in the belief that the matter has been already decided upon by the Fates and Destinies in some dark tribunal in which they sit together to regulate the future of nations. The destiny of every Englishman is in his own heart; the destiny of England is in the great heart of England; and to that, and not to dreams and omens, I look as the arbiter of her fate.

65   War against all superiority

From a speech by Robert Lowe, *Hansard*, 26 April 1866. See note
to 64 above.

Does not the right hon. Gentleman know what democracy is? Whatever we learnt at Oxford, we learnt that democracy was a form of
Government in which the poor, being many, governed the whole
country, including the rich, who were few, and for the benefit of the
poor. The question is—Is not that the form of Government which the
right hon. Gentleman is seeking to introduce? It is not, then, liberty or
vice; it is the government of the rich by the poor. Why should not
we call it by its right name at once? That is a very short, but for my
purpose a sufficient, analysis of the argument of the Chancellor of the
Exchequer at Liverpool, because I do not pretend in the least to
answer it. I simply deny that justice has anything to do with the matter;
it is purely a question of State policy. We are told that we are bound
to forge our own fetters, while we shut our eyes to the consequences
of what we do; but the essence of my theory is that you are bound to
look most strictly to the results we may reasonably anticipate. From
the sweeping nature of this Bill when carefully looked at, from the
manner in which it has been forced upon the House, and from the
arguments by which it has been supported by the right hon. Gentleman, I maintain that it is founded upon the principles I have mentioned,
and I may state that not one person who has spoken on it in connection
with the Government has taken a view of it different from his, or has
endeavoured in the least to qualify the principle upon which it is
based; and that is that the franchise is due to everyone whom you
cannot show to be unfit. But that principle followed up leads straight
to ruin; it asserts that the franchise is a thing we are bound to pay;
and so clear is our obligation that we are desired to shut our eyes and
disregard all expediency, and to leave the constituencies so created to
take care of us and of themselves. We are told that we are under no
more obligation to see what use they would make of the franchise
than we are to inquire what use a creditor would make of a payment

of money justly due to him. Anything more dangerous, more utterly subversive, I cannot conceive. . . .

. . . There is another matter with which my hon. Friend has not dealt. I mean the point of combination among the working classes. To many persons there appears great danger that the machinery which at present exists for strikes and trade unions may be used for political purposes. . . .

Why is it that those various organisations have not been so made use of? The hon. Gentleman asked that question in 1860, and I admit that hitherto he has received no answer. Why? I will tell you why. The working classes, to use his own expression, are the lever. But they must have a fulcrum before they can act. They have not got it. Give them the majority of the voters in a number of boroughs, and it is supplied to them. It is not by passing resolutions and making speeches they coerce their masters. They watch their opportunity—they wait for the time when large orders are in, and they refuse to work. That is the fulcrum they work on. Give them the majority of voters—that will be their political fulcrum; and if the hon. Gentleman repeats his advice, no doubt they will use it with avidity. I want to call the attention of the House in a few words to the condition of the trade unions, because we are all anxious to discover, if we can, the future of that democracy which, I believe, this Bill will be the first means of establishing. . . .

The truth is—and of this I want to convince the House—that these trades unions are far more unions against the best, the most skilful, the most industrious, and most capable of the labourers themselves, than they are against their masters. Listen to [a] rule which is taken from the printed book of the co-operative society of masons—

Working overtime, tending to our general injury by keeping members out of employment, shall be abolished, excepting in case of accident or necessity.

This is your future political organisation. Again—

It is also requested that lodges harassed by piecework or sub-contracting, do apply at a reasonable time for a grant to abolish it.

That is to say, men are first to be driven into these unions, . . . and then, once they are got within the limits, whatever their necessities, whatever the pressure of their families, they are not to be allowed to eke out their income by working overtime. To do so might enable a man, a poor man, to raise himself out of that sphere of life, and furnish him with some still better occupation. But although his good conduct may have invited the confidence and attracted the notice of his master, he is not to be allowed to take a sub-contract, to make a little money in that way. The object of all these proceedings is obvious. It is to enclose as many men as can be got into these societies, and then to apply to them the strictest democratic principle, and that is to make war against all superiority, to keep down skill, industry, and capacity, and make them the slaves of clumsiness, idleness, and ignorance. . . .

66 Not our equals, but certainly our masters

From *Quarterly Review*, July 1867. Unsigned, but certainly Lowe. See note to 64 above.

Essays on Reform. London, 1867.
Questions for a Reformed Parliament. London, 1867.

The two volumes of essays that lie before us are the work of different authors, each of whom disclaims any responsibility except for that which bears his name. . . . The writers seem almost all to have received a good classical education; none of them display any considerable knowledge of English history or constitutional principles; all are fervent advocates of democratic change, and none, so far as we are able to gather, possess any practical experience of the manner in which public business is carried on, or any very clear views as to the limits of legislation or of the action of Government. These volumes were only printed in the present year, and yet many subjects on which they treat are for all practical purposes obsolete. They are relics of a period when reform in Parliament was considered a matter of reason, and when a necessity was felt and acknowledged for doing away with the general effect of the debate of last year, which seemed at the time so discouraging to the cause of democracy. The question has now been decided the other way, but certainly not in consequence of any superiority in argument. Still we think even now some service may be done by a detailed examination of the arguments which it was thought worth while to bring forward in the early part of this year on behalf of a parliamentary reform, once denounced as extreme, but moderate indeed when compared with that which has been determined on. It is curious to observe that almost all the writers of these essays are much more employed in defence than in attack, in answering objections than in bringing forward charges. There is an anxiety to hedge and qualify, to limit the sweeping nature of assertions, and to guard against possible misconstructions, which denotes anything rather than an assured confidence in the truth of their position. The constitution is assailed, but it is much more the object of the besiegers to guard against dangerous sorties than to assault the place themselves. All this timidity and circumspection are very curious, as compared with the utter abandonment of all attempts to defend our ancient constitution, which so speedily followed the publication of these volumes, and may serve as one proof among many how entirely independent of controversial considerations was the surrender by the Government to the cry for large organic changes. It is curious, also, to observe how little effect the teaching of our public schools and universities has had on the minds of our ablest young men, and how little the study of ancient languages and literature tends in modern times to inculcate the conservative cast of thought which used to be the distinguishing mark of our great universities. . . .

. . . It is indeed a melancholy spectacle to see that the best education the country has to give, the society and associations of our places of learning, lead to no higher and better result than a species of Philistinism, a systematic depreciation of culture and its effects, a marked preference for what is mean and vulgar, and, we are sorry to say, a scarcely disguised hostility to our institutions. The object in most of these essays is rather the destruction than the amelioration of the Constitution. Every little defect in it is magnified, while the state of things that is to replace the present is spoken of with a revolting recklessness. It is not to make our Constitution work better, it is towards a democracy with a single imperial head that their suggestions tend—America is spoken of, but France is meant. Yet conscious as we are of the very moderate amount of ability, literary or political, which in these volumes is devoted to the maintenance of these subversive theories, we think these essayists are entitled to all the respect and courtesy with which they are here treated. They are after all the advocates of the winning cause. Flimsy as is the intellectual texture they have spun, it is only the covering that veils the gigantic limbs of what is daily more and more clearly recognised as the second and by far the greater English Revolution. In these days when all men are absorbed in the worship of success denuded of all those attributes of consistency, probity, and honour, which make a losing cause respectable, and the absence of which makes a winning cause despicable, we, like every one else, must pay our homage to superior fortune, and assume a moderation that suits the position of the advocates of a vanquished and ruined cause. Argument has nothing to do with the decision of this most important matter. Contrary to the teaching of all history, more especially contrary to the teaching of the history of England, we have flung aside all moderation, all foresight, all prudence. Last year the attempt was to enfranchise the class whose leading principles and ideas are illustrated by the transactions of Trades Unions. This year we have at least in some degree avoided this risk by swamping the skilled artisan in an element of which we do not even know that it has in it any political life at all. We seek to escape the evils of unbridled democracy by the evils of unbounded corruption. Our last hope is, that our future rulers may choose to sell us the power we are giving them, instead of exercising it for their ruin and our own. Mr Gladstone is terrified, Mr Bright stands aghast. We call upon the Radicals to save us, we blush to say it, from the Tory Government, and they are gradually taking up the position of a Conservative opposition against the measures of Lord Derby and Mr Disraeli. When such is the state of things, we owe some respect to the writers who alone have endeavoured to put into a permanent form the principles of the new order of things, and we take leave of them with the frank admission that though we cannot accept them for our teachers, they are undoubtedly our masters.

67   Calculations in cabinet

From a memo sent by Disraeli to Lord Derby on 30 January 1868
(quoted in the two-volume 1929 edition of Monypenny and
Buckle's life of Disraeli, vol. II, pp. 313–14).

Confidential. Downing Street, Jan 30, 1868.
I am in receipt of your letter on the Education measure. . . . Any
forced decisions, at this moment, on conscience clauses and rating, and
boards of managers, would break up the Cabinet.

What the Cabinet decided on, I may say unanimously, was that
legislation was necessary; that it should be preliminary, not definitive;
that, to be preliminary and not insignificant, the institution of an
Education Minister was necessary, whose duties should be very large—
no longer confined to the application of the Revised Code, but
harmonising the system of lower class with pauper education; dealing
with the distribution of endowments, which the forthcoming Report
on Middle Class Education will render necessary; supervising all the
departments of art and science, and, as proposed by Lord Stanley, and
much approved, controlling generally Irish education. It was felt that,
if our Bill were limited to census and incorporation, the Opposition
would successfully start Mr Bruce's Bill, and the question of the day
would be taken out of our hands. It was felt that, if our action was
limited to extending aid to the poor schools, a minute to be laid on the
table would be sufficient, and that in the present temper of Parliament
and the country that would not suffice.

68   Democracy, alas: now educate the masters

From a speech by Robert Lowe given to the Liverpool
Philomathic Society, 22 January 1868. See note to 64 above.

What do we mean by middle-class education? What I mean is, the
education of a class that would not think of sending its children to primary schools supported by the State, and yet is not in the condition of
life to think of sending its children to universities, or public schools.
Now, gentlemen, that class has in it something very peculiar. It was
until last year the depository of political power in this country in the
last resort; and yet, strange to say, although it exercised that power in a
manner which extorted from its many adversaries admiration, and to
which I never have failed to give my humble testimony, it has so
contrived as to do little or nothing for itself. This country is full of
endowments, designed for the education of these middle classes; and
yet somehow or other the middle classes have allowed these endowments to pass altogether from their hands, and to be applied to other
purposes; so that when you look around for the means of supporting
the education of the middle classes, you find that these means are gone,
that they are reappropriated, and have in fact gone to classes above
them, who receive education at their expense. Then there is another
most remarkable thing. Up to last year, as I have already said, the
middle classes were the depository of political power in this country.
During that year political power was taken from them, and transferred
elsewhere—whether for good or for evil I do not say—posterity will
tell; but the curious thing is this, that it was done without a remonstrance on their part. I was one of those—they were very few indeed—
who lifted their voices in favour of the middle class, not so much for
their sake as for the sake of the country, and pointed to what had been
done under their rule, what happiness the country had experienced
from it; and, gentlemen, I never met with the slightest encouragement
or support from those whose cause I was pleading. There was no
meeting, no demonstration, no sympathy of movement on their part.

They treated the matter, as to whether they should be virtually the sovereign power in this country, or have that power transferred to others, as a matter of perfect indifference, in which they had no concern; and, having received it without having asked for it, they allowed it to be taken from them without a word of complaint or remonstrance—without even asking in what they had offended. This phenomena I attribute very much to the defects of middle-class education. I trace the negligence and apathy as to the common interests of the class to the want of common culture, to the want of something that should have raised men's minds above the business of every-day cares, and made them take a more large, a more elevated, a more expanded view of their own position, in a society in which they occupy so important a place. But every man was thinking too much of his own business, of his own affairs, of his till and his counting-house, and too little of the great events passing around him. They discharged very well the duty thrown on them, as individuals, of electing members of Parliament, but they seem incapable of combined action. The education this class as a whole has received is founded on a radical mistake and an entire misconception. As I understand it, the sort of education peculiar to this class, is what may be called a technical education; that is to say, children are sent to what are called commercial academies, to read, write, and cypher, to read business letters, understand bills of parcels, and keep books by single and double entry—in fact to do at school precisely those things they will be called upon to do in after life. The consequence is, that when they leave school they go to business, without any education except that which the business itself to which they go would have given them. They have had no culture, no mental discipline; they don't approach business from the vantage ground of more extensive knowledge than its detail, and the consequence is they don't rise above their position, they shew no power of combined exertion, no conception of their duties as members of an influential class, although capable of discharging their duties in their individual capacity. They seem to want altogether that most common attribute of Englishmen—common and united action, even for objects in which they are most concerned, and which to them would be most beneficial. Well, gentlemen, if that be a correct view of middle-class education in general, I think I need say no more to show that the subject requires careful revision.

What education should we desire that the class I allude to—shop-keepers, or persons engaged in business, neither requiring great capital nor transcendent skill—should receive? I suppose all will agree with me, that we should like them to be taught something practical, and useful to them in after life; and besides that, that we should submit them to a good, sound mental discipline, such as a man requires for the purposes of business. What a man wants in business, is, in the first instance, a keen observation of all things bearing upon it, and then caution and discretion; that he is not to believe everything he is told. He ought to see things as they are according to the actual state of affairs, and not through the medium of his own wishes and prejudices, or he will make serious mistakes. His mind ought to be trained to estimate probabilities, to draw sound practical conclusions from them; this is the sort of training which education should give to a man, if he is to be a really prosperous and successful man of business. . . . I think we have arrived at a point in education where we really must quit the path of mere expediency, of merely devising contrivances which may carry us on from day to day, must search out some definite principle, and must apply that principle boldly to the system of education in this country. We have been dealing now for twenty-two years with tentative measures; we have been feeling our way, and now I think we should march on to a more decided object. I hold it is too late now to enter into the question whether the State has anything to do with regard to education. It seems to me that after the State has been for twenty-two years assisting schools in all parts of the country, it is admitted so entirely that the admission can never be taken back that the State has a duty to perform to education. Well, then, if the State has a duty with regard to popular education, I apprehend it is perfectly clear that it is not discharging that duty now. If the State undertakes this matter, it ought to go through with it; whatever be the object it has in view, it ought not to rest, it ought not to take its hand from the plough until it has attained that object. Supposing the State undertook the defence of the country, it is bound to provide an army and navy sufficient for that defence; if it does not do that, they who undertook the charge of it fail in their duty. So, if it undertakes to provide for education, it ought to take the necessary measures to provide education, and if it does not do that, why it fails in its duty. What does the State now do? It occupies a position which is purely subordinate and ancillary. We have no Minister of education—we have no Department of education. What we have is a department whose duty it is to wait and see what private enterprise and benevolence will do, and when private enterprise and benevolence have done what they think proper, then to step in and aid them. It is quite intelligible to say that the State has nothing to do with education, and that it should be left to free trade altogether. But having once left that ground as we have, I hold it is impossible to stop short; we are bound to see that education is offered to all, and that it is not confined to those places where persons are benevolent and kind enough to step forward and give it. And that is the cardinal fault of the present system—it is partial. The State aid is given wherever persons are willing to come forward, wherever there is such a willingness for education that it would probably be supplied if the State withheld its hand. But where there is no willingness, persons are allowed to grow up in barbarism; that which is the duty of the State is neglected; where it ought to intervene more willingly than where persons are ready to come forward and educate the poor, there the State does nothing at all. That I hold to be an intolerable state of things, only to be excused by religious difficulties, and by the jealousy naturally felt of a new system working its way in the country. I think, for political reasons to which I shall not further allude, that the time has arrived when we should make some decided move in this direction. . . .

We must make up our minds what the educational unit of the country is to be. I have no particular view on that subject; perhaps in the town we may say the municipal boundaries, and in the country the poor-law union. Perhaps these districts are too large. That must be settled by Parliament. Taking those as the future educational districts, I should like to have a clause empowering guardians and municipal councils to make rates for education. Then I should like a second clause enabling the Committee of Council, including as it does the Chancellor of the Exchequer, the Secretary of State for the Home Department, and other high officers of State, in case the local authorities refused to make a rate, to make that rate for them. I should like to have as a third clause, a conscience clause—that is to provide what is now provided with the assent of the bishops in all the grammar schools—a clause protecting the faith of those children who are not of the faith taught in the school. That is all I should require, and I think that with that and the machinery of the Privy Council, I could work out the rest. I say the machinery of the Privy Council, because the rule I would go upon is this, that all schools, when once called into existence, whether by voluntary contributions or by rate, should be treated by the Privy Council in the same manner, that is, all inspected and examined, and receive grants. No matter how they were established, I would give grants to those called into existence by the rates as well as to those that were originated by voluntary contributions. So that, though the schools would be diverse in their origin, when they came to be brought under the central department they would be treated exactly alike with complete simplicity of management. In the next place I think it would be very desirable, if the change were to be effected, though I am afraid I cannot get all my audience to agree with me, that we should undenominationalise our inspection. . . .

I think the next step is to call upon persons resident in the place to come forward and supply, if they think proper, these schools by voluntary contribution; but every fresh denominational school must be placed under the conscience clause. If they were unwilling to do that, the next thing would be to call upon the local authorities to make a rate for the support of such schools, and if they would not make a rate, to make a rate for them. With that simple machinery I am satisfied that, with a little firmness, a little management, and a little consideration, and with the power of giving or withholding grants, the system could be brought into effect without deranging, at least at present, the existing schools. I would not touch one of them; I would go on as before inspecting the denominational schools. It would be my earnest wish to preserve them, and so avoid an educational revolution. . . .

The question of compelling children to attend schools appears to me not yet ripe for decision, for the simple reason that we have not yet in many parts of the country, schools to compel them to go to. There is that very serious difficulty in the general question. I myself should object entirely to passing any law for compelling children to attend schools till we have got, in the first place, a thorough educational survey of the country, and knew exactly how things stand, and until, in the second place, we had covered the country with schools which the children could attend. I cannot conceive any greater absurdity than to ask people to make bricks without straw, and it would be much the same thing to punish people for not going to schools that do not exist. . . .

The question divides itself into two branches—one town, and the other country. As to the country, I have not the least doubt in the present state of our agricultural population, that it would be impracticable to compel attendance at schools—that is, to punish parents for not sending children to schools, or to refuse the child employment if not sent there. There is a good deal of employment for children during some parts of the year, and a great deal of backwardness, sluggishness, and inertness in some parts of the country; parents would not yield without compulsion, and I am satisfied that such a measure would only tend to make educational martyrs. The case is different when you come to places like Liverpool and Manchester, where you have a large population of children on the streets. I am not prepared to say that they should not, perhaps, form the subject of legislation; but it does not appear to me that the case of those children really forms part of the national education question as I conceive it. The national education I have in my mind, is an education founded on the notion of paying for the efficiency of schools, and does not apply to the case of those street arabs, schools for whom must be to a great extent of a different character. I do not know how it would be possible to adopt entire, the same system of schools for children of that kind, and for the children of the respectable classes. I, myself, am not prepared to say even when this machinery is universal, that there ought to be any law whatever to compel children to go to school. Whether anything ought to be done with regard to children wandering about—whether their parents ought to be permitted to bring up children to crime and misery in that way, and what the remedy ought to be, is a question of the first importance, and one which the Legislature, if it can see its way, ought to deal with. It is a question not so much of education as of police or of poor-relief.

69   Education and continuity

From a speech by A. C. Weir, 'Primary Education Considered in Relation to the State', delivered before the Philosophical Institution, Edinburgh on 1 November 1868.

A. C. Weir described himself as Secretary to the Educational Institute of Scotland. This was one of the many answers to speeches made by Lowe in 1868, when Lowe had decided to come to terms with the new democracy whether he liked it or not.

I now proceed to consider Mr Lowe's plan. Mr Lowe said, 'We are all aware that the Government of the country—the *voice potential* in the Government—is placed in the hands of persons in a lower position of life than has hitherto been the case'. 'It is not merely desirable, it is of the utmost importance, it is necessary for the preservation of the institutions of the country, that those people should be able properly and intelligently to discharge the duties devolving on them.' 'We cannot suffer any large number of our citizens, now that they have obtained the right of influencing the destinies of the country, to remain uneducated.' 'I am going to show you how, with such experience as I have, this can be effected.' 'The first sacrifice the advocates and friends of the present system must make is, that they must give up the denominational system of education.' 'I think the State will have to confine itself to the secular part of education, to give what is at present a sort of joint-partnership in inspectors with the different denominations.' In this manner Mr Lowe 'vindicates for the State its proper function in education'. He proposes, *first*, that inspectors shall cease to be denominational; *second*, that the State shall pay no money to any school that has not a conscience clause; *third*, that the inspectors shall make a parochial survey to ascertain the extent of the educational wants of the country; and, *fourth*, that the Committee of Council—the Secretary of State, or some other great responsible public officer— shall have power to order a school rate to be levied to meet the extent of the reported educational destitution. Such is Mr Lowe's plan, proposed to meet the necessities of the country, and 'to vindicate for the State its proper function in the matter'.

On this plan I remark, *first*, that it is not original; that it is borrowed wholly, in thought and expression, from the report of the Royal Commissioners on Scottish Education, issued in May, 1867. . . .

. . . I remark, *second*, that Mr Lowe's plan (if it can be called Mr Lowe's, after appearing first in the Commissioners' Report) is not, in any sense whatever, a large, comprehensive scheme of national education. It is a mere modification of the present mode of distributing aid to schools, with a considerable enlargement of the present anomalous, arbitrary powers of the Committee of Council—a system based entirely upon denominationalism—a basis which Mr Lowe now proposes, in vindication of the State's function, to kick away from beneath the system, but without disturbing the superstructure, which he desires still to stand, if not more *stable*, at least more *extended*, and exercising an influence on the education of the country far more *absolute*. . . .

No taxation without representation is one of the best established principles of the Constitution; yet Mr Lowe would destroy this principle, and hand over to an arbitrary Committee, who are under few restraints of law, the power of levying a local rate for education. The Whigs found Mr Lowe to be a dangerous colleague—the Jonah of the storm—and they pitched him overboard. Mr Lowe betook himself thereafter to prophesying, and the Conservatives found him to be a dangerous opponent, to be kept at bay. Latterly, Mr Lowe has taken to volunteering, and his dangerous propensities still manifest themselves in his attempting to destroy the very Constitution which he has volunteered to defend and preserve, and to do battle for which he has entered the breach against the enfranchised masses.

I remark, *third*, that Mr Lowe's proposals are crude and unstatesman-like, and not at all calculated to effect even the objects which he himself has in view. Their crudeness is manifest in that they are not thought out. This is obvious. The modifications proposed in the system of inspection, and in the introduction of a conscience clause, are comparatively harmless as regards the Committee of Council, and they could be carried out, in the aided schools even, by a simple order of the Committee, if not opposed in Parliament; but, what effect would the change have on the religious convictions, or prejudices even, of the recipients of the grants? What effect would they have on the amount of the voluntary contributions, and, indeed, on the continued accept-ance of the grants? Has Mr Lowe calculated how such changes will affect the school managers and their future course of action in relation to the Committee of Council, and to the aid granted on such condi-tions? If he has, he has given no indication of it in his Address. . . .

I remark, *fourth*, that on no account ought the people of Scotland to give up the rich inheritance bequeathed to them in their parish schools. In all earnestness my counsel would be, preserve them, enlarge them, improve them, raise their standard, and increase their usefulness; but do not be induced to part with them, do not part with any important feature of them much less destroy them, and do not substi-tute for the system of teaching therein practised—that has made them what they are—a cramming, mechanical routine, without sense or soul; based upon arbitrary rules, without reason; formed upon the crudest theories, more suited to knaves than honest men, and changed so frequently that no one knows what a day will bring forth.

70   Education for anarchy?

From Herbert Vaughan's *Popular Education in England*, 1868.

Vaughan was born in 1832 at Ross, and educated at Stonyhurst, Downside and Rome. In his long connection with education he founded several colleges for home and foreign missions, and when he delivered the paper from which this was taken he was Superior to St Joseph's Missionary Church. In 1872 he was made Bishop of Salford. Twenty years later he became Archbishop of Westminster, and in 1895 laid the first stone of Westminster Cathedral. Died 1903.

It does not require an eagle's eye to discern the general track and direction taken in politics by the people of England. In 1829 they laid the basis of religious toleration and equality; in 1848 they consecrated the principle of Free Trade and got cheap bread; in 1867 they secured to themselves in the mass the representation and government of the country. And now all parties are agreed upon the necessity of an extensive system of education; the battle is to be fought regarding the *nature* of that system. There are three issues; though the third is more properly a mere compromise, which lets in the main principle in dispute. In the course of a few years, the nation will have finally committed itself to a path along which there will be no returning. The crucial and vital importance of the choice of that path; of the lot which must await the people along its way; of the bourne to which it infallibly leads, no one can exaggerate.

Which, then, are those two distinct systems of education, and what that compromise, for which men are beginning to contend? One party urges that education shall be purely secular, that is, without the admixture of religious and doctrinal teaching. Their actual example of such a system is the United States' National Common School.

The other party defends an education that shall continue to be religious and strictly and exclusively denominational, according to the principles adopted by the Committee of Council in the year 1839.

But between these two parties, which are perfectly distinct and consistent, comes in a third. It is a kind of *mezzo termine*, one of those numerous compromises so dear to practical, illogical Englishmen when in perplexity. It is the 'conscience-clause' and the 'rating-clause' party.

The effect of the 'conscience-clause' is to remove the authority whereby a clergyman can require the ordinary course of religious instruction to be given to the whole of his school, and to vest an absolute right in parents or guardians to *send* their children indeed to the school, but to *forbid* their receiving any religious instruction whatever, or frequenting any church or chapel. Under this system the children of professed secularists might claim exemption from learning even the Lord's Prayer, the Ten Commandments, the History of the Bible, or the Life of Christ. . . .

Such, then, is the momentous question which politicians are hastening the people of this empire to consider and decide. It is time that all should awake to a perception of its gravity. We have all of us influence; we have all a voice in the verdict and final judgement to be pronounced by the nation. A direct responsibility in this matter rests upon every Christian. We are bound to come to a conscientious decision as to the course of our future conduct. It too often happens, indeed, in communities and societies in which all have equal rights and powers, that the many are passive and otiose, while the energetic few rule and decide. Nothing can be more disastrous than such apathy. . . .

. . . But when the time shall come (and it is at hand) for a trial in this country of the great question of popular education, the Catholics of the empire will know how to act. We are confident that they will be found active in general and local meetings, in canvassing for members of Parliament, in elections at the hustings, organising petitions, setting in motion the engine of the press; above all, by wisely and heartily co-operating with all the denominations who will work with them. . . . But let us suppose for a moment that the secularists were so far to win the day as to obtain a 'local rating Education Bill'; that the management of the schools, as the *Pall Mall Gazette* says, was entrusted no longer to the clergy who represent religion, but to a Committee of ratepayers who represent temporal ends. . . .

We believe the natural consequences would be as follows. (1) Shocking as it may be to say so, to attach the Royal signature to such a measure would be to sign the national apostasy from Christianity. A country which adopts and proclaims the principle of education without religion, proclaims the destruction of religion together with its own apostasy.

(2) It would be the formal return of the nation, through an act o its Legislature, to an unmythological Paganism.

(3) It would be the eradication of the last great Catholic principle which still remains rooted in the foundations of our time-honoured Constitution. That principle was supported by Lord Derby when he declared, in the words of Chief Justice Twining in the time of Henry IV:— 'La doctrine et information des enfants est chose spirituelle;' and in the later decision of Chief Justice Holt in the time of William III, that 'without doubt, schoolmasters are, in a great measure, intrusted with the education of youth in principles, and therefore it is necessary they should be of sound doctrine.' This declaration was a corollary. But to what great principle was it a corollary? To no other than to this, that the education of man is the education of an immortal soul, and that the secular arm has a duty to acknowledge and protect the spiritual arm. It is the principle embodied in the union of those familiar words, 'Church and State'.

This is a question for the serious consideration of Anglicans rather than for ourselves. It is certain that, if the nation divest the higher education of the land of a religious character, . . . then, as in all consistency bound, declare that the primary school system shall, like that of the universities, be secular and not religious, it will not be able to stop short of its next legitimate conclusion.

And what would that be? It would be the destruction of the national Church. If the State does not pay for the religious instruction of children, why should it pay for the religious instruction of adults? If it is the duty of the State, as Lord Russell avers, 'to educate the people without reference to their religious opinions', how can it be the duty of the State to pay for the maintenance of religious opinions? In a word, Liberals and Radicals, and all who may be educated under the secular system, will demand as a logical and just conclusion the destruction of the national Church. They will say: We have godless universities, godless colleges, and godless schools. Let the State be also godless; therefore sweep away towards secular purposes the eight or nine millions a year which are paid to a national Church. The educational scheme of the secularists would inflict a blow indeed upon all forms of religion, but on the national Church it would be the blow preparatory only to its death-blow.

(4) It would be the beginning—and this is a point not contemplated by its more respectable abettors—of the breaking up of our empire.

H

Banish religion, and you let loose disorder and revolution. And be sure that the break-up of the British Empire, with its dense population and brutal passions, would be second only for anarchy, horror, and immorality to the last days of the Roman Empire. . . .

If we have taken a serious view of the state of parties in England, especially in reference to the vital question of education, let it not be supposed that we are alarmists. . . .

Consider the position of the country at the present moment: the lower classes have fallen into formidable organisations against their employers. The Trades' Unions, we are told, have 'embittered the relations subsisting between employers and employed; the breach is perpetually widening; the antagonism between the interests of capital and labour ever increasing'. . . . Now, if the tendency of the Trades' Unions is to destroy the immense trade of this country and to transfer it to the Continent, whence will be drawn the hundreds of millions for the payment of wages to our workmen? And if they are not paid, and the resources used during the cotton famine fail also with the capital of the country, how terrific will be the internal revolution which will inevitably follow! . . .

But, worse even than Trades' Unions, we have growing up around us leagues and revolutionary associations—the brethren of Mazzini, Garibaldi, Louis Blanc, and the blasphemous revolutionists of the continent of Europe. The masses are sapped by scepticism and infidelity, and are penetrated with 'hatred of the Churches'—and we are told that in many large populations not above 1 in 500 are baptised or attend any place of worship. The Reform Bill has raised many of these to a political power in the kingdom; and their views on education are certainly not higher than those of Mr John S. Mill, Mr Lowe, and others who maintain absolutely the *purely secular* system. In the presence, therefore, of such dangers threatening us ahead—of dispositions so hostile to religion pervading great masses of the people, does not an imperative duty weigh upon every Catholic to take his part in the coming struggle, and to endeavour by every means within his power to secure the permanence of the denominational or religious system? Who need it more than those who protest against it? Whose children are more completely dependent upon us, for their welfare and for our peace, than the children of those who reject the teaching of Christianity, and appeal first to the 'goddess of reason', and then to the authority of violence and brute force?

A few months ago, the writer was speaking to three or four stalwart and intelligent working-men; they declared, that 'the upper classes had taught them to read and write, and that now they should *govern* them no longer. We have learnt our rights, and will secure them by force.'

71 National education: but not for democracy?

From William Pound's *Remarks upon the Best Mode of Carrying out a National Education*, 1868.

The Rev. William Pound was principal of Appuldurcombe School, Isle of Wight.

In the following remarks all allusion to religion in the outset is omitted, in order that men's minds may approach the difficulties of the subject discussed upon a smoother road than religious controversy affords.

National Education is defined to be that training which confers upon the youth of the realm a dexterous handicraft, a suitable technical knowledge, and a sound moral principle. An education which fails in one of these requirements produces a man incompetent to fulfil the duties of his station in life. Dexterity of workmanship is most valuable, when under the guidance of scientific knowledge. But this combination, however profitable in itself, fails in promoting the social advancement and happiness of the people unless it be associated with the balance of a sound, conscientious, and moral principle. The iniquities of trades'-unions and the late enormities of commercial delinquencies are the result of a partial education, in which the balance of principle has been too much neglected. There arise, therefore, three distinct departments in which the successful Educator must work—the hand, the mind, the conscience.

A development of such education is not optional in the nineteenth century. The moral principle cannot be neglected in a country which aspires to a prominent position among the nations, and seeks to take a lead in the guidance of the human family. This leadership must be secured by Commercial integrity, as well as by Mechanical ingenuity.

The ever-extending ramifications of commerce bring the inhabitants of the whole world within one universal influence, by which north and south, east and west, are more or less dependent upon each other, not only for the embellishments and luxuries of life, but even for the comforts and necessaries of daily existence. The question is no longer, shall we educate the masses in this 'great Babylon'? but, how shall we educate a great and moral people, whose principles and whose intelligence shall be as it were 'the morning star' in civilising the world?

72   Mental treasures for all

From Alfred Dewes's 'Letter to Oliver Heywood', 1868.

The Rev. Alfred Dewes was Vicar of Christ Church, Pendelbury.

If then education means the training up of a child to be what it was meant to be, it seems of necessity to follow, that it is the duty of the State either to educate the child, or to see that others do it. It is for the good of those it governs that Government exists: I know no other ground on which Government can claim to exist at all. . . .

Each Government is bound to see that all children born within its dominions have provided for them the necessaries of life. Nor is this all. Mere life itself is no great boon: not merely the necessaries of life should be provided, but that which alone makes life worth having should be provided too. The mental and spiritual needs, if not so urgent as those which touch the body, must not be overlooked. Ignorance itself is no light evil, but it is a far greater evil still to have a nature hard and stern, with all the better feelings undeveloped. The great truth is not yet fully understood, that all men in essence are the same, however much in accidents they differ. It may be that, to the end of time, many will have to toil hard at coarse, uninteresting work, to provide for themselves and those who must look to them for the necessaries of life, but surely it need not be that they should toil on in the ignorance and its companion vices that so much beset them now. Possibly the comforts and luxuries which wealth procures never may be theirs; but if this be so indeed, we, to whom those luxuries and comforts are familiar things, may well be anxious to bring within their power those higher, truer joys, to which the mind and the affections alone can lead us, and which wealth can never give. The old theory used to be, that the hewers of wood and drawers of water had but little or nothing to do with any such things as these. For them the whole duty of man was thus defined: they must learn to labour hard, that they might not become burdensome to those above them, to be skilful handicraftsmen, to touch their hats to all their betters, and keep the peace. That theory is lingering still, and that too amongst earnest Christian men . . . the theory has not yet vanished into that place of doom whither all such hateful theories shall one day surely go. Men will still gravely tell us that all should be taught to read (for otherwise how can they read their Bibles?), and perhaps to write; but beyond these, and things like these, they go on with all gravity to ask, What need have the working classes of mental cultivation. It is hard to hear such questions asked, and not feel one's blood begin to boil with indignation. Are they not men of like passions with ourselves? as capable of enjoying the blessings life can give? . . . Next to the joys that spring from the affections, and the joy that springs from faithfulness to conscience, I know no joys for a moment to be compared with those which spring from mental exercise:—the joy of overcoming some difficulty which sore perplexed us, of clearing up some doubt which long had troubled us; the joy of finding at last some clue to guide us through the labyrinth in which we had wandered almost without hope, of seeing at last a light that leads along what had proved to us a dark and dreary way; the joy of holding fellowship with the noble thoughts of noble minds, and that greatest joy of all (greatest because most rare), the joy that we too have evolved a thought well worth preserving, which proves our kinship with the noblest minds. To all that follow after knowledge for the sake of knowledge itself, and not for the sake of the advantages at the command of those who gain it, to all such I am sure that the increase of knowledge is, and ever must be, the increase of joy.

73   The spirit of the age and the wants of the country

From Captain Maxse's 'The Education of the Agricultural Poor', an address to a meeting of Botley and South Hants Farmers' Club, 1868.

Captain Maxse, RN, was born in 1833 in Bristol; he had a distinguished career as an admiral, and wrote on political topics. His views on Home Rule and on women's suffrage were tenaciously conservative, but he was otherwise a radical, and tried unsuccessfully to enter Parliament as such. His idiosyncratic temperament interested his friend George Meredith. In many ways, a very typical Englishman of his times.

The logical result of the non-compulsory theory is that we acquiesce in the right of some to generate criminals and paupers. If you may not insist upon the labourer's children receiving education, you are bound to acquiesce in the existence of those foul nurseries—gardens of guilt they have been called—which are planted (we have been told it over and over again) in great cities, where children are actually bred up in infamy. That is, from earliest infancy they are taught and trained to regard vice as virtue,—that it is *good* to be *bad*.

We step in with legislative measures to arrest the spread of contagion. No difficulties are too great, no details too vexatious to which we will not submit to preserve our cattle, for instance. But a far more prolific source of contagion, one from which the whole people suffer from year to year both in happiness and wealth, we hesitate to deal with.

That compulsory education is consistent with liberty may be proved by observing that it has been established in none but countries where there is representative government. . . .

I trust this . . . will dispel any illusion as to the principle of compulsory education being an unsound one, or an eccentric one. I trust it will urge us to comply with the spirit of the age and the wants of the country.

There are scruples about interfering with parental responsibility. But I maintain that private benevolence has already, and with most encouraging results, to a considerable extent superseded this. And if it had not, we have to inquire whether experience proves we can rely upon parental responsibility for the fulfilment of its duty in this respect. We know we can *not*.

74   The way ahead

From the Taunton Report, 1868.

The Taunton Report, also called the Schools' Inquiry, is considered by many to be the most influential of the great nineteenth-century enquiries on education. It was set up on 28 December 1864 to 'inquire into the education given in schools' (other than schools dealt with by Newcastle and Clarendon), and to report on measures that could be taken to improve education, given the available endowments. Signed by Taunton and others on 2 December 1867; published 1868.

With regard to educational endowments (to which our attention was more especially called by Your Majesty's commands), we have desired to maintain them, so far as they could be rendered really and adequately useful, for the great purposes for which they were intended; but to provide a complete and durable remedy for those wide-spread abuses which have been abundantly proved to exist in these institutions. It is true that the principle itself of educational endowments has sometimes been questioned on high authority, and we are disposed to admit that, unless they shall be so re-organised as to aid, they will positively obstruct the improvement of education; but, besides the fact that we find them in existence, we are of opinion that however liable they may be to perversion without vigilant and constant supervision, yet that they often give a character of dignity and permanence to schools which produces the most beneficial effect on the minds both of instructors and of scholars. We have also desired in various ways to encourage the systematic improvement of private schools, and the establishment of others of a more public character throughout the country, by the instrumentality of local bodies, without interfering unduly with that freedom of private action which is so wisely valued by Englishmen, and for the absence of which we believe that no exertions on the part of the State could adequately make up. . . .

The result of our inquiry has been to show that there are very many English parents who, though they are willing to pay the fair price of their children's education, yet have no suitable schools within their reach where they can be sure of efficient teaching, and that consequently great numbers of the youth of the middle class, and especially of its lower divisions, are insufficiently prepared for the duties of life, or for the ready and intelligent acquisition of that technical instruction, the want of which is alleged to threaten such injurious consequences to some of our great industrial interests. We were of opinion that the subject either of technical or of professional education of any kind did not properly come within the scope of our inquiry, but, as it was brought incidentally before us, we considered it of so much consequence as applied to the arts of industry in this country that we thought it right to call special attention to it. . . .

We believe that schools, above most other institutions, require thorough concert among themselves for their requisite efficiency; but there is in this country neither organisation, nor supervision, nor even effective tests to distinguish the incompetent from the truly successful; and we cannot but regard this state of things as alike unjust to all good schools and schoolmasters, and discreditable and injurious to the country itself.

75 A liberal education, and where to find it

From T. H. Huxley's 'A Liberal Education.', given as an address in 1868.

T. H. Huxley was born in 1825 in Ealing. He graduated at London, and became a surgeon, with pronounced philosophic interests. Darwin's *Origin of Species* (1859) greatly influenced him, and he became famous later as a free-thinker. His interest in education led to his appointment among the first members of the school board for London set up in 1870. He stressed the value of literature to education, and was a strong champion of the idea of universities as places where knowledge was honoured and pursued for its own sake, and not for vocational or any other secondary ends.

The business which the South London Working Men's College has undertaken is a great work: indeed, I might say, that Education, with which that college proposes to grapple, is the greatest work of all those which lie ready to a man's hand just at present.

And, at length, this fact is becoming generally recognised. You cannot go anywhere without hearing a buzz of more or less confused and contradictory talk on this subject—nor can you fail to notice that, in one point at any rate, there is a very decided advance upon like discussions in former days. Nobody outside the agricultural interest now dares to say that education is a bad thing. If any representative of the once large and powerful party, which, in former days, proclaimed this opinion, still exists in a semi-fossil state, he keeps his thoughts to himself. In fact, there is a chorus of voices, almost distressing in their harmony, raised in favour of the doctrine that education is the great panacea for human troubles, and that, if the country is not shortly to go to the dogs, everybody must be educated.

The politicians tell us, 'You must educate the masses because they are going to be masters'. The clergy join in the cry for education, for they affirm that the people are drifting away from church and chapel into the broadest infidelity. The manufacturers and the capitalists swell the chorus lustily. They declare that ignorance makes bad workmen;

H*

that England will soon be unable to turn out cotton goods, or steam engines, cheaper than other people; and then, Ichabod! Ichabod! the glory will be departed from us. And a few voices are lifted up in favour of the doctrine that the masses should be educated because they are men and women with unlimited capacities of being, doing, and suffering, and that it is as true now, as ever it was, that the people perish for lack of knowledge.

These members of the minority, with whom I confess I have a good deal of sympathy, are doubtful whether any of the other reasons urged in favour of the education of the people are of much value—whether, indeed, some of them are based upon either wise or noble grounds of action. They question if it be wise to tell people that you will do for them, out of fear of their power, what you have left undone, so long as your only motive was compassion for their weakness and their sorrows. And, if ignorance of everything which it is needful a ruler should know is likely to do so much harm in the governing classes of the future, why is it, they ask reasonably enough, that such ignorance in the governing classes of the past has not been viewed with equal horror?

Compare the average artisan and the average country squire, and it may be doubted if you will find a pin to choose between the two in point of ignorance, class feeling, or prejudice. It is true that the ignorance is of a different sort—that the class feeling is in favour of a different class—and that the prejudice has a distinct savour of wrong-headedness in each case—but it is questionable if the one is either a bit better, or a bit worse, than the other. The old protectionist theory is the doctrine of trades unions as applied by the squires, and the modern trades unionism is the doctrine of the squires applied by the artisans. Why should we be worse off under one *régime* than under the other?

Again, this sceptical minority asks the clergy to think whether it is really want of education which keeps the masses away from their ministrations—whether the most completely educated men are not as open to reproach on this score as the workmen; and whether, perchance, this may not indicate that it is not education which lies at the bottom of the matter?

Once more, these people, whom there is no pleasing, venture to doubt whether the glory, which rests upon being able to undersell all the rest of the world, is a very safe kind of glory—whether we may not purchase it too dear; especially if we allow education, which ought to be directed to the making of men, to be diverted into a process of manufacturing human tools, wonderfully adroit in the exercise of some technical industry, but good for nothing else.

And, finally, these people inquire whether it is the masses alone who need a reformed and improved education. They ask whether the richest of our public schools might not well be made to supply knowledge, as well as gentlemanly habits, a strong class feeling, and eminent proficiency in cricket. They seem to think that the noble foundations of our old universities are hardly fulfilling their functions in their present posture of half clerical seminaries, half racecourses, where men are trained to win a senior wrangleship, or a double-first, as horses are trained to win a cup, with as little reference to the needs of after-life in the case of the man as in that of the racer. And, while as zealous for education as the rest, they affirm that, if the education of the richer classes were such as to fit them to be the leaders and the governors of the poorer; and, if the education of the poorer classes were such as to enable them to appreciate really wise guidance and good governance, the politicians need not fear mob-law, nor the clergy lament their want of flocks, nor the capitalists prognosticate the annihilation of the prosperity of the country.

Such is the diversity of opinion upon the why and the wherefore of education. And my hearers will be prepared to expect that the practical recommendations which are put forward are not less discordant. There is a loud cry for compulsory education. We English, in spite of constant experience to the contrary, preserve a touching faith in the efficacy of acts of Parliament; and I believe we should have compulsory education in the course of next session, if there were the least probability that half a dozen leading statesmen of different parties would agree what that education should be.

Some hold that education without theology is worse than none. Others maintain, quite as strongly, that education with theology is in the same predicament. But this is certain, that those who hold the first opinion can by no means agree what theology should be taught; and that those who maintain the second are in a small minority.

At any rate 'make people learn to read, write, and cipher', say a great many; and the advice is undoubtedly sensible as far as it goes. But, as has happened to me in former days, those who, in despair of getting anything better, advocate this measure, are·met with the objection that it is very like making a child practise the use of a knife, fork, and spoon, without giving it a particle of meat. I really don't know what reply is to be made to such an objection. . . .

76   Will the past be safe with us?

From George Eliot's 'Felix Holt, Radical', in *Blackwood's Magazine*, 1868.

George Eliot (born Mary Ann Evans, 1819) became a leading Victorian novelist and a distinguished exponent of liberal agnosticism. She wrote *Felix Holt* in 1865 and 1866, studying a radical from the earlier century, but with the current situation clearly in mind. In 1868, after the passing of the Reform Act, she resurrected her fictional hero to offer these contemporary reflections.

This strikes us, as we say in the Introduction, as one of the most important contributions to our debate (along with 77 following).

George Eliot died in 1880.

ADDRESS TO WORKING MEN,
BY FELIX HOLT.

FELLOW-WORKMEN,—I am not going to take up your time by complimenting you. It has been the fashion to compliment kings and other authorities when they have come into power, and to tell them that, under their wise and beneficent rule, happiness would certainly overflow the land. But the end has not always corresponded to that beginning. If it were true that we who work for wages had more of the wisdom and virtue necessary to the right use of power than has been shown by the aristocratic and mercantile classes, we should not glory much in that fact, or consider that it carried with it any near approach to infallibility.

In my opinion, there has been too much complimenting of that sort; and whenever a speaker, whether he is one of ourselves or not, wastes our time in boasting or flattery, I say, let us hiss him. If we have the beginning of wisdom, which is, to know a little truth about ourselves, we know that as a body we are neither very wise nor very virtuous. And to prove this, I will not point specially to our own habits and doings, but to the general state of the country. Any nation that had within it a majority of men—and we are the majority—

possessed of much wisdom and virtue, would not tolerate the bad practices, the commercial lying and swindling, the poisonous adulteration of goods, the retail cheating, and the political bribery, which are carried on boldly in the midst of us. A majority has the power of creating a public opinion. We could groan and hiss before we had the franchise: if we had groaned and hissed in the right place, if we had discerned better between good and evil, if the multitude of us artisans, and factory hands, and miners, and labourers of all sorts, had been skilful, faithful, well-judging, industrious, sober—and I don't see how there can be wisdom and virtue anywhere without those qualities— we should have made an audience that would have shamed the other classes out of their share in the national vices. . . . Therefore, let us have done with this nonsense about our being much better than the rest of our countrymen, or the pretence that that was a reason why we ought to have such an extension of the franchise as has been given to us. The reason for our having the franchise, as I want presently to show, lies somewhere else than in our personal good qualities, and does not in the least lie in any high betting chance that a delegate is a better man than a duke, or that a Sheffield grinder is a better man than any one of the firm he works for.

However, we have got our franchise now. We have been sarcastically called in the House of Commons the future masters of the country; and if that sarcasm contains any truth, it seems to me that the first thing we had better think of is, our heavy responsibility; that is to say, the terrible risk we run of working mischief and missing good, as others have done before us. . . . Whether our political power will be any good to us now we have got it, must depend entirely on the means and materials—the knowledge, ability, and honesty—we have at command. . . .

We have reason to be discontented with many things, and, looking back either through the history of England to much earlier generations or to the legislation and administration of later times, we are justified in saying that many of the evils under which our country now suffers are the consequences of folly, ignorance, neglect, or self-seeking in those who, at different times, have wielded the powers of rank, office, and money. But the more bitterly we feel this, the more loudly we utter it, the stronger is the obligation we lay on ourselves to beware lest we also, by a too hasty wresting of measures which seem to promise an immediate partial relief, make a worse time of it for our own generation, and leave a bad inheritance to our children. . . .

I come back to this: that, in our old society, there are old institutions, and among them the various distinctions and inherited advantages of classes, which have shaped themselves along with all the wonderful slow-growing system of things made up of our laws, our commerce, and our stores of all sorts, whether in material objects, such as buildings and machinery, or in knowledge, such as scientific thought and professional skill. . . . Now the only safe way by which society can be steadily improved and our worst evils reduced, is not by any attempt to do away directly with the actually existing class distinctions and advantages, as if everybody could have the same sort of work, or lead the same sort of life (which none of my hearers are stupid enough to suppose), but by the turning of Class Interests into Class Functions or duties. What I mean is, that each class should be urged by the surrounding conditions to perform its particular work under the strong pressure of responsibility to the nation at large; that our public affairs should be got into a state in which there should be no impunity for foolish or faithless conduct. . . .

Now changes can only be good in proportion as they help to bring about this sort of result: in proportion as they put knowledge in the place of ignorance, and fellow-feeling in the place of selfishness. In the course of that substitution class distinctions must inevitably change their character, and represent the varying Duties of men, not their varying Interests. But this end will not come by impatience. . . . Still less will it come by mere undoing, or change merely as change. And moreover, if we believed that it would be unconditionally hastened by our getting the franchise, we should be what I call superstitious men, believing in magic, or the production of a result by hocus-pocus. Our getting the franchise will greatly hasten that good end in proportion only as every one of us has the knowledge, the foresight, the conscience, that will make him well-judging and scrupulous in the use of it. The nature of things in this world has been determined for us beforehand, and in such a way that no ship can be expected to sail well on a difficult voyage, and reach the right port, unless it is well manned: the nature of the winds and the waves, of the timbers, the sails and the cordage, will not accommodate itself to drunken, mutinous sailors. . . .

We have all to see to it that we do not help to rouse what I may call the savage beast in the breasts of our generation—that we do not help to poison the nation's blood, and make richer provision for bestiality to come. We know well enough that oppressors have sinned in this way—that oppression has notoriously made men mad; and we are determined to resist oppression. But let us, if possible, show that we can keep sane in our resistance, and shape our means more and more reasonably towards the least harmful, and therefore the speediest, attainment of our end. Let us, I say, show that our spirits are too strong to be driven mad, but can keep that sober determination which alone gives mastery over the adaptation of means. And a first guarantee of this sanity will be to act as if we understood that the fundamental duty of a Government is to preserve order, to enforce obedience of the laws. It has been held hitherto that a man can be depended on as a guardian of order only when he has much money and comfort to lose. But a better state of things would be, that men who had little money and not much comfort should still be guardians of order, because they had sense to see that disorder would do no good, and had a heart of justice, pity, and fortitude, to keep them from making more misery only because they felt some misery themselves. There are thousands of artisans who have already shown this fine spirit, and have endured much with patient heroism. If such a spirit spread, and penetrated us all, we should soon become the masters of the country in the best sense and to the best ends. For, the public order being preserved, there can be no government in future that will not be determined by our insistence on our fair and practicable demands. It is only by disorder that our demands will be choked, that we shall find ourselves lost amongst a brutal rabble, with all the intelligence of the country opposed to us, and see government in the shape of guns that will sweep us down in the ignoble martyrdom of fools.

It has been a too common notion that to insist much on the preservation of order is the part of a selfish aristocracy and a selfish commercial class. . . . Does anybody set out *meaning* to ruin himself, or to drink himself to death, or to waste his life so that he becomes a despicable old man, a superannuated nuisance, like a fly in winter? Yet there are plenty, of whose lot this is the pitiable story. Well now, supposing us all to have the best intentions, we working men, as a body, run some risk of bringing evil on the nation in that unconscious manner—half-hurrying, half-pushed in a jostling march towards an end we are not thinking of. For just as there are many things which we know better and feel much more strongly than the richer, softer-handed classes can know or feel them; so there are many things—many precious benefits —which we, by the very fact'of our privations, our lack of leisure and instruction, are not so likely to be aware of and take into our account. Those precious benefits form a chief part of what I may call the common estate of society: a wealth over and above buildings, machinery, produce, shipping, and so on, though closely connected with these; a wealth of a more delicate kind, that we may more unconsciously bring into danger, doing harm and not knowing that we do it. I mean that treasure of knowledge, science, poetry, refinement of thought, feeling, and manners, great memories, and the interpretation of great records, which is carried on from the minds of one generation to the minds of another. This is something distinct from the indulgences of luxury and the pursuit of vain finery; and one of the hardships in the lot of working men is that they have been for the most part shut out from sharing in this treasure. It can make a man's life very great, very full of delight, though he has no smart furniture and no horses: it also yields a great deal of discovery that corrects error, and of invention that lessens bodily pain, and must at last make life easier for all.

Now the security of this treasure demands, not only the preservation of order, but a certain patience on our part with many institutions and facts of various kinds, especially touching the accumulation of wealth, which, from the light we stand in, we are more likely to discern the evil than the good of. It is constantly the task of practical wisdom not to say, 'This is good, and I will have it,' but to say, 'This is the less of two unavoidable evils, and I will bear it.' And this treasure of knowledge, which consists in the fine activity, the exalted vision of many minds, is bound up at present with conditions which have much evil in them. Just as in the case of material wealth and its distribution we are obliged to take the selfishness and weaknesses of human nature into account, and, however we insist that men might act better, are forced, unless we are fanatical simpletons, to consider how they are likely to act; so in this matter of the wealth that is carried in men's minds, we have to reflect that the too absolute predominance of a class whose wants have been of a common sort, who are chiefly struggling to get better and more food, clothing, shelter, and bodily recreation, may lead to hasty measures for the sake of having things more fairly shared, which, even if they did not fail of their object, would at last debase the life of the nation. Do anything which will throw the classes who hold the treasures of knowledge—nay, I may say, the treasure of refined needs—into the background, cause them to withdraw from public affairs, stop too suddenly any of the sources by which their leisure and ease are furnished, rob them of the chances by which they may be influential and pre-eminent, and you do something as short-sighted as the acts of France and Spain when in jealousy and wrath, not altogether unprovoked, they drove from among them races and classes that held the traditions of handicraft and agriculture. You injure your own inheritance and the inheritance of your children.

You may truly say that this which I call the common estate of society
has been anything but common to you; but the same may be said, by
many of us, of the sunlight and the air, of the sky and the fields, of
parks and holiday games. Nevertheless, that these blessings exist makes
life worthier to us, and urges us the more to energetic, likely means
of getting our share in them; and I say, let us watch carefully, lest we
do anything to lessen this treasure which is held in the minds of men,
while we exert ourselves first of all, and to the very utmost, that we and
our children may share in all its benefits. Yes; exert ourselves to the
utmost, to break the yoke of ignorance. If we demand more leisure,
more ease in our lives, let us show that we don't deserve the reproach
of wanting to shirk that industry which, in some form or other, every
man, whether rich or poor, should feel himself as much bound to as he
is bound to decency. Let us show that we want to have some time and
strength left to us, that we may use it, not for brutal indulgence, but
for the rational exercise of the faculties which make us men. Without
this no political measures can benefit us. No political institution will
alter the nature of Ignorance, or hinder it from producing vice and
misery. Let Ignorance start how it will, it must run the same round of
low appetites, poverty, slavery, and superstition. Some of us know
this well—nay, I will say, feel it; for knowledge of this kind cuts deep;
and to us it is one of the most painful facts belonging to our condition
that there are numbers of our fellow-workmen who are so far from
feeling in the same way, that they never use the imperfect opportunities
already offered them for giving their children some schooling, but
turn their little ones of tender age into bread-winners, often at cruel
tasks, exposed to the horrible infection of childish vice. Of course, the
causes of these hideous things go a long way back. Parents' misery has
made parents' wickedness. But we, who are still blessed with the
hearts of fathers and the consciences of men—we who have some
knowledge of the curse entailed on broods of creatures in human
shape, whose enfeebled bodies and dull perverted minds are mere
centres of uneasiness, in whom even appetite is feeble, and joy
impossible,—I say we are bound to use all the means at our command
to help in putting a stop to this horror. Here, it seems to me, is a way in
which we may use extended co-operation among us to the most
momentous of all purposes, and make conditions of enrolment that
would strengthen all educational measures. . . .

If we have any false ideas about our common good, our rules will
be wrong, and we shall be co-operating to damage each other. But
now, here is a part of our good, without which everything else we

strive for will be worthless,—I mean the rescue of our children. Let us demand from the members of our Unions that they fulfil their duty as parents in this definite matter, which rules can reach. Let us demand that they send their children to school, so as not to go on recklessly breeding a moral pestilence among us, just as strictly as we demand that they pay their contributions to a common fund, understood to be for a common benefit. While we watch our public men, let us watch one another as to this duty, which is also public, and more momentous even than obedience to sanitary regulations. While we resolutely declare against the wickedness in high places, let us set ourselves also against the wickedness in low places; not quarrelling which came first, or which is the worst of the two,—not trying to settle the miserable precedence of plague or famine, but insisting unflinchingly on remedies once ascertained, and summoning those who hold the treasure of knowledge to remember that they hold it in trust, and that with them lies the task of searching for new remedies, and finding the right methods of applying them. . . .

To get the chief power into the hands of the wisest, which means to get our life regulated according to the truest principles mankind is in possession of, is a problem as old as the very notion of wisdom. The solution comes slowly, because men collectively can only be made to embrace principles, and to act on them, by the slow stupendous teaching of the world's events. . . . Selfishness, stupidity, sloth, persist in trying to adapt the world to their desires, till a time comes when the world manifests itself as too decidedly inconvenient to them. Wisdom stands outside of man and urges itself upon him, like the marks of the changing seasons, before it finds a home within him, directs his actions, and from the precious effects of obedience begets a corresponding love. . . .

But now, for our own part, we have seriously to consider this outside wisdom which lies in the supreme unalterable nature of things, and watch to give it a home within us and obey it. If the claims of the unendowed multitude of working men hold within them principles which must shape the future, it is not less true that the endowed classes, in their inheritance from the past, hold the precious material without which no worthy, noble future can be moulded. Many of the highest uses of life are in their keeping; and if privilege has often been abused, it has also been the nurse of excellence. Here again we have to submit ourselves to the great law of inheritance. If we quarrel with the way in which the labours and earnings of the past have been preserved and handed down, we are just as bigoted, just as narrow, just as wanting in that religion which keeps an open ear and an obedient mind to the teachings of fact, as we accuse those of being who quarrel with the new truths and new needs which are disclosed in the present. The deeper insight we get into the causes of human trouble, and the ways by which men are made better and happier, the less we shall be inclined to the unprofitable spirit and practice of reproaching classes as such in a wholesale fashion. Not all the evils of our condition are such as we can justly blame others for; and, I repeat, many of them are such as no change of institutions can quickly remedy. To discern between the evils that energy can remove and the evils that patience must bear, makes the difference between manliness and childishness, between good sense and folly. And more than that, without such discernment, seeing that we have grave duties towards our own body and the country at large, we can hardly escape acts of fatal rashness and injustice. . . .

77   The great divide

From Matthew Arnold's *Culture and Anarchy*, 1869.

For a note on Arnold, see 54 above.

Arnold gives the names of 'Barbarians', 'Philistines' and 'Populace' to the three main classes in English society, seeing in the first two of these classes a characteristic mingling of strengths and weaknesses, and in the third—and largest—an apocalyptic challenge.

The Barbarians, 'to whom we all owe so much', are the aristocracy—sturdy individualists, full of bodily health and grace, good looks and good nature, full of charm but closed to ideas. The Philistines are the middle-classes, sturdy individualists too, in their way; wedded to hard work, thrift, money-making, machines, and the vigorous self-seeking radicalism associated with such names as Bright's and Cobden's. They have drive, energy, puritan virtues, ideals of a kind, but no charm; no love of high culture; no spiritual affinity with 'the best that has been said and thought in the world'.

While Arnold sees the great challenge and hope for education in the pursuit of perfection, he is acutely aware that neither of the two powerful classes in English society embodies this ideal in a dynamic form. But the dramatic and irresistible challenge comes from the third class, the Populace—now coming into their own, through revolutionary action and the tide of democracy, unlighted by ideals of any kind. Sunk in the most basic deprivations, material as well as mental and spiritual, they threaten to overthrow the ideals and achievements of human aspiration and culture along with the material possessions and privileges of their immediate oppressors. Can they, too, be raised somehow by education towards love of perfection; how much money, how much effort, how much time would be needed for this?

Culture and Anarchy must be read as a whole; these extracts are the best we can offer in limited space.

(i) *The basic challenge.*

For a long time . . . the strong feudal habits of subordination and deference continued to tell upon the working class. The modern spirit has now almost entirely dissolved those habits, and the anarchical tendency of our worship of freedom in and for itself, of our superstitious faith, as I say, in machinery, is becoming very manifest. More and more, because of our want of light to enable us to look beyond machinery to the end for which machinery is valuable, this and that man, and this and that body of men, all over the country, are beginning to assert and put in practice an Englishman's right to do what he likes; his right to march where he likes, meet where he likes, enter where he likes, hoot as he likes, threaten as he likes, smash as he likes. All this, I say, tends to anarchy . . . (*from* Chapter II).

(ii) *The immediate challenge; and the ultimate hope.*
It is obvious that that part of the working class which, working diligently by the light of Mrs Gooch's Golden Rule, looks forward to the happy day when it will sit on thrones with Mr Bazley and other middle-class potentates, to survey, as Mr Bright beautifully says, 'the cities it has built, the railroads it has made, the manufactures it has produced, the cargoes which freight the ships of the greatest mercantile navy the world has ever seen'—it is obvious, I say, that this part of the working class is, or is in a fair way to be, one in spirit with the industrial middle class. It is notorious that our middle-class Liberals have long looked forward to this consummation, when the working-class shall join forces with them, aid them heartily to carry forward their good works, go in a body to their tea-meetings, and, in short, enable them to bring about their millennium. That part of the working class, therefore, which does really seem to lend itself to these great aims, may, with propriety, be numbered by us among the Philistines. That part of it, again, which so much occupies the attention of philanthropists at present,—the part which gives all its energies to organising itself, through trades' unions and other means, so as to constitute, first, a great working-class power, independent of the middle and aristocratic classes, and then, by dint of numbers, give the law to them, and itself reign absolutely,—this lively and interesting part must also, according to our definition, go with the Philistines; because it is its class and its class-instinct which it seeks to affirm, its ordinary self, not its best self; and it is a machinery, an industrial machinery, and power and pre-eminence and other external goods, which fill its thoughts, and not an inward perfection. . . . But that vast portion, lastly, of the working class which, raw and half-developed, has long lain half-hidden amidst its poverty and squalor, and is now issuing from its hiding-place to assert an Englishman's heaven-born privilege of doing as he likes, and

is beginning to perplex us by marching where it likes, meeting where
it likes, bawling what it likes, breaking what it likes,—to this vast
residuum we may with great propriety give the name of *Populace*. . . .

But, in using this new, and, I hope, convenient division of English
society, two things are to be borne in mind. The first is, that since,
under all our class divisions, there is a common basis of human nature,
therefore, in every one of us, whether we be properly Barbarians,
Philistines or Populace, there exists, sometimes only in germ and
potentially, sometimes more or less developed, the same tendencies
and passions which have made our fellow-citizens of other classes
what they are. . . . And as to the Populace, who, whether he be
Barbarian or Philistine, can look at them without sympathy, when he
remembers how often,—every time that we snatch up a vehement
opinion in ignorance and passion, every time that we long to crush an
adversary by sheer violence, every time that we are envious, every time
that we are brutal, every time that we adore mere power or success,
every time that we add our voice to swell a blind clamour against
some unpopular personage, every time that we trample savagely on
the fallen,—he has found in his own bosom the eternal spirit of the
Populace, and that there needs only a little help from circumstances to
make it triumph in him untameably?

The second thing to be borne in mind . . . is this. All of us, so far as
we are Barbarians, Philistines, or Populace, imagine happiness to
consist in doing what one's ordinary self likes. . . . But in each class
there are a certain number of natures with a curiosity about their best
self, with a bent for seeing things as they are, for disentangling themselves from machinery, for simply concerning themselves with reason
and the will of God, and doing their best to make these prevail; for the
pursuit, in a word, of perfection. To certain manifestations of this
love for perfection mankind have accustomed themselves to give the
name of genius; implying, by this name, something original and
heaven-bestowed in the passion. But the passion is to be found far
beyond those manifestations of it to which the world usually gives
the name of genius, and in which there is, for the most part, a *talent* of
some kind or other, a special and striking faculty of execution, informed by the heaven-bestowed ardour, or genius. It is to be found in
many manifestations besides these, and may best be called, as we have
called it, the love and pursuit of perfection; culture being the true
nurse of the pursuing love, and sweetness and light the true character
of the pursued perfection. Natures with this bent emerge in all classes,
—among the Barbarians, among the Philistines, among the Populace.

And this bent always tends to take them out of their class, and to make their distinguishing characteristic not their Barbarianism or their Philistinism, but their *humanity*. . . .

Therefore, when we speak of ourselves as divided into Barbarians, Philistines, and Populace, we must be understood always to imply that within each of these classes there are a certain number of *aliens*, if we may so call them,—persons who are mainly led, not by their class spirit, but by a general *humane* spirit, by the love of human perfection; and that this number is capable of being diminished or augmented. I mean, the number of those who will succeed in developing this happy instinct will be greater or smaller, in proportion both to the force of the original instinct within them, and to the hindrance or encouragement which it meets with from without. . . . At a moment, therefore, when it is agreed that we want a source of authority, and when it seems probable that the right source is our best self, it becomes of vast importance to see whether or not the things around us are, in general, such as to help and elicit our best self, and if they are not, to see why they are not, and the most promising way of mending them (*from* Chapter III).

(*iii*) *The humane and practical challenge.*
I remember, only the other day, a good man looking with me upon a multitude of children who were gathered before us in one of the most miserable regions of London,—children eaten up with disease, half-sized, half-fed, half-clothed, neglected by their parents, without health, without home, without hope,—said to me: 'The one thing really needful is to teach these little ones to succour one another, if only with a cup of cold water; but now, from one end of the country to the other, one hears nothing but the cry for knowledge, knowledge, knowledge!' And yet surely, so long as these children are there in these festering masses, without health, without home, without hope, and so long as their multitude is perpetually swelling, charged with misery they must still be for themselves, charged with misery they must still be for us, whether they help one another with a cup of cold water or no; and the knowledge how to prevent their accumulating is necessary, even to give their moral life and growth a fair chance! (*from* Chapter VI).

(*iv*) *The educational ideal.*
The pursuit of perfection, then, is the pursuit of sweetness and light . . . Culture looks beyond machinery, culture hates hatred; culture has one

great passion, the passion for sweetness and light. It has one even yet greater!—the passion for making them *prevail*. It is not satisfied till we *all* come to a perfect man; it knows that the sweetness and light of the few must be imperfect until the raw and unkindled masses of humanity are touched with sweetness and light. If I have not shrunk from saying that we must work for sweetness and light, so neither have I shrunk from saying that we must have a broad basis, must have sweetness and light for as many as possible. Again and again I have insisted how those are the happy moments of humanity, how those are the marking epochs of a people's life, how those are the flowering times for literature and art and all the creative power of genius, when there is a *national* glow of life and thought, when the whole of society is in the fullest measure permeated by thought, sensible to beauty, intelligent and alive. Only it must be *real* thought and *real* beauty; *real* sweetness and *real* light. Plenty of people will try to give the masses, as they call them, an intellectual food prepared and adapted in the way they think proper for the actual condition of the masses. The ordinary popular literature is an example of this way of working on the masses. Plenty of people will try to indoctrinate the masses with the set of ideas and judgments constituting the creed of their own profession or party. Our religious and political organisations give an example of this way of working on the masses. I condemn neither way; but culture works differently. It does not try to teach down to the level of inferior classes; it does not try to win them for this or that sect of its own, with ready-made judgments and watchwords. It seeks to do away with classes; to make the best that has been thought and known in the world current everywhere; to make all men live in an atmosphere of sweetness and light, where they may use ideas, as it uses them itself, freely,— nourished and not bound by them.

This is the *social idea*; and the men of culture are the true apostles of equality. The great men of culture are those who have had a passion for diffusing, for making prevail, for carrying from one end of society to the other, the best knowledge, the best ideas of their time; who have laboured to divest knowledge of all that was harsh, uncouth, difficult, abstract, professional, exclusive; to humanise it, to make it efficient outside the clique of the cultivated and learned, yet still remaining the *best* knowledge and thought of the time, and a true source, therefore, of sweetness and light (*from* Chapter I).

78 All seekers still

From Matthew Arnold's Preface to *Essays in Criticism*, 1869. See note on 54 above.

. . . No, we are all seekers still! seekers often make mistakes, and I wish mine to redound to my own discredit only, and not to touch Oxford. Beautiful city! so venerable, so lovely, so unravaged by the fierce intellectual life of our century, so serene!

There are our young barbarians all at play!

And yet, steeped in sentiment as she lies, spreading her gardens to the moonlight, and whispering from her towers the last enchantments of the Middle Age, who will deny that Oxford, by her ineffable charm, keeps ever calling us nearer to the true goal of all of us, to the ideal, to perfection,—to beauty, in a word, which is only truth seen from another side?—nearer, perhaps, than all the science of Tubingen. Adorable dreamer, whose heart has been so romantic! who hast given thyself so prodigally, given thyself to sides and to heroes not mine, only never to the Philistines! home of lost causes, and forsaken beliefs, and unpopular names, and impossible loyalties! what example could ever so inspire us to keep down the Philistine in ourselves, what teacher could ever so save us from that bondage to which we are all prone, that bondage which Goethe, in those incomparable lines on the death of Schiller, makes it his friend's highest praise (and nobly did Schiller deserve the praise) to have left miles out of sight behind him;—the bondage of '*was uns alle bändigt*, DAS GEMEINE!' She will forgive me, even if I have unwittingly drawn upon her a shot or two aimed at her unworthy son; for she is generous, and the cause in which I fight is, after all, hers. Apparitions of a day, what is our puny warfare against the Philistines, compared with the warfare which this queen of romance has been waging against them for centuries, and will wage after we are gone?

79   Education for the democracy

From W. E. Forster's speech on his Education Act, *Hansard*,
17 February 1870.

W. E. Forster was born in 1818 in Dorsetshire, and became a
leading liberal politician, with special commitment to the causes of
democracy and of education. He carried the 1870 Act triumphantly,
despite bitter sectarian battles over finance which threatened to
wreck it. In many ways the Bill was a compromise, creating more
problems than it solved, but it marks the moment when elementary
education for all was finally accepted as a national responsibility.

More or less imperfectly about 1,500,000 children are educated in the
schools that we help—that is, they are simply on the registers. But, as
I had the honour of stating last year, only two-fifths of the children
of the working classes between the ages of six and ten years are on the
registers of the Government schools, and only one-third of those
between the ages of ten and twelve. Consequently, of those between
six and ten, we have helped about 700,000 more or less, but we have
left unhelped 1,000,000; while of those between ten and twelve, we
have helped 250,000, and left unhelped at least 500,000. Some hon.
members will think, I daresay, that I leave out of consideration the
unaided schools. I do not, however, leave them out of consideration;
but it so happens—and we cannot blame them for it—that the schools
which do not receive Government assistance are, generally speaking,
the worst schools, and those least fitted to give a good education to the
children of the working classes. . . .

The first problem, then, is, 'How can we cover the country with
good schools?' Now, in trying to solve that problem there are certain
conditions which I think hon. members on both sides of the House
will acknowledge we must abide by. First of all, we must not forget
the duty of the parents. Then we must not forget our duty to our
constituencies, our duty to the taxpayers. Though our constituencies
almost, I believe, to a man would spend money, and large sums of
money, rather than not do the work, still we must remember that it is

upon them that the burden will fall. And, thirdly, we must take care not to destroy in building up—not to destroy the existing system in introducing a new one. In solving this problem there must be, consistently with the attainment of our object, the least possible expenditure of public money, the utmost endeavour not to injure existing and efficient schools, and the most careful absence of all encouragement to parents to neglect their children. . . . Our object is to complete the present voluntary system, to fill up gaps, sparing the public money where it can be done without, procuring as much as we can the assistance of the parents, and welcoming as much as we rightly can the co-operation and aid of those benevolent men who desire to assist their neighbours. . . .

. . . I have said that this is a very serious question; I would further say that whatever we do in the matter should be done quickly. We must not delay. Upon the speedy provision of elementary education depends our industrial prosperity. It is of no use trying to give technical teaching to our artisans without elementary education; uneducated labourers—and many of our labourers are utterly uneducated—are, for the most part, unskilled labourers, and if we leave our work-folk any longer unskilled, notwithstanding their strong sinews and determined energy, they will become over-matched in the competition of the world. Upon this speedy provision depends also, I fully believe, the good, the safe working of our constitutional system. To its honour, Parliament has lately decided that England shall in future be governed by popular government. I am one of those who would not wait until the people were educated before I would trust them with political power. If we had thus waited we might have waited long for education; but now that we have given them political power we must not wait any longer to give them education. There are questions demanding answers, problems which must be solved, which ignorant constituencies are ill-fitted to solve. Upon this speedy provision of education depends also our national power. Civilised communities throughout the world are massing themselves together, each mass being measured by its force; and if we are to hold our position among men of our own race or among the nations of the world we must make up the smallness of our numbers by increasing the intellectual force of the individual.

Four 1870–1916: Equality of opportunity or egalitarianism? Towards the great divide

We start with F. D. Maurice (80), a clergyman who has the courage to talk of real Christian equality, the ideal which democracy perhaps most of all needs if it is to ward off envy. Unlike most of our contributors, Maurice speaks in the New Testament spirit, highlighting one crisis of his times. If men are to opt for material goods and for a mere cult of possessions, where can social 'equality' point, but to envy and greed? How can a church enmeshed in worldliness proclaim its message, and if it does, how can it hope to be believed?

This remaining section has two further official landmarks, the Bryce Report on Secondary Education in 1895, and the Balfour Education Act of 1902. After 1870, the battle tended to fragment into points of detail and warring interests—sectarianism, bureaucracy, taxation and the rest. The Act of 1876 introduced compulsory education up to the age of twelve, but not free education; there was also provision for exemptions at an earlier age. Disraeli's pioneering spirit in the 1860s led to no mad radicalism; as Robert Blake has said in his biography of Disraeli, 'Indeed, the Education Act of 1876 can be interpreted largely as an attempt to prevent the incursion of rate-aided "boards" into the counties, and at the same time to preserve as far as possible the position of the voluntary denominational schools. Conservatives were equally reluctant to spend the taxpayer's money . . .' (p. 554).

If there is, through this period now to concern us, a central theme, it is the slow triumph of the movement to open to merit and industry many doors that had previously been closed to them, the movement towards 'equality of opportunity' as it can justly be called. On this journey, the Balfour Education Act of 1902 was a notable milestone, and the later emergence of universal secondary education, with schools attuned to talent and ability, was the logical end.

But there are two educational flowers, not one, in the garden of democracy, each fighting and strangling the other by the laws of its growth. Which will be tended and nurtured with the greater love? Will 'equality of opportunity' or will 'egalitarianism' be the favoured flower? If the democracy hankers not after equality of opportunity but after equality of performance, it might decree that traditional education is *in itself* an intolerable wrong. Much will depend on the truth or otherwise of the hopes of the utopians, that the majority will in fact excel if it is given the fullest chance. But suppose that the majority fails to achieve excellence, or fails even to acknowledge it? How then will its democratic powers be used? Privilege won by merit might come to seem even more hateful than privilege given by 'family', just as earned income might rouse more envy than a win on the pools.

Our remaining section is in the form of scattered insights, a cross-section of complexities to come. The real battle for the soul of education comes later and is a different story, but there were some Victorians who foresaw what form it might take, and who pointed the way.

Walter Bagehot (81) offers a warning: 'The characteristic danger of great nations, like the Romans or the English, which have a long history of continuous creation, is that they may at last fail from not comprehending the great institutions which they have created.' He interprets the 1832 Reform Act as an attack on the rule of trained intelligence, and 1867 as an all too fitting sequel in this respect. Of the original reformers, he says, 'They thus by conspicuous action, which is the most influential of political instruction, taught mankind that an increase in the power of numbers was the change most to be desired in England. And of course the mass of mankind are only too ready to think so. They are always prone to believe their own knowledge to be "for all practical purposes" sufficient, and to wish to be emancipated from the authority of the higher culture.' James's novel *The Princess Casamassima* dramatises such forebodings with more subtlety than our extracts can do justice to (82), though even these indicate problems that must prove particularly difficult to solve and distasteful to face.

Matthew Arnold consoles himself, in his retirement, with thoughts of the elementary teachers (83) and of their general response to children as to a sacred trust. Sydney Olivier (84), in a Fabian context, hopes that elementary education will unlock to all children those basic skills which make learning a natural delight for the rest of one's life. When the motivation for learning is general, adult education will be widely and inexpensively available, and 'the reproach of proletarian coarseness' will be done away.

In Morris's imaginary future (85) we come across yet another hope—this time of a de-schooled world, where children, freed from social injustice and social inequality, learn by experience and desire. This blueprint for the ultra-progressive in education anticipates a day when the ladder of ability, at that moment being painfully constructed and slowly hoisted into place, will be knocked away again, and the liberated children will pick up literacy, languages and skills with perfect ease.

1895 sees the fifth and last of the great government reports, Bryce on Secondary Education (86), with its recommendation in favour of secondary education for all. This, the Report urges, would represent the final stage in the building of a great national system of education, which is 'among the first subjects with which social legislation ought to deal'. In this year, however, Hardy dramatises the position of a sensitive working-class boy (87) for whom educational help of any kind at all was yet to arrive. *Jude the Obscure* is set in the past, but its sensibility was contemporary (so much so, that it was burnt by a Bishop, and fairly generally denounced as obscene). In our extracts, Jude writes to the Masters of several Christminster (i.e. Oxford) Colleges, and receives one reply, brutal in tone, but devastatingly honest in its advice. He gets drunk, and alternates between a mood in which the ordinary, illiterate, drunken and randy life of 'the people' seems to him permanent truth, with the world of education a mere irrelevance, and a mood when, deeply wounded, he scrawls his protest on the walls of the College which rejected him, using the resonant words of Job. Interestingly, Hardy implies elsewhere in the novel that if Jude had been born fifty years later, things might have been better for him—both touching his opportunities for education, and his muddled and deeply unhappy experience of love and sex. Is this true? Fifty years later Jude would have had a chance to go to a grammar school and from there to a university, perhaps even to Oxford itself. But suppose his talent had not after all proved sufficient, or his staying-power had not been enough? From what we see of him in the novel he is sensitive but muddled, and unable to organise his life; he is at the mercy of sensuality and strongly tempted by drink. If his opportunity had led him to a secondary modern school and to academic failure, would he have been more or less bitter than he actually was? This question is by no means rhetorical, and the answer can only be a guess. Jude has the integrity and honesty that might have accepted failure; but the scrawling of graffiti need not stop with the book of Job.

There is a particular interest in this crux for modern readers, since it also pinpoints a major change of values that was shortly to come. The great majority of Victorians took for granted that one of the major benefits of education would be growing self-control and self-discipline, and an escape from the bondage of animality and of drink. But Hardy already shows signs of a new attitude to sex (though not to alcohol) which is a pointer to the changes to come. One aspect of the democracy has been a cult of sensuality, which has stood many traditional values on their head. Freudian and other psychological insights have of course greatly contributed, though in 1895 these were still being formulated, mostly well out of sight. D. H. Lawrence, writing on *Jude the Obscure* only a few years later, was able to identify Jude's sensuality as a strength, and his attempted rejection of it as among his greatest mistakes. And it is a fact that the later upsurge of egalitarianism in the 1960s and 1970s has been accompanied by a glorification of sensuality and eroticism—arts where universal achievement, of a kind, is indeed open to most. Whether this is liberation or enslavement is open to question, but it belongs to that strange entanglement of democracy and education in the area that Hardy probes. The fascination of Hardy's last novel for modern readers is a tested phenomenon, a perception perhaps of complexities still far from resolved.

In 1896 the young Bernard Shaw looked at a more fortunate Jude (88) through the eyes of his father, adapting these issues to a light play of wit.

In 1900, the Parliamentary Committee of the TUC (89) alleged that the government was regressing on the educational question, and demanded a fulfilment of the 1870 hopes. Its explicit ideal is equality of opportunity, not egalitarianism, and this remains true of the later TUC report of 1921 (100). By and large, TUC and Labour thinking was along these lines in the first half of the present century, and the Labour governments of 1945–51 were its natural heirs. The great change came somewhere between 1951 and 1964, for immensely complex reasons (though there are seeds of change in the Butler Act of 1944, and the logic of egalitarianism has not been confined to the political left).

In 1902, Balfour introduced the Education Act which completed the progress, as we have been tracing it, from wholly piecemeal education, privately financed, to compulsory education supervised and increasingly paid for by the state. Most of Balfour's speech was a tight-rope walk between various factions, but the peroration (90) announced for education 'the complete, radical and final cure'. Two commentators, both less than enthusiastic (91 and 92) openly doubt this, but recognise a measure of educational advance. The ladder of ability is at last ready to be placed in position. From now on—for some time at least—the pressure will be to set as many feet as possible on the lower rungs.

Balfour was still, of course, contentious (97) and, like educational legislators before and after him, did not lack detractors of a virulent kind.

Our final documents can be a mere epilogue; the rise and fall of the great twentieth-century grammar schools is another tale. At this stage, English and American ideals began to cross-fertilise, so it seems appropriate to broaden out from the purely English scene. Dewey (93) writes of the 'organic, positive principle involved in democracy', and charts that way towards those demands for 'consultation' and 'participation' which have become so much a feature of our modern way of life. Democracy will spread its claims to all kinds of institution, and by no means to central government alone. If this happens, we shall move away from democratic 'representatives', towards a society where men more and more desire to direct their own affairs. How will *this* come to terms with informed opinion, or with the claims of skill and merit to a special place? Optimists will hope that men will measure up to their opportunities, pessimists will naturally fear the reverse. Does Dewey's thinking bring Bagehot's 'tyranny of the commonplace' (47) a little nearer, or even the tyranny of determined minorities as foreseen by Vaughan (70)?

In 1905, the *Blue Book* advice to teachers has a certain interest (95); in 1908, Shaw (96) outlines the dangers touched on by Mill as early as 1832 (20). But before this, more sombrely original, Shaw (94) had faced, in the Preface to *Man and Superman* (1903), the possibility of a war to the death developing between egalitarianism and heredity. Suppose that glaring inequalities are in fact prescribed by nature, and that no known or possible educational process can iron them out? For a thoroughgoing egalitarian, there may then be two possibilities only, both apocalyptic in implication if in different ways.

One solution is to pretend that the inequalities do not exist, and to make this pretence obligatory; genetic scientists might be discouraged, or even put to death. The other solution is to accept that differences exist, but to go beyond education, relying on selective breeding, genetic engineering and the like when all else fails. To most men, both of these notions are profoundly distasteful, but egalitarianism might find itself forced to make a choice between the two. With characteristic forthrightness, Shaw opts for the second, setting out the case for selective breeding in its starkest form.

Adams (98) puts his finger on certain other, looming problems, but tantalisingly refrains from pursuing them to their implied ends. If the fully educated will, in fact, always be a minority, what will their status be as the democracy matures? If they are not to be identified with 'the ruling classes', how will they relate to their rulers in practical fact? Will they offer skills and services of the kind which society needs to utilise, but which might become increasingly envied and disliked? If they are felt to have advantages due to genetic or other unequal causes, on what terms will these be honoured and encouraged, if indeed on any at all? Would a society which equalised wealth and salaries solve the problem, by making service an area for sacrifice, and not for reward? But if it did this, how would human nature operate? Would ambition or idealism or inner prompting still lead men to be surgeons or scientists or vice-chancellors or aeroplane pilots, even if there were no social and financial gains and perhaps even the reverse?

Dewey (99) is assured that the 'devotion of democracy to education is a familiar fact', but he too hits on a problem, or contradiction, at a sensitive point. Put very bluntly, who is to do the dirty jobs in an equal society? How are educational or even democratic 'rights' to be equated with *them*? This may seem a point to take off into science fiction, in search of a society where machines do all the work, and produce wealth enough for the human population and to spare. At a homelier level, one can note that democratic cities are in fact finding it harder and harder to man the unattractive social services, and that the underlying problem is still tacitly exiled from most public debate.

We end with an Epilogue from D. H. Lawrence, and with an extravagance only slightly further from the centre of our theme. Democracy for the body, education for the mind and spirit: is *this* the solution, and the way ahead?

80   Equality in Christ

From F. D. Maurice's *Christian Education: Two Sermons* (preached on behalf of the Old Schools at Cambridge on Sunday 20 November 1870, and published as a pamphlet).

The Rev. F. D. Maurice, born 1805, became a leading member of a group of clergy and laymen who sought to infuse working-class movements with practical Christianity and to campaign for political reform against class legislation. They wrote novels, pamphlets, etc., and formed working-class co-operatives and societies. Though no great practical achievements can be pointed to, they had a considerable general influence through their organic theory of society and their hatred of anti-human political economy.

There are many serious and benevolent persons who desire for our country what they call a purely secular education. They say that what we want above all things is teaching which shall not split us into sects and classes, which shall be good for the whole nation. They say that rich and poor alike need to be instructed in their duties as citizens, to be grounded in a practical morality. They dread the influence of us clergymen. We are apt, they say, to adopt a very imperfect theory of civic obligations; our morality is wont to be partial and conventional.

To hear such statements must do us good if they touch us ever so closely. Whatever education will do most to cultivate a sound morality in men, women, and children; whatever education will most associate personal morality with political; whatever education will most help to form a united people, to break down the barriers which separate us; must be the best. Certainly we should watch and suspect ourselves with the utmost diligence, lest, under any pretext, we should hinder the accomplishment of these objects.

Because I entertain that conviction, because I wish to make it effectual, I say it behoves us to maintain our Christian Education; to make it more, not less, distinctly Christian than it has been hitherto. When we confess Christ to be the Lord our righteousness, we cannot bear to connect Him with any sect or school: even to speak of Him as the head of the Christian sect must be profane. We regard Him as the Lord of our nation, of every nation. When we proclaim Him to be the Son of God, one with the Father, the express image of His person, we affirm God to be the righteous being. All religious notions and theories which represent Him as arbitrary—as a mere sovereign ruling at His pleasure—we solemnly repudiate when we say that the perfect manifestation of Him was in one who emptied Himself of power; who took upon Him the form of a servant; who sacrificed Himself for men. The proclamation of Christ as divine has this effect upon morality; and yet without the proclamation of Him as human it would be of little worth: the righteousness would stand apart from us, a grand object for devout men to contemplate; it would have nothing to do with the life of those who toil and groan; it would not enable any one of us to feel, 'I am meant to be right and to do right, it is possible for me to be right and to do right.'

If you want the rich man not practically to worship his riches, not to bow down to them as the Kings of Kings and Lords of Lords; you must tell him plainly and directly that a poor man, one who was called a carpenter's son, is truly and indeed his Lord, and will be shewn to be so at the last. If you would convince the poor man that he need not envy and hate the rich man for his superiority to him, you must bring the same message home to him; you must shew him that the kingdom of Heaven and its righteousness are for him, seeing the King of Heaven who for our sakes became poor revealed the true righteousness which all may partake together. . . .

That is what I mean, what I think our fathers meant, by a Christian education. That it may be the root of a national education; that upon it may grow all practical lessons of conduct adapted to the circumstances of every new period; that it can never become obsolete; that the more there is of strife and division among us, the more need we have of it; you will, I hope, feel inwardly; you will try to express your feelings in acts.

81   1832 and 1867: a rake's progress to destruction?

From Walter Bagehot's 'Lord Althorpe and the Reform Act of 1832' in *Fortnightly Review*, November 1876. See note on 47 above.

But if ever Lord Althorpe's life is well written, it will, I think, go far to explain not only why the [1832] Reform Bill was carried, but why that Bill is what it was. He embodies all the characteristic virtues which enable Englishmen to effect well and easily great changes in politics: their essential fairness, their 'large roundabout common sense', their courage, and their disposition rather to give up something than to take the uttermost farthing. But on the other hand also he has all the characteristic English defects: their want of intellectual and guiding principle, their even completer want of the culture which would give that principle, their absorption in the present difficulty, and their hand-to-mouth readiness to take what solves it without thinking of other consequences. And I am afraid the moral of those times is that these English qualities as a whole—merits and defects together—are better suited to an early age of politics than to a later. . . . The instantaneous origination of obvious expedients is of no use when the field is already covered with the heterogeneous growth of complex past expedients; bit-by-bit development is out of place unless you are sure which bit should and which bit should not be developed; the extension of customs may easily mislead when there are so many customs; no immense and involved subject can be set right except by faculties which can grasp what is immense and scrutinise what is involved. But mere common sense is here matched with more than it can comprehend, like a schoolboy in the differential calculus;—and absorption in the present difficulty is an evil, not a good, for what is wanted is that you should be able to see many things at once, and take in their bearings, not fasten yourself on one thing. The characteristic danger of great nations, like the Romans or the English, which have a long history of continuous creation, is that they may at last fail from not comprehending the great institutions which they have created.

No doubt it would be a great exaggeration to say that this calamity happened in its fulness in the year 1832, and it would be most unfair to Lord Althorpe to cite him as a complete example of the characteristics which may cause it; but there was something in him of those qualities, and some trace in 1832 of that calamity—enough in both cases to be a warning. . . .

We must remember that if now we feel these evils we must expect ere long to feel them much more. The Reform Act of 1867 followed in the main the precedent of 1832; and year by year we shall feel its consequences more and more. The two precedents which have been set will of necessity, in the English world, which is so much guided by precedent, determine the character of future Reform Acts. And if they do the supremacy of the central group of trained and educated men which our old system of parliamentary choice created, will be completely destroyed, for it is already half gone.

I know it is thought that we can revive this intellectual influence. Many thoughtful reformers believe that by means of Mr Hare's system of voting, by the cumulative suffrage, the limited suffrage, or by some others like them, we may be able to replace that which the legislation of 1832 began to destroy, and that which those who follow them are destroying. And I do not wish to say a word against this hope. On the contrary, I think that it is one of the most important duties of English politicians to frame these plans into the best form of which they are capable, and to try to obtain the assent of the country to them. But the difficulty is immense. The reformers of 1832 destroyed intellectual constituencies in great numbers without creating any new ones, and without saying, indeed without thinking, that it was desirable to create any. They thus by conspicuous action, which is the most influential of political instruction, taught mankind that an increase in the power of numbers was the change most to be desired in England. And of course the mass of mankind are only too ready to think so. They are always prone to believe their own knowledge to be 'for all practical purposes' sufficient, and to wish to be emancipated from the authority of the higher culture. What we have now to do, therefore, is to induce this self-satisfied, stupid, inert mass of men to admit its own insufficiency, which is very hard; to understand fine schemes for supplying that insufficiency, which is harder; and to exert itself to get those ideas adopted, which is hardest of all. Such is the duty which the reformers of 1832 have cast upon us.

And this is what of necessity must happen if you set men like Lord Althorpe to guide legislative changes in complex institutions. Being without culture, they do not know how these institutions grew; being without insight, they only see one half their effect; being without foresight, they do not know what will happen if they are enlarged; being without originality, they cannot devise anything new to supply if necessary the place of what is old. Common sense no doubt they have, but common sense without instruction can no more wisely revise old institutions than it can write the Nautical Almanac. Probably they will do some present palpable good, but they will do so at a heavy cost; years after they have passed away, the bad effects of that which they did, and of the precedents which they set, will be hard to bear and difficult to change. . . .

82   Justice or envy?

From Henry James's *The Princess Casamassima*, 1886.

Henry James was born in 1843 in New York City. He was educated privately, and from the age of twelve enjoyed extensive travels in Europe. A major novelist who, more than any other of the great Victorian novelists, relied solely on his art to convey effective social criticism.

The Princess Casamassima was suggested to him, he says, by his habit of walking the London streets and reflecting upon the possible lot of a young man who should have been produced by this civilisation and yet should be condemned to witness it as an outsider. The dilemma crystallises when the hero, who has joined an anarchist organisation working for revolution, realises that he loves the culture he has vowed to destroy. In the end, he chooses self-destruction; and James, through this unusually sensational plot, dramatises a clash of emotions which would be central to many sensitive children from poor homes in the years ahead.

(i) . . . He was liable to moods in which the sense of exclusion from all he would have liked most to enjoy in life settled on him like a pall. They had a bitterness, but they were not invidious—they were not moods of vengeance, of imaginary spoliation: they were simply states of paralysing melancholy, of infinite sad reflection, in which he felt how in this world of effort and suffering life was endurable, the spirit able to expand, only in the best conditions, and how a sordid struggle in which one should go down to the grave without having tasted them was not worth the misery it would cost, the dull demoralisation it would involve.

In such hours the great roaring indifferent world of London seemed to him a huge organisation for mocking at his poverty. . . . He felt, moreover, that there was neither consolation nor refutation in saying to himself that the immense majority of mankind were out of it with him and appeared to put up well enough with the annoyance. That was their own affair; he knew nothing of their reasons or their resignation, and if they chose neither to rebel nor to compare he at least, among the disinherited, would keep up the standard. When these fits were on our young man his brothers of the people fared, collectively, very ill at his hands; their function then was to represent in massive shape precisely the grovelling interests which attracted one's contempt, and the only acknowledgement one owed them was for the completeness of the illustration. Everything which in a great city could touch the sentient faculty of a youth on whom nothing was lost ministered to his conviction that there was no possible good fortune in life of too 'quiet' an order for him to appreciate—no privilege, no opportunity, no luxury to which he mightn't do full justice. It was not so much that he wanted to enjoy as that he wanted to know; his desire wasn't to be pampered but to be initiated. . . .

And this was· not the fruit of a morbid vanity on his part, or of a jealousy that couldn't be intelligent; his personal discomfort was the result of an intense admiration for what he had missed. There were individuals whom he followed with his eyes, with his thoughts, some-times even with his steps; they seemed to tell him what it was to be the flower of a high civilisation. . . . It made him even rather faint to think that he must choose; that he couldn't (with any respect for his own consistency) work underground for the enthronement of the demo-cracy and yet continue to enjoy in however platonic a manner a spectacle which rested on a hideous social inequality. He must either suffer with the people as he had suffered before, or he must apologise to others, as he sometimes came so near doing to himself, for the rich; inasmuch as the day was certainly near when these two mighty forces would come to a death-grapple. . . . There were times when he said to himself that it might very well be his fate to be divided to the point of torture, to be split open by sympathies that pulled him in different ways; for hadn't he an extraordinary mingled current in his blood, and from the time he could remember wasn't there one half of him always either playing tricks on the other or getting snubs and pinches from it? (from Chapter XI).

(ii) . . . He was aware the people were direfully wretched—more aware, it often seemed to him, than they themselves were; so frequently was he struck with their brutal insensibility, a grossness proof against the taste of better things and against any desire for them . . . In these hours the poverty and ignorance of the multitude seemed so vast and preponderant, and so much the law of life, that those who had managed to escape from the black gulf were only the happy few, spirits of resource as well as children of luck: they inspired in some degree the interest and sympathy that one should feel for survivors and victors, those who have come safely out of a shipwreck or a battle. What was most in Hyacinth's mind was the idea, of which every pulsation of the general life of his time was a syllable, that the flood of democracy was rising over the world; that it would sweep all the traditions of the past before it; that, whatever it might fail to bring, it would at least carry in its bosom a magnificent energy; and that it might be trusted to look after its own. When this high, healing, uplifting tide should cover the world and float in the new era, it would be its own fault (whose else?) if want and suffering and crime should continue to be ingredients of the human lot. With his mixed, divided nature, his conflicting sympathies, his eternal habit of swinging from one point of view to another, he regarded the prospect in different moods with different intensities. In spite of the example Eustache Poupin gave him of the reconcilement of disparities, he was afraid the democracy wouldn't care for perfect bindings or for the finer sorts of conversation. . . . At the same time there was joy and exultation in the thought of surrendering one's self to the wash of the wave, of being carried higher on the sun-touched crests of wild billows than one could ever be by a dry, lonely effort of one's own. That vision could deepen to ecstasy; make it indifferent if one's ultimate fate, in such a heaving sea, were not almost certainly to be submerged in bottomless depths or dashed to pieces on immovable rocks. Hyacinth felt that, whether his personal sympathy should finally rest with the victors or the vanquished, the victorious force was potentially infinite and would require no testimony from the irresolute (from Chapter XXXVIII).

83   Hope in the teachers

From Matthew Arnold's retirement speech, 12 November 1886.
See note on 54 above.

My reflection is one to comfort and cheer myself, and I hope others, at this our parting. We are entering upon new times, where many influences, once potent to guide and restrain, are failing. Some people think the prospect of the reign of democracy, as they call it, very gloomy. This is unwise, but no one can regard it quite without anxiety. It is nearly 150 years since the wisest of English clergymen told the Lord Mayor and Sheriffs of London in a hospital sermon that the poor are very much what the rich make them. (Hear, hear.) That is profoundly true, though perhaps it rather startles us to hear it. On the other hand, it is almost a commonplace that children are very much what their teachers make them. I will not ask what our masses are likely to be if the rich have the making of them. I prefer to ask what they are likely to be so far as the teachers have the making of them. And on the whole—and here is the consoling reflection with which I shall end—though the teachers have, of course, their faults as individuals, though they have also their faults as a class, yet, on the whole, their action is, I do think and believe, powerful for good. (Hear, hear.) And not in England only, but in other countries as well, countries where the teachers have been much spoken against, I have found it so. I find plenty of deleterious and detestable influences at work, but they are influences of journalism in one place, in another influences of politicians, in some places both the one and the other; they are not the influences of teachers. The influence of the elementary teacher, so far as my observation extends, is for good; it helps morality and virtue. I do not give the teacher too much praise for this; the child in his hands so appeals to his conscience, his responsibility is so direct and palpable. But the fact is none the less consoling, and the fact is, I believe, as I have stated it. Burke speaks of the ancient and inbred integrity and piety of the English people; where should this influence of the teachers for good be so strong sustained as here? Thus, in conclusion, we are carried beyond and above the question of my personal gratitude, although that, too, is very deep and real. I love to think of the elementary teachers, to whom I owe so much and am so grateful, as more and more proving themselves to deserve, and more and more coming to possess, in the days which are now at hand for us, the esteem and gratitude of the entire country. (Cheers.)

84   An end to the reproach of coarseness

From Sydney Olivier's contribution to *Fabian Essays*, 1889.

Sydney Olivier was born in 1859 in Colchester, and had a· distinguished career as civil servant and statesman. In 1885 he joined the Fabian Society, and contributed an essay on its moral basis, from which this is taken. He later joined Ramsay MacDonald's first Labour government, and was created a Baron. Died 1943.

But though it is not envy or resentment at this tribute that mostly moves us to our warfare, this tribute we must certainly resume if the ideal of the school is to effect its social purpose. For the ideal of the school implies, in the first place, leisure to learn: that is to say, the release of children from all non-educational labour until mind and physique have had a fair start and training, and the abolition of compulsion on the adult to work any more than the socially necessary stint. The actual expenditure on public education must also be considerably increased, at any rate until parents are more generally in a position to instruct their own children. But as soon as the mind has been trained to appreciate the inexhaustible interest and beauty of the world, and to distinguish good literature from bad, the remainder of education, granted leisure, is a comparatively inexpensive matter. Literature has become dirt-cheap; and all the other educational arts can be communally enjoyed. The schools of the adult are the journal and the library, social intercourse, fresh air, clean and beautiful cities, the joy of the fields, the museum, the art-gallery, the lecture-hall, the drama, and the opera; and only when these schools are free and accessible to all will the reproach of proletarian coarseness be done away. . . .

85   Picking things up in the democracy

From William Morris's *News From Nowhere*, 1890.

William Morris was born in 1834 in Walthamstow, and became poet, novelist, artist, medievalist, manufacturer, prophet and socialist, all on an extensive scale. In his later years he became disillusioned with liberalism, which failed to arrest man's dehumanisation; he joined the Democratic Federation—a league of London working-men's radical clubs—in 1883, and his mind turned towards state socialism. His most enduring work is likely to be the poetry, but *News From Nowhere* is perhaps the most widely known, a fantasy of the communist and pastoral new society of the future. Its educational views, a blue-print for extreme progressivism in the context of communist democracy, have had a success in our own very different society of the early 1970s which might have surprised their author. Morris died in 1896.

... I saw that I was likely to get out of my depth again, and so merely for the sake of tiding over an awkwardness and to say something, I said:

'Well, the youngsters here will be all the fresher for school when the summer gets over and they have to go back again.'

'School?' he said; 'yes, what do you mean by that word? I don't see how it can have anything to do with children. We talk, indeed, of a school of herring, and a school of painting, and in the former sense we might talk of a school of children—but otherwise,' said he, laughing, 'I must own myself beaten.'

Hang it! thought I, I can't open my mouth without digging up some new complexity. I wouldn't try to set my friend right in his etymology; and I thought I had best say nothing about the boy-farms which I had been used to call schools, as I saw pretty clearly that they had disappeared; and so I said after a little fumbling, 'I was using the word in the sense of a system of education.'

'Education?' said he, meditatively, 'I know enough Latin to know that the word must come from *educere*, to lead out; and I have heard it used; but I have never met anybody who could give me a clear explanation of what it means.'

You may imagine how my new friends fell in my esteem when I heard this frank avowal; and I said, rather contemptuously, 'Well, education means a system of teaching young people.'

'Why not old people also?' said he with a twinkle in his eye. 'But,' he went on, 'I can assure you our children learn, whether they go through a "system of teaching" or not. Why, you will not find one of these children about here, boy or girl, who cannot swim, and every one of them has been used to tumbling about the little forest ponies— there's one of them now! They all of them know how to cook; the bigger lads can mow; many can thatch and do odd jobs at carpentering; or they know how to keep shop. I can tell you they know plenty of things.'

'Yes, but their mental education, the teaching of their minds', said I, kindly translating my phrase.

'Guest,' said he, 'perhaps you have not learned to do these things I have been speaking about; and if that's the case, don't run away with the idea that it doesn't take some skill to do them, and doesn't give plenty of work for one's mind: you would change your opinion if you saw a Dorsetshire lad thatching, for instance. But, however, I understand you to be speaking of book-learning; and as to that, it is a simple affair. Most children, seeing books lying about, manage to read by the time they are four years old; though I am told it has not always been so. As to writing, we do not encourage them to scrawl too early (though scrawl a little they will), because it gets them into a habit of ugly writing; and what's the use of a lot of ugly writing being done, when rough printing can be done so easily. You understand that handsome writing we like, and many people will write their books out when they make them, or get them written; I mean books of which only a few copies are needed—poems, and such like, you know. However, I am wandering from my lambs; but you must excuse me, for I am interested in this matter of writing, being myself a fair writer.'

'Well,' said I, 'about the children; when they know how to read and write, don't they learn something else—languages, for instance?'

'Of course,' he said; 'sometimes even before they can read, they can talk French, which is the nearest language talked on the other side of the water; and they soon get to know German also, which is talked by a huge number of communes and colleges on the mainland. These are the principal languages we speak in these islands, along with English or Welsh, or Irish, which is another form of Welsh; and children pick them up very quickly, because their elders all know them; and besides our guests from oversea often bring their children with them, and the little ones get together, and rub their speech into one another.'

'And the older languages?' said I.

'O yes,' said he, 'they mostly learn Latin and Greek along with the modern ones, when they do anything more than merely pick up the latter.'

'And history?' said I; 'how do you teach history?'

'Well,' said he, 'when a person can read, of course he reads what he likes to; and he can easily get some one to tell him what are the best books to read on such or such a subject, or to explain what he doesn't understand in the books when he is reading them.'

'Well,' said I, 'what else do they learn? I suppose they don't all learn history?'

'No, no,' said he; 'some don't care about it; in fact, I don't think many do. I have heard my great-grandfather say that it is mostly in periods of turmoil and strife and confusion that people care much about history; and you know,' said my friend, with an amiable smile, 'we are not like that now. No; many people study facts about the make of things and the matters of cause and effect, so that knowledge increases on us, if that be good; and some, as you heard about friend Bob yonder, will spend time over mathematics. 'Tis no use forcing people's tastes.'

Said I: 'But you don't mean that children learn all these things?'

Said he: 'That depends on what you mean by children; and also you must remember how much they differ. As a rule, they don't do much reading, except for a few story-books, till they are about fifteen years old; we don't encourage early bookishness, though you will find some children who *will* take to books very early; which perhaps is not good for them; but it's no use thwarting them; and very often it doesn't last long with them, and they find their level before they are twenty years old. You see, children are mostly given to imitating their elders, and when they see most people about them engaged in genuinely amusing work, like house-building and street-paving, and gardening, and the like, that is what they want to be doing; so I don't think we need fear having too many book-learned men.'

86   Much, much more might be done

From the Bryce Report, 1895.

The Bryce Report was signed by Bryce and others on 13 August
1895. The commission had been set up on 2 March 1894 to enquire
into the organisation of secondary education. It was specifically
concerned with matters of administration, not with curricula, but
its investigations and comments were comprehensive and of
far-reaching importance.

Things have improved within the last thirty years. . . . But the educational opportunities offered in most of our towns, and in nearly all
our country districts, to boys or girls who do not proceed to the
universities, but leave school at sixteen, are still far behind the requirements of our time, and far less ample than the incomes of the parents
and the public funds available might well provide. More than twenty
years ago, a very distinguished writer (now unhappily lost to us), who
did more than any one else to call the attention of his countrymen to
this topic, and was often disheartened by what seemed their apathy,
dwelt forcibly upon this point.

'Our energies and our prosperity will be more fruitful and safer,
the more we add intelligence to them; and here, if anywhere, is an
occasion of applying the words of the wise man:—"If the iron be
blunt, and the man do not whet the edge, then must he put forth more
strength; but wisdom is profitable to direct." ' (Matthew Arnold,
Higher Schools and Universities in Germany, 1874.)

More, much more, than is now done might be done, not merely to
fit such boys and girls for the practical work of their respective future
careers, but to make them care for knowledge, to give them habits of
application and reflection, to implant in them tastes which may give
them delights or solaces outside the range of their work-a-day lives.
Not a few censors have dilated upon the disadvantages from which
young Englishmen suffer in industry and commerce owing to the
superior preparation of their competitors in several countries of
continental Europe. These disadvantages are real. But we attach no

less importance to the faults of dulness and barrenness to which so many lives are condemned by the absence of those capacities for intellectual enjoyment which ought to be awakened in youth. In an age of increasing leisure and luxury, when men have more time and opportunity for pleasure, and pursue it more eagerly, it becomes all the more desirable that they should be induced to draw it from the best sources. Thus, it is not merely in the interest of the material prosperity and intellectual activity of the nation, but no less in that of its happiness and its moral strength, that the extension and reorganisation of Secondary Education seem entitled to a place among the first subjects with which social legislation ought to deal.

87   Not inferior

From Hardy's *Jude the Obscure*, 1895.

Thomas Hardy was born in 1840 in Dorset, and privately educated. He attained fame as a novelist, but always wanted chiefly to be a poet. *Jude the Obscure*, his last novel, was published thirty-three years before his death. In the twentieth century, he became a major poet, achieving his wish. Died 1928.

It was decidedly necessary to consider facts a little more closely than he had done of late. What was the good, after all, of using up his spare hours in a vague labour called 'private study' without giving an outlook on practicabilities?

'I ought to have thought of this before', he said, as he journeyed back. 'It would have been better never to have embarked on the scheme at all than to do it without seeing clearly where I am going, or what I am aiming at. . . . This hovering outside the walls of the colleges, as if expecting some arm to be stretched out from them to lift me inside, won't do! I must get special information'. . . .

During the next week or two he accordingly placed himself in such positions about the city as would afford him glimpses of several of the most distinguished among the Provosts, Wardens, and other Heads of Houses; and from those he ultimately selected five whose physiognomies seemed to say to him that they were appreciative and far-seeing men. To these five he addressed letters, briefly stating his difficulties, and asking their opinion on his stranded situation.

When the letters were posted Jude mentally began to criticise them; he wished they had not been sent. 'It is just one of those intrusive, vulgar, pushing, applications which are so common in these days', he thought. 'Why couldn't I know better than address utter strangers in such a way? I may be an imposter, an idle scamp, a man with a bad character, for all that they know to the contrary. . . . Perhaps that's what I am!'

Nevertheless, he found himself clinging to the hope of some reply as to his one last chance of redemption. He waited day after day, saying that it was perfectly absurd to expect, yet expecting. . . .

By the light of the flickering lamps he rambled home to supper, and had not long been sitting at table when his landlady brought up a letter that had just arrived for him. She laid it down as if impressed with a sense of its possible importance, and on looking at it Jude perceived that it bore the embossed stamp of one of the Colleges whose heads he had addressed. '*One*—at last!' cried Jude.

The communication was brief, and not exactly what he had expected; though it really was from the Master in person. It ran thus:

Biblioll College.

'SIR,—I have read your letter with interest; and, judging from your description of yourself as a working-man, I venture to think that you will have a much better chance of success in life by remaining in your own sphere and sticking to your trade than by adopting any other course. That, therefore, is what I advise you to do. Yours faithfully,
T. Tetuphenay.
To Mr J. Fawley, Stone-mason.

This terribly sensible advice exasperated Jude. He had known all that before. He knew it was true. Yet it seemed a hard slap after ten years of labour, and its effect upon him just now was to make him rise recklessly from the table, and, instead of reading as usual, to go downstairs and into the street. He stood at a bar and tossed off two or three glasses, then unconsciously sauntered along till he came to a spot called The Fourways in the middle of the city, gazing abstractedly at the groups of people like one in a trance, till, coming to himself, he began talking to the policeman fixed there.

That officer yawned, stretched out his elbows, elevated himself an inch and a half on the balls of his toes, smiled, and looking humorously at Jude, said, 'You've had a wet, young man'.

'No; I've only begun', he replied cynically.

Whatever his wetness, his brains were dry enough. He only heard in part the policeman's further remarks, having fallen into thought on what struggling people like himself had stood at that Crossway, whom nobody ever thought of now. It had more history than the oldest college in the city. It was literally teeming, stratified, with the shades of human groups, who had met there for tragedy, comedy, farce; real enactments of the intensest kind. At Fourways men had stood and talked of Napoleon, the loss of America, the execution of King Charles, the burning of the Martyrs, the Crusades, the Norman Conquest, possibly of the arrival of Caesar. Here the two sexes had met for loving, hating, coupling, parting; had waited, had suffered for each other; had triumphed over each other; cursed each other in jealousy, blessed each other in forgiveness.

He began to see that the town life was a book of humanity infinitely more palpitating, varied, and compendious than the gown life. These struggling men and women before him were the reality of Christminster, though they knew little of Christ or Minster. That was one of the humours of things. The floating population of students and teachers, who did know both in a way, were not Christminster in a local sense at all.

He looked at his watch, and, in pursuit of this idea, he went on till he came to a public hall, where a promenade concert was in progress. Jude entered, and found the room full of shop youths and girls, soldiers, apprentices, boys of eleven smoking cigarettes, and light women of the more respectable and amateur class. He had tapped the real Christminster life. A band was playing, and the crowd walked about and jostled each other, and every now and then a man got upon a platform and sang a comic song.

The spirit of Sue seemed to hover round him and prevent his flirting and drinking with the frolicsome girls who made advances— wistful to gain a little joy. At ten o'clock he came away, choosing a circuitous route homeward to pass the gates of the College whose Head had just sent him the note.

The gates were shut, and, by an impulse, he took from his pocket the lump of chalk which as a workman he usually carried there, and wrote along the wall:

'*I have understanding as well as you; I am not inferior to you; yea, who knoweth not such things as these?*—Job XII. 3.

88   Democracy, or education?

From G. Bernard Shaw's *You Never Can Tell*, 1896.

Shaw was born in 1856 in Dublin, and became famous in his lifetime
as Fabian, dramatist, wit and social prophet. His educational views
were tinged with paradox, and illustrate (notably 94 below) the
totalitarian tug of his brand of élitism. Died 1950.

Dolly	Is your son a waiter too, William?
Waiter	Oh no, miss: he's too impetuous. He's at the Bar.
M'Comas	A potman, eh?
Waiter	No, sir: the other bar. Your profession, sir. A Q.C., sir.
M'Comas	I'm sure I beg your pardon.
Waiter	Not at all, sir. Very natural mistake, I'm sure, sir. I've often wished he was a potman, sir. Would have been off my hands ever so much sooner, sir. . . . Yes, sir: had to support him until he was thirty-seven, sir. But doing well now, sir: very satisfactory indeed, sir. Nothing less than fifty guineas, sir.
M'Comas	Democracy, Crampton! Modern democracy!
Waiter	No, sir, not democracy: only education, sir. Scholarships, sir. Cambridge Local, sir. Sidney Sussex College, sir. . . . Very good thing for him, sir: he never had any turn for real work, sir.

89 Educational regress?

From the circular from the Parliamentary Committee of the TUC,
August 1900.

This circular started with the words: 'The time has come to draw
your attention to the conspiracy against the education of your
children which has been developing during the last five years.' It
attacks the whole motives of Tory policy. The peroration, which is
our present extract, is also quoted in a valuable chapter in Brian
Simon's *Education and the Labour Movement 1870–1920* (1965), p. 199.

The retrograde steps of the last few years have revealed the weakness
of our position, and before the ruin of all the slowly-built edifice of
popular education is accomplished we appeal to the workers of
England and Wales to speak out.

The education of the nation is a national interest. Equality of
opportunity free and ungrudgingly given to every child is of vital
concern. The rights of those of humble birth are too precious to be
left at the mercy of warring sects or social prejudices. The only safeguard of democratic interest is a democratic franchise and a free,
direct, and efficient popular control. We therefore demand that:

(1) The scheme of National Education foreshadowed by the Act of
1870 shall be completed and made secure by the appointment in every
district of Education Authorities elected as freely and democratically
as other municipal bodies.

(2) That they shall be empowered to provide efficient and suitable
education to all who require it.

(3) That the clerical managers and clerical organisations shall not be
allowed to control the education of the people to serve sectarian
purposes.

(4) That the elementary and higher education of the people shall be
at the public expense, free, unsectarian, and under the management of
the elected representatives of the people.

90   The complete, radical, and final cure

From A. J. Balfour's speech introducing his Education Act, *Hansard*,
24 March 1902.

A. J. Balfour was born in 1848 in East Lothian, and became a
philosopher and statesman. In 1896, the failure of an Education Bill
during his stint of leadership in the Commons caused him to
reappraise the extreme political complexities of the issue at this time.
He had more success with this famous Act of 1902 introduced
very shortly before he became Prime Minister. He died in 1930.

The political pressure for a new Act had mounted not only from
trade unions and from political radicals but from the church. One
incidental effect of the 1870 Act had been that while Board schools
were entitled to finances from rates, church schools were not.
Within a decade or so the latter were becoming desperate for
money. Another factor pointing towards change was a famous
judgment of 1901, which declared that under the 1870 Act, board
schools were not entitled to produce 'higher grade' classes. This new
Act, even more than Forster's, was a tight-rope walk over various
abysses. In the outcome, the church seemed to have won back lost
ground, and militant enemies of 1902, such as the nonconformist
minister James Hirst Hollowell (see 97 below) much stressed this
aspect. In retrospect, however, it seems more important as the serious
acceptance of secondary education, and of some—though by no
means all—of the major Bryce recommendations.

To the educationist, I think I need make no apologies and offer no
excuses. From him I anticipate, and I believe I shall obtain, the heartiest
support. He has long seen a vast expenditure of public money, which
has yet left this country behind all its Continental and American rivals
in the matter of education. He has seen a huge average cost per child
in our elementary schools, and yet at the same time many of those
schools half starved, inadequately equipped, imperfectly staffed. He
has seen in the last ten or fifteen years a development of University life
by private liberality which has no parallel except in America, which has

covered, and is still covering, our great industrial centres with Universities and University colleges where the very highest type of University instruction is given by men well qualified for their duty. He has seen technological institutions which I am afraid do not yet rival those which America and Germany have produced, but which yet in their measure and within their limits are admirable. He has seen them erected at a vast cost in every great industrial centre. Yet these University colleges and these great technological institutions do not, cannot, and never will effect all they might do so long as our secondary education, which is their necessary preparation, is in the imperfect condition in which we find it. Therefore I think I may make my appeal, to the educationist at least, with perfect confidence. I think I might go further. It is not upon the opinions or wishes of any particular section of opinion in this House or in the country that the fate of this Bill depends. It depends upon the common-sense of the great body of the people, on their growing perception of the need of a really national system of education. If the country is determined on reform in this matter—and I believe its determination to be unalterable—then I say with some confidence that it is upon the lines of this Bill, and only upon the lines of this Bill, that that great reform can proceed. No other scheme—be it what you like—will give to the educational evils of this country the complete, radical, and final cure which this Bill will give. I count upon the support of our countrymen to enable us to close for ever these barren controversies which for too long have occupied our time, and in the interests alike of parental liberty and of educational efficiency to terminate the present system of costly confusion.

91 Towards the ladder of ability

From an unsigned article in *Blackwood's Edinburgh Magazine*, May 1902.

The Education Bill itself, being the work of human hands, is not perfect. But it aims at carrying out what has long been advocated by educational reformers of every shade of opinion, and that is the establishment of a great system of primary and secondary education, the one leading up to the other, and placed under the control, both in town and country, of one local authority. If the primary schools are to be made stepping-stones to the secondary schools, so that 'the upper edge of the one shall be adjusted to the lower edge of the other', they must clearly be under one management. There are many other arguments in favour of the 'one authority' principle, but that by itself is sufficient. In the present bill, as far as secondary education is concerned, we get little more than the recognition of the principle. But that is all-important, and may serve as the starting-point for further legislation on some future occasion. . . .

92   Distaste for complexities

From an unsigned article in *Edinburgh Review*, July 1902.

It may be safely said that nothing is more distasteful than educational legislation, alike to the average man who takes part in public affairs and to the man who is specially concerned with education. . . . An Education Bill, if it is a large constructive measure, is not only encompassed with difficulties of principle and filled with contentious minutiæ of local and educational government: it is haunted by the contrast of lofty motives and great ideals with small ambitions and untoward prejudices. To one man the subject presents itself as one of pedagogy, to another of local self-government, to another of religious freedom, to another of local or imperial finance. The teacher, the minister of religion, the ratepayer, the taxpayer, all have something to say: there are not wanting those who would sooner the whole country was left untaught than that the machinery of local control or the conditions of religious teaching were not arranged to their liking. Amid these cross-currents of opinion and purpose an Education Bill labours slowly on its way.

What are the defects which most urgently call for treatment? First and foremost, there is the religious difficulty, which dislocates our system of elementary education. Next, there is the debateable ground of higher elementary and lower secondary education—the teaching of boys and girls with a view, more or less immediate, to the practice of a trade or profession. Perhaps of all educational problems this is the most important to the future of the country. Thirdly, we need fuller provision for the training of teachers, and last, though not least, we need the adjustment of our secondary education, not only to that kind which may be described as higher elementary, but to the requirements of the Universities and the professions.

93   The organic positive principle in democracy

From John Dewey's article 'Democracy in Education', in *The Elementary School Teacher*, December 1903.

John Dewey, born in 1959 in Vermont, USA, became a psychologist and philosopher with a particular interest in education. His ideas became important in the subsequent history of 'progressive education', particularly through his emphasis on the importance of freedom of movement and activity in the learning process. But he always rejected extreme progressivism, especially in its 'child-centred' form, when this seemed to him to neglect the importance of social roles and relationships. Died 1952.

Modern life means democracy, democracy means freeing intelligence for independent effectiveness—the emancipation of mind as an individual organ to do its own work. We naturally associate democracy, to be sure, with freedom of action, but freedom of action without freed capacity of thought behind it is only chaos. If external authority in action is given up, it must be because internal authority of truth, discovered and known to reason, is substituted.

How does the school stand with reference to this matter? Does the school as an accredited representative exhibit this trait of democracy as a spiritual force? Does it lead and direct the movement? Does it lag behind and work at cross-purposes? I find the fundamental need of the school today dependent upon its limited recognition of the principle of freedom of intelligence. This limitation appears to me to affect both of the elements of school life: teacher and pupil. As to both, the school has lagged behind the general contemporary social movement; and much that is unsatisfactory, much of conflict and defect, comes from the discrepancy between the relatively undemocratic organisation of the school, as it affects the mind of both teacher and pupil, and the growth and extension of the democratic principle in life beyond school doors. . . .

Politically we have found that this country could not endure half free and half slave. We shall find equally great difficulty in encouraging freedom, independence, and initiative in every sphere of social life, while perpetuating in the school dependence upon external authority. The forces of social life are already encroaching upon the school institutions which we have inherited from the past, so that many of its mainstays are crumbling. Unless the outcome is to be chaotic, we must take hold of the organic, positive principle involved in democracy, and put that in entire possession of the spirit and work of the school.

In education meet the three most powerful motives of human activity. Here are found sympathy and affection, the going out of the emotions to the most appealing and the most rewarding object of love —a little child. Here is found also the flowering of the social and institutional motive, interest in the welfare of society and in its progress and reform by the surest and shortest means. Here, too, is found the intellectual and scientific motive, the interest in knowledge, in scholarship, in truth for its own sake, unhampered and unmixed with any alien ideal. Co-partnership of these three motives—of affection, of social growth, and of scientific inquiry—must prove as nearly irresistible as anything human when they are once united. And, above all else, recognition of the spiritual basis of democracy, the efficacy and responsibility of freed intelligence, is necessary to secure this union.

94 Democracy and breeding: a new alliance?

From the Preface to Shaw's *Man and Superman*, 1903. See note to 88 above.

The need for the Superman is, in its most imperative aspect, a political one. We have been driven to Proletarian Democracy by the failure of all the alternative systems; for these depended on the existence of Supermen acting as despots or oligarchs; and not only were these Supermen not always or even often forthcoming at the right moment and in an eligible social position, but when they were forthcoming they could not, except for a short time and by morally suicidal coercive methods, impose superhumanity on those whom they governed; so, by mere force of 'human nature', government by consent of the governed has supplanted the old plan of governing the citizen as a public-schoolboy is governed.

Now we have yet to see the man who, having any practical experience of Proletarian Democracy, has any belief in its capacity for solving great political problems, or even for doing ordinary parochial work intelligently and economically. Only under despotisms and oligarchies has the Radical faith in 'universal suffrage' as a political panacea arisen. It withers the moment it is exposed to practical trial, because Democracy cannot rise above the level of the human material of which its voters are made. . . . Australia and Canada, which are virtually protected democratic republics, and France and the United States, which are avowedly independent democratic republics, are neither healthy, wealthy, nor wise; and they would be worse instead of better if their popular ministers were not experts in the art of dodging popular enthusiasms and duping popular ignorance. The politician who once had to learn how to flatter Kings has now to learn how to fascinate, amuse, coax, humbug, frighten, or otherwise strike the fancy of the electorate; and though in advanced modern States, where the artisan is better educated than the King, it takes a much bigger man to be a successful demagogue than to be a successful courtier, yet he

who holds popular convictions with prodigious energy is the man for
the mob, whilst the frailer sceptic who is cautiously feeling his way
towards the next century has no chance unless he happens by accident
to have the specific artistic talent of the mountebank as well, in which
case it is as a mountebank that he catches votes, and not as a meliorist. . . .

Our only hope, then, is in evolution. We must replace the man by
the superman. It is frightful for the citizen, as the years pass him, to see
his own contemporaries so exactly reproduced by the younger
generation. . . . All hope of advance dies in his bosom as he watches
them: he knows that they will do just what their fathers did, and that
the few voices which will still, as always before, exhort them to do
something else and be something better, might as well spare their
breath to cool their porridge (if they can get any). . . .

And so we arrive at the end of the Socialist's dream of 'the socialisation of the means of production and exchange', of the Positivist's
dream of moralising the capitalist, and of the ethical professor's,
legislator's, educator's dream of putting commandments and codes
and lessons and examination marks on a man as harness is put on a
horse, ermine on a judge, pipeclay on a soldier, or a wig on an actor,
and pretending that his nature has been changed. The only fundamental
and possible Socialism is the socialisation of the selective breeding of
Man: in other terms, of human evolution. We must eliminate the
Yahoo, or his vote will wreck the commonwealth.

As to the method, what can be said as yet except that where there is a
will, there is a way? . . . That may mean that we must establish a State
Department of Evolution, with a seat in the Cabinet for its chief, and
a revenue to defray the cost of direct State experiments, and provide
inducements to private persons to achieve successful results. It may
mean a private society or a chartered company for the improvement
of human live stock. But for the present it is far more likely to mean a
blatant repudiation of such proposals as indecent and immoral, with,
nevertheless, a general secret pushing of the human will in the repu-
diated direction; so that all sorts of institutions and public authorities
will under some pretext or other feel their way furtively towards the
Superman. . . .

The novelty of any such experiment, however, is only in the scale
of it. . . . Let those who think the whole conception of intelligent
breeding absurd and scandalous ask themselves why George IV was
not allowed to choose his own wife whilst any tinker could marry
whom he pleased? Simply because it did not matter a rap politically

whom the tinker married, whereas it mattered very much whom the king married. . . . Well, nowadays it is not the King that rules, but the tinker. Dynastic wars are no longer feared, dynastic alliances no longer valued. Marriages in royal families are becoming rapidly less political, and more popular, domestic, and romantic. . . . On the other hand a sense of the social importance of the tinker's marriage has been steadily growing. We have made a public matter of his wife's health in the month after her confinement. We have taken the minds of his children out of his hands and put them into those of our State schoolmaster. We shall presently make their bodily nourishment independent of him. But they are still riff-raff; and to hand the country over to riff-raff is national suicide, since riff-raff can neither govern nor will let anyone else govern except the highest bidder of bread and circuses. There is no public enthusiast alive of twenty years' practical democratic experience who believes in the political adequacy of the electorate or of the bodies it elects. The overthrow of the aristocrat has created the necessity for the Superman. . . .

King Demos must be bred like all other Kings; and with Must there is no arguing.

95   Suggestions for teachers

From the Board of Education *Blue Book*, 1905.

Handbook of Suggestions for the Consideration of Teachers and others concerned in the work of Public Elementary Schools.

The teacher must know the children and must sympathise with them, for it is of the essence of teaching that the mind of the teacher should touch the mind of the pupil. He will seek at each stage to adjust his mind to theirs, to draw upon their experience as a supplement to his own, and so take them as it were into partnership for the acquisition of knowledge. Every fact on which he concentrates the attention of the children should be exhibited not in isolation but in relation to the past experience of the child; each lesson must be a renewal and an increase of that connected store of experience which becomes knowledge.

Finally all the efforts of the teacher must be pervaded by a desire to impress upon the scholars, especially when they reach the highest class, the dignity of knowledge, the duty of each pupil to use his powers to the best advantage, and the truth that life is a serious as well as a pleasant thing.

The work of the public elementary school is the preparation of the scholars for life; character and the power of acquiring knowledge are valuable alike for the lower and for the higher purposes of life, and though the teachers can influence only a short period of the lives of the scholars, yet it is the period when human nature is most plastic, when good influence is most fruitful, and when teaching, if well bestowed, is most sure of permanent result.

96   Governing by the ignorance of majorities

From the Preface to Shaw's *Getting Married*, 1908. See note to 88 above.

The modern notion that democracy means governing a country according to the ignorance of its majorities is never more disastrous than when there is some question of sexual morals to be dealt with. The business of a democratic statesman is not, as some of us seem to think, to convince the voters that he knows no better than they as to the methods of attaining their common ends, but on the contrary to convince them that he knows much better than they do, and therefore differs from them on every possible question of method. The voter's duty is to take care that the Government consists of men whom he can trust to devise or support institutions making for the common welfare. This is highly skilled work; and to be governed by people who set about it as the man in the street would set about it is to make straight for 'red ruin and the breaking up of laws'. Voltaire said that Mr Everybody is wiser than anybody; and whether he is or not, it is his will that must prevail; but the will and the way are two very different things. . . . When Mrs Squeers opened an abscess on her pupil's head with an inky penknife, her object was entirely laudable: her heart was in the right place: a statesman interfering with her on the ground that he did not want the boy cured would have deserved impeachment for gross tyranny. But a statesman tolerating amateur surgical practice with inky penknives in school would be a very bad Minister of Education. It is on the question of method that your expert comes in; and though I am democrat enough to insist that he must first convince a representative body of amateurs that his way is the right way and Mrs Squeers's way the wrong way, yet I would not have them assume that Mrs Squeers's amateur way is likely to be the right way because she belongs to the democracy. . . .

97   Rallying the people for secularism?

From William Evans's *James Hirst Hollowell*, 1911.

The Rev. William Evans's account of Hollowell is a fascinating period piece. Hollowell was born in Northampton in 1851, and ordained to the congregationalist ministry in 1875 at Bedford Chapel, Camden Town, London. His dislike of the established church led him into fierce campaigns of the kind described here in favour of an educational system where the church would be totally neutral towards denominations. His argument was that the financing of church schools played into the hands of secularism, but we might think, with hindsight, that the secularists could hardly have wanted a better champion for their cause. Hollowell died in 1909.

A meeting of supporters of National Education under popular control was called in the Philosophical Hall, Leeds, on November 16th, 1896, and after condemnation of the Education Bill of 1896, unless 'genuine public control by representatives of the rate and tax payers is at the same time established', and declaring 'that no settlement of the Education question will be considered just or accepted as final that does not create Universal School Boards as in Scotland', the meeting resolved, with the view of obtaining the objects set forth in the resolutions, to form a Northern Counties Education League. . . .

The basis upon which the League was founded was:—
   1. To defend the existing Board School System in England and Wales against the attacks of Ecclesiastical parties.

2. To demand that all Elementary Schools receiving Government grants or local rates shall be brought under popular control.
3. To secure throughout England and Wales a Universal Board School system such as already exists in Scotland.
4. To secure that Training Colleges and the offices of Teacher and Pupil Teacher now maintained at the public cost, shall be thrown open to all without test of creed or denomination, and that teachers shall be engaged solely for the work of Education, and shall not be required to undertake or perform extraneous duties.

This programme found immediate favour, promising as it did the settlement of the Education question, and embodying the principles of the Progressives. The common justice of the proposals, the integrity of the leaders of this new movement, the enthusiasm of Mr Hollowell's advocacy of the plain way, all served to rally around the League a large number of ardent workers, and from the very first its success was assured. . . .

. . . 1902 was the most arduous year in Hirst Hollowell's life. . . . He had for some time seen the approach of this crisis and had been prophesying the near advent of the great sale of the people's schools to the clerical bidders, so that when in March the 'Single issue government' proposed to meet the desires of those who had so willingly seen the Party through a discreditable war crisis, by abolishing School Boards and *ad hoc* elections, and placing all Schools—Board, Church, and Roman Catholic—on the rates with a modicum of Municipal control, which meant nothing—when this wonderful proposal appeared Hirst Hollowell was not taken unawares by any means.

'After seven years of preparation, intrigues and minor experiments in reaction, the Government, in March, 1902 . . . was clearing the ground for a general attack upon the best parts of the settlement of 1870, and for a vast extension and the endowment of the denominational system. These anticipations were confirmed on March 24th.'

Hirst Hollowell's judgment, foresight and sagacity were unhappily fully justified. He and a few other 'alarmists and extremists' proved themselves to be the only sane leaders. . . .

'It is impossible', so he writes, 'to enumerate the whole of the meetings held or addressed in the Northern and other counties during the agitation. The number has been legion.' . . . In the matter of literature he writes pamphlets, edits the magazine, issues cartoons, reprints letters, publishes analyses of the Bill, and in all sends out 280,200 copies of publications, work which in itself would ordinarily have been deemed sufficient for one man's day. But in addition to all

this, we have the arranging of demonstrations on a large scale. . . .
Woodhouse Moor being the climax of the whole. . . . From 70,000
to 100,000 people attended, and the procession took two hours in
moving through the city of Leeds. . . . For this occasion Hirst Hollowell,
who was always making 'verse', wrote the Battle Song of the Schools.
A song which became quite popular at many demonstrations, and of
which 33,000 copies were sold.

England, rouse thy legions,
   Ere it be too late,
Foes of right, and foes of light,
   Would storm the schoolhouse gate,

CHORUS
   Children's voices call thee,
     Call thee to the fight;
   Do thy bravest; do it now!
   And God defend the Right!

Thirty years have come and gone,
   Since, with valiant hand,
Gladstone, Forster, Bright, upreared
   Free schools throughout thy land.

While our sons were over-sea,
   While the soldier fought,
Priest and traitor sought to bring
   The people's schools to nought . . .

Rally, then, from sea to sea,
   England, in thy might!
Win for men—more Liberty!
   Win for the child—more Light!

98   The new cultured and the new line of cleavage

From John Adams's *The Evolution of Educational Theory*, 1912.

John Adams was born in 1857 in Glasgow. He taught in grammar schools and colleges of education, lectured in the evenings very often, and from 1902 to 1922 was Professor of Education in the University of London. Knighted 1925. Died 1934.

With regard to the improvement of the moral conditions of the world by means of education, Kant's naif recommendation to prepare for a slightly better world than that of the period at which the educands are being trained cannot be taken seriously. Is it not true that we have always trained our educands for a much higher moral state than they are ever likely to meet with in this world? The general complaint indeed is that the theoretical school morality is unworkable in the great world, and none too workable in school. There is a danger in fact that in day schools in poor districts there may be set up a double morality: the morality of the home and the morality of the school. . . .

What prevents moral disaster in the matter is the fact that the direct teachers break the shock of the contrast. Here we have one of the great advantages of the average nature of the ordinary direct teacher. He is not so high above the ordinary run of humanity as to make him a hopelessly lofty model. Yet from his responsible position with regard to his educands he puts his best aspect to them, and thus maintains a high level of conduct. His occasional lapses, however, are such as to demonstrate his common humanity, and the educand by comparing his educator's normal goodness with very occasional lapses gets at a practical working code of morals that enables him to give and take in society without falling to a low ideal.

There is one aspect of education that in the past has received little attention, and has had small chance of leading to practical applications. This may be called the disinterested aspect. It is sometimes said that education should be sought for its own sake, and not for any material, social or other secondary advantage. As a matter of fact education has been nearly always sought either for the personal advantage of the educand, or for the benefit of the society for which he is being prepared. No doubt there have been many cases in which culture has been sought for its own sake, for the delights of scholarship, for the joy of mere knowledge. But the love of learning for its own sake is rare, and is more frequently the result of long training than of original inclination. In any case, learning and education are not to be confounded. Education must always have an end to serve, and cannot therefore be regarded as quite disinterested. What writers like Comte and Ruskin complain of is the tendency to regard education as a mere means of enabling the educand to raise himself from his present social position to a higher, instead of merely fitting him to make the best of himself in whatever position he may be placed. Ruskin becomes violent in denouncing the use of education as a mere stepping-stone to social advancement:

> The idea of an education which is to fit everybody to be
> Emperor of Russia, and provoke a boy, wherever he is, to want
> to be something better, and wherever he was born to think it a
> disgrace to die, is the most entirely and directly diabolic of all the
> countless stupidities into which the British nation has been of
> late betrayed by its avarice and irreligion.

Making due obeisance to the ideal underlying this protest, we may consider whether as a working principle it is practicable. Is it possible for people to be educated, as the phrase goes, 'above their station' without seeking to move upwards? Let it be noted that there is a certain begging of the question here. It is assumed that there is an education suitable for each social grade. Now this is the very point at issue. No doubt as matters stand at present there is a certain amount of specific preparation necessary to enable the educand to be quite at home in any given social grade. But what is really implied above is that the various social strata have each its level of culture above which it cannot rise. But there is no real causal connection between social status and capacity for culture. Opportunity is a different matter.

The interested motive in education has always been of fundamental importance in the world, but it may not be too extravagant to say that in the immediate future it is likely to reach its zenith. . . . There remains, however, one final step to be taken in the education of the people, a step that will not be taken till the demand comes from the people themselves, and when the demand is made and granted, we

K

shall have one of the most important experiments ever made in the working out of educational theory.

> It is not yet clearly perceived by the people that there is not any more natural and lasting distinction between the *educated* and the *uneducated* classes of which we hear so much nowadays, than there has been between the other classes in the past. Citizen and slave, patrician and plebeian, feudal lord and serf, privileged classes and common people, leisured classes and working masses, have been steps in a process of development. In the 'educated classes' and the 'uneducated classes' we have only the same distinction under a subtler and even less defensible form; for the right to education in its highest forms now remains largely independent of any other qualification than the possession of mere riches to secure it; it constitutes, in fact, one of the most exclusive, and at the same time one of the most influential, of the privileges of wealth.*

The ready answer to this is that at present the scholarship system enables every child of intellectual promise to obtain the best education available in the country. Huxley's figure has captured the popular imagination. He describes an ideal school organisation as 'a great educational ladder with one end in the gutter and the other in the university'. *The educational ladder* is a recognised phrase in our educational vocabulary. We are rather proud of it. One of our English educational monthly magazines has a permanent section under this title. The general opinion is that the ladder is more than sufficient. Educational authorities point out to each other that so far from there being any difficulty in a poor boy obtaining a scholarship, it is impossible to get candidates of sufficient ability to warrant the awarding of scholarships, and in some cases the number of scholarships originally offered has had to be reduced, on the ground that there was not a sufficient supply of candidates qualified for them. . . .

In a democracy, a higher education, as we understand that term, may cease to have its present social prestige, and may therefore lose all but its intrinsic attractions. With specific education carried to a high pitch, each man may feel that his store of knowledge is sufficient to maintain his self-respect, even though he has not acquired certain kinds of knowledge that at present are regarded as essential to anyone who claims to rank as educated. There will always remain a floating mass of knowledge of a general kind that is supposed to be common to all

* Benjamin Kidd: *Social Evolution.*

intelligent people. There must be this fringe of Humanity if people are to maintain the amenities of life. But relief will no doubt be found in the introduction here of division of labour. People will not be called upon to pretend to be grounded in all the humanities as at present— to know the ancient classics, to be familiar with literature ancient and modern, to have a mastery of two or three modern languages, to be well acquainted with the drama, and to have an adequate command of the technique of criticism in art and music. The serious study of these subjects will no doubt in the future as in the past demand a great expenditure of time, and those only who start with the advantage of wealth will be able to afford the necessary time, except in the case of those who master those subjects as professional crafts. . . .

Democracy will claim, and will no doubt receive, perfect equality in the matter of higher education, and when this comes about it will be true to say that the distinction between the educated and the uneducated classes has disappeared, since all will have an education suitable to the state to which their inclinations and capacities have called them. There will remain as before the distinction between the cultured and uncultured classes as determined by the appreciation of humanistic instruction. But there will be cultured people in all grades of society, and every grade of society will have then, as now, its uncultured section. The line of cleavage will not be caused by wealth or social distinction, but by capacity and inclination.

99   Democracy devoted to education

From John Dewey's *Democracy and Education*, 1916. See note to 93 above.

The devotion of democracy to education is a familiar fact. The superficial explanation is that a government resting upon popular suffrage cannot be successful unless those who elect and who obey their governors are educated. Since a democratic society repudiates the principle of external authority, it must find a substitute in voluntary disposition and interest; these can be created only by education. But there is a deeper explanation. A democracy is more than a form of government; it is primarily a mode of associated living, of conjoint communicated experience. The extension in space of the number of individuals who participate in an interest so that each has to refer his own action to that of others, and to consider the action of others to give point and direction to his own, is equivalent to the breaking down of those barriers of class, race, and national territory which kept men from perceiving the full import of their activity. These more numerous and more varied points of contact denote a greater diversity of stimuli to which an individual has to respond; they consequently put a premium on variation in his action. They secure a liberation of powers which remain suppressed as long as the incitations to action are partial, as they must be in a group which in its exclusiveness shuts out many interests.

The widening of the area of shared concerns, and the liberation of a greater diversity of personal capacities which characterise a democracy, are not of course the product of deliberation and conscious effort. On the contrary, they were caused by the development of modes of manufacture and commerce, travel, migration, and intercommunication which flowed from the command of science over natural energy. But after greater individualisation on one hand, and a broader community of interest on the other have come into existence, it is a matter of deliberate effort to sustain and extend them. Obviously a society to which stratification into separate classes would be fatal, must see to it that intellectual opportunities are accessible to all on equable and easy terms. A society marked off into classes need be specially attentive only to the education of its ruling elements. A society which is mobile, which is full of channels for the distribution of a change occurring anywhere, must see to it that its members are educated to personal initiative and adaptability. Otherwise, they will be overwhelmed by the changes in which they are caught and whose significance or connections they do not perceive. The result will be a confusion in which a few will appropriate to themselves the results of the blind and externally directed activities of others . . .

Democratic society is peculiarly dependent for its maintenance upon the use in forming a course of study of criteria which are broadly human. Democracy cannot flourish where the chief influences in selecting subject matter of instruction are utilitarian ends narrowly conceived for the masses, and, for the higher education of the few, the traditions of a specialised cultivated class. The notion that the 'essentials' of elementary education are the three R's mechanically treated, is based upon ignorance of the essentials needed for realisation of democratic ideals. Unconsciously it assumes that these ideals are unrealisable; it assumes that in the future, as in the past, getting a livelihood, 'making a living', must signify for most men and women doing things which are not significant, freely chosen, and ennobling to those who do them; doing things which serve ends unrecognised by those engaged in them, carried on under the direction of others for the sake of pecuniary reward. For preparation of large numbers for a life of this sort, and only for this purpose, are mechanical efficiency in reading, writing, spelling and figuring, together with attainment of a certain amount of muscular dexterity, 'essentials'. Such conditions also infect the education called liberal, with illiberality. They imply a somewhat parasitic cultivation bought at the expense of not having the enlightenment and discipline which come from concern with the deepest problems of common humanity. A curriculum which acknowledges the social responsibilities of education must present situations where problems are relevant to the problems of living together, and where observation and information are calculated to develop social insight and interest. . . .

. . . We lose rather than gain in change from serfdom to free citizenship if the most prized result of the change is simply an increase in the mechanical efficiency of the human tools of production. . . . The increased political and economic emancipation of the 'masses' has shown itself in education; it has effected the development of a common school system of education, public and free. It has destroyed the idea that learning is properly a monopoly of the few who are predestined by nature to govern social affairs. But the revolution is still incomplete. The idea still prevails that a truly cultural or liberal education cannot have anything in common, directly at least, with industrial affairs, and that the education which is fit for the masses must be a useful or practical education in a sense which opposes useful and practical to nurture of appreciation and liberation of thought. . . .

100   Negotiations, strikes and mental calibre

From *Report of the Trade Union Education Enquiry Committee*, 1921 (subsequently adopted by the TUC).

The progress of working class organisation and outlook foreshadows the approach of fundamental changes in our social and industrial relations and gives education a new meaning to trade unionists. It is therefore becoming more urgent that, so far as possible, trade unionists, but more especially those holding positions of responsibility in executive, district, and branch organisations, should be men and women having a wide range of knowledge germane to economic and political problems, and such trained capacity as will enable them not only to understand the immediate results of decisions and actions but also to foresee possible ultimate results.

Apart from these general considerations, the increasing activities of trade unions have called into existence a series of educational problems which can only be satisfactorily dealt with by trade unions accepting responsibility for the provision of suitable facilities.

A brief comparison between the activities of trade union branches and district organisations thirty years ago with those that obtain today will illustrate this striking change. Trade union government involves an ever-increasing responsibility. The administration of trade union rules and regulations has become more intricate and difficult, and each new amalgamation and federation increases these complexities.

Branch records require to be kept with greater accuracy than appeared to be necessary at the beginning of the period we are considering. Friendly benefit and unemployed benefit require to be administered, not only in compliance with the rules of the union, but also with the regulations governing the administration of the National Health Insurance and Unemployment Acts. In view of the equipment in secretarial staff and machinery of the modern employers' organisation, not only a practical and technical knowledge of the trade or industry, but mental alertness and trained minds are more and more essential if trade unions are to hold their own in negotiations around the conference table or before the arbitration court in dealing with thousands of matters affecting their members' standard of life. Vital questions of policy and principle tend to shift more and more from national executives to branch and district committees, and executive officers require to rely to an increasing extent on branch and district officers for such interpretation of their decisions as will maintain harmony and unity within the union.

The success of both trade negotiations and strikes is today a far truer measure of the intelligent loyalty of the members and the tact and trained judgment of branch and district officers than it was three decades ago. In addition, a greatly increased complexity in business organisations, necessitating a corresponding growth in the industrial and political activities of trade unions, both local and national, during the last twenty years, is one of the most significant developments of the century.

All this clearly points to the need for a corresponding development in educational activities. Many negotiations and strikes that have failed would have succeeded, and much other useful work might have been accomplished by the trade unions, if only a small portion of the money that has been spent in these struggles had been devoted to training the latent mental capacity of the men engaged in them.

The power, prestige, and influence of trade unionism rests on the mental calibre of its membership.

Epilogue   For the body, democracy; for mind and soul, education

From 'Democracy', an essay by D. H. Lawrence written at an unknown date; first published in *Phoenix*, 1936.

D. H. Lawrence, born in Nottingham 1885, died 1930. Too well known as novelist and social prophet to require notes.

The Law of the Average is well known to us. Upon this law rests all the vague dissertation concerning equality and social perfection. Rights of Man, Equality of Man, Social Perfectibility of Man: all these sweet abstractions, once so inspiring, rest upon the fatal little hypothesis of the Average.

What is the Average? As we are well aware, there is no such animal. It is a pure abstraction. It is the reduction of the human being to a mathematical unit. . . . The average human being: put him on the table, the little monster, and let us see what his works are like. He is just a little monster. He has two legs, two eyes, one nose—all exact. He has a stomach and a penis. . . . Since he has a mouth, he is made for eating. Since he has feet, he is made for walking. Since he has a penis, he is made for reproducing his species. And so on, and so on.

What a loathsome little beast he is, this Average, this Unit, this Homunculus. Yet he has his purposes. He is useful to measure by. That's the purpose of all averages. An average is not invented to be an Archetype. What a really comical mistake we have made about him. . . . He is invented to serve as a standard, just like any other standard, like the metre, or the gramme, or the English pound sterling. . . . He was never intended to be worshipped. . . .

What are the purposes? Merely for the comparing of one *living* man with another *living* man, in case of necessity: just as money is merely a contrivance for comparing a leg of mutton with a volume of Keats's poems. . . .

The Average Man is somehow very unsatisfactory. He is not sufficiently worked out. . . . How could we scientifically establish the Average, whilst he had to stand draped upon a pedestal, as an Ideal? Haul him down at once. He is no Ideal. He is just a Standard. . . . This is all your Man-in-the-street amounts to: this tailor's dummy of an average. He is the image and effigy of all your equality. Men are not equal, and never were, and never will be, save by the arbitrary determination of some ridiculous human Ideal. . . .

Now we will settle for ever the Equality of Man, and the Rights of Man. Society means people living together. People *must* live together. And to live together, they must have some Standard, some *Material* Standard. This is where the Average comes in. And this is where Socialism and Modern Democracy come in. For Democracy and Socialism rest upon the Equality of Man, which is the Average. And this is sound enough, so long as the Average represents the real basic material needs of mankind: basic material needs: we insist and insist again. For Society, or Democracy, or any Political State or Community exists not for the sake of the individual, nor should ever exist for the sake of the individual, but simply to establish the Average, in order to make living together possible: that is, to make proper facilities for every man's clothing, feeding, housing himself, working, sleeping, mating, playing, according to his necessity as a common unit, an average. Everything beyond that common necessity depends on himself alone.

The proper adjustment of material means of existence: for this the State exists, but for nothing further. The State is a dead ideal. *Nation* is a dead ideal. Democracy and Socialism are dead ideals. They are one and all just *contrivances* for the supplying of the lowest material needs of a people. . . . But once more we have mistaken the means for the end: so that Presidents, those representatives of the collected masses, instead of being accounted the chief machine-section of society, which they are, are revered as ideal things. The thing to do is not to raise the idea of Nation, or even of Internationalism, higher. The need is to take away every scrap of ideal drapery from nationalism and from internationalism, to show it all as a material contrivance for housing and feeding and conveying innumerable people. . . .

Each human self is single, incommutable, and unique. This is its *first* reality. Each self is unique, and therefore incomparable. It is a single well-head of creation, unquestionable: it cannot be compared with another self, another well-head, because, in its prime or creative reality, it can never be comprehended by any other self.

The living self has one purpose only: to come into its own fullness of being, as a tree comes into full blossom, or a bird into spring beauty, or a tiger into lustre.

But this coming into full, spontaneous being is the most difficult thing of all. Man's nature is balanced between spontaneous creativity and mechanical-material activity. Spontaneous being is subject to no law. But mechanical-material existence is subject to all the laws of the mechanical-physical world. Man has almost half his nature in the material world. His spontaneous nature *just* takes precedence.

The only thing man has to trust to in coming to himself is his desire and his impulse. But both desire and impulse tend to fall into mechanical automatism: to fall from spontaneous reality into dead or material reality. . . .

All education must tend against this fall; and all our efforts in all our life must be to preserve the soul free and spontaneous. The whole soul of man must *never* be subjected to one motion or emotion, the life activity must never be degraded into a fixed activity, there must be *no fixed direction*.

There can be no ideal goal for human life. Any ideal goal means mechanisation, materialism, and nullity. There is no pulling open the buds to see what the blossom will be. Leaves must unroll, buds swell and open, and *then* the blossom. And even after that, when the flower dies and the leaves fall, *still* we shall not know. There will be more leaves, more buds, more blossoms: and again, a blossom is an unfolding of the creative unknown. Impossible, utterly impossible to preconceive the unrevealed blossom. You cannot forestall it from the last blossom. We know the flower of today, but the flower of tomorrow is all beyond us. Only in the material-mechanical world can man foresee, foreknow, calculate, and establish laws.

So, we more or less grasp the first term of the new Democracy. We see something of what a man will be unto himself.

Next, what will a man be unto his neighbour?—Since every individual is, in his first reality, a single, incommutable soul, not to be calculated or defined in terms of any other soul, there can be no establishing of a mathematical ratio. We cannot say that all men are equal. We cannot say A=B. Nor can we say that men are unequal. We may not declare that A=B+C.

Where each thing is unique in itself, there can be no comparison made. One man is neither equal nor unequal to another man. When I stand in the presence of another man, and I am my own pure self, am I aware of the presence of an equal, or of an inferior, or of a superior? I am not. When I stand with another man, who is himself, and when I am truly myself, then I am only aware of a Presence, and of the strange reality of Otherness.

Select Bibliography

We have had to be extremely selective in our editing of documents, and serious students will want to return to the sources. In particular, Matthew Arnold's *Culture and Anarchy* is essential reading.

For a general background to the nineteenth century, students might consult the following:

David Thomson, *England in the Nineteenth Century*, Penguin, 1950.
G. M. Young, *Portrait of an Age*, Oxford University Press, 1936.
Asa Briggs, *Victorian People*, Odhams, 1954; Penguin, 1965.
Asa Briggs, *Victorian Cities*, Odhams, 1963; Penguin, 1968.

The first gives an adequate summary of the major events and trends, for students new to the period. The second is a classic short social history, compressed and vivid. The third and fourth are lively, highly readable accounts of some of the mid-century's leading reformers, and cities, respectively.

For more detailed history, we particularly recommend:

Elie Halévy, *History of the English People in the Nineteenth Century*, 6 vols, Benn, 1913–32 (all available in English translation, in paperback).
Asa Briggs, *The Age of Improvement, 1783–1867*, Longmans, 1959.

For the history of working-class movements in Britain, two important books which continually throw light on our theme are:

G. D. H. Cole and Raymond Postgate, *The Common People, 1746–1946*, Methuen, 1938; now a Methuen university paperback; also published by Barnes & Noble, New York.
E. P. Thompson, *The Making of the English Working Class*, Gollancz, 1964.

Of the many books specifically on Chartism, the three we have found most helpful are:

Mark Hovell, *The Chartist Movement*, Manchester University Press, 1918.

G. D. H. Cole, *Chartist Portraits*, Macmillan, 1941.
Asa Briggs, *Chartist Studies*, Macmillan, 1959.

On the two great Reform Acts of 1832 and 1867, we recommend the following:

G. M. Trevelyan, *Lord Grey of the Reform Bill*, Longmans, Green, 1920.
Maurice Cowling, *1867, Disraeli, Gladstone and Revolution: the Passing of the Second Reform Bill*, Cambridge University Press, 1967.
F. B. Smith, *The Making of the Second Reform Bill*, Cambridge University Press, 1966.

The first is intensely readable, and gives an excellent account of the pressures in the early nineteenth century. The other two were specially prepared for the centenary of 1867.

For a background to nineteenth-century education, the following are specially recommended, out of an enormous possible list:

H. C. Barnard, *A Short History of English Education 1760–1944*, University of London Press, second edition 1968.
H. B. Binns, *A Century of Education 1808–1908*, Dent, 1908.
S. J. Curtis, *History of Education in Great Britain*, University Tutorial Press, 5th edn, 1965.
John Hurt, *Education in Evolution 1800–1870*, Hart-Davies, 1971.
A. D. C. Peterson, *A Hundred Years of Education*, Duckworth, 1952.
Brian Simon, *Studies in the History of Education 1780–1870*, Lawrence & Wishart, 1960.
Brian Simon, *Education and the Labour Movement 1870–1920*, Lawrence & Wishart, 1965.

All of these have their particular emphases. Binns has the turn of the century as his standpoint; in Curtis's book, the educational achievements and disappointments are placed in a wider context. Brian Simon's books are lively, readable, and the best full account of the history of events in the period, but some of his interpretations have a marked commitment to one side of the case.

For a recent and very challenging study of Victorian politics with a direct bearing on our theme and a radical reappraisal of current assumptions, we strongly recommend:

George Watson, *The English Ideology*, Allen Lane, 1973.

Readers of this volume will find fruitful cross-references in other volumes of the Birth of Modern Britain series, notably:

David M. Thompson, *Nonconformity in the Nineteenth Century*,
Routledge & Kegan Paul, 1972.
Patricia Hollis, *Class and Conflict in Nineteenth-Century England
1815–1850*, Routledge & Kegan Paul, 1973.
Michael Sanderson, *The Universities in the Nineteenth Century*,
Routledge & Kegan Paul, 1975.

One other collection of documents which students will find helpful
is:

G. D. H. Cole and A. W. Filson, *British Working Class Movements,
Selected Documents 1789–1875*, Macmillan, 1951 and St Martin's
Press, New York; also available as a Papermac.

The debate central to nineteenth-century education continues
today, with continuing polemics from opposed sides. Here, we list
the following contributions—with personal interests to declare in
two of them, but a virtuous sense of fairness in mentioning the
others:

C. B. Cox and A. E. Dyson (eds), *The Black Papers on Education*,
Davis-Poynter, 1971.
Ivan D. Illich, *Deschooling Society*, Calder & Boyars, 1971.
National Council for Educational Standards (ed.), *The Basic Unity
of Education*, Critical Quarterly Society, 1972.
A. S. Neill, *Summerhill*, Penguin, 1968.
David Rubinstein and Colin Stoneman (eds), *Education for
Democracy*, Penguin, 1970.

Index

Index